PHILOSOPHY OF EDUCATION:
CLASSICAL AND
CONTEMPORARY

PHILOSOPHY OF EDUCATION: CLASSICAL AND CONTEMPORARY

John L. Elias
Fordham University
New York

KRIEGER PUBLISHING COMPANY
MALABAR, FLORIDA
1995

Original Edition 1995

Printed and Published by
KRIEGER PUBLISHING COMPANY
KRIEGER DRIVE
MALABAR, FLORIDA 32950

FROM A DECLARATION OF PRINCIPLES JOINTLY ADOPTED BY A COM-
MITTEE OF THE AMERICAN BAR ASSOCIATION AND COMMITTEE OF
PUBLISHERS:

This Publication is designed to provide accurate and authoritative information in regard to the subject matter covered. It is sold with the understanding that the publisher
is not engaged in rendering legal, accounting, or other professional service. If legal advice or other expert assistance is required, the services of a competent professional person should be sought.

Library of Congress Cataloging-In-Publication Data

Elias, John L.
    Philosophy of education : classical and contemporary / John L.
Elias.
        p.   cm.
    Includes bibliographical references and index.
    ISBN 0-89464-898-5 (alk. paper)
    1. Education—Philosophy.   2. Education—Philosophy—History.
I. Title.
LB17.E4   1995
370'.1—dc20   95-8059
                                                                CIP

10 9 8 7 6 5 4 3 2

CONTENTS

PREFACE

When I first began teaching courses in philosophy of education in the 1970s, the approach I used was a treatment of the various schools of philosophy, such as liberal, progressive, behaviorist, humanistic, reconstructionist, and analytic. Having written a text in the philosophy of adult education along these lines, I searched for another way to introduce students to this subject. The approach which I have found most helpful in recent years is the one I use in this book: an inquiry into philosophical ideas, both classical and contemporary, in the various curricular areas.

Although there are many excellent books in philosophy of education, I believe that this book has a number of unique features that will recommend it to both professors and students. This book treats the history of philosophical ideas in education, including classical theories and contemporary discussions. It is also one of the few books to deal both historically and philosophically with the full range of curricular areas in education. The book is organized to provide an introduction to many forms of education: intellectual, moral, aesthetic, physical, vocational, religious, and political. One chapter covers the history and philosophy of special education, a subject rarely treated in books in this field.

I owe a debt of gratitude to many persons who over the years have influenced my thinking about philosophy of education. I was introduced to this field in the 1970s at Temple University by two esteemed professors, James McClellan and Paul Komisar. Courses in history of education under Professor William Cutler of Temple University encouraged me to situate philosophical ideas in their broader historical context. In the 1980s conversations with Professors John Hull and Richard Dearden, as well as Dr. Michael Grimmitt, all of the University of Birmingham, enriched my perspectives. More recently students and colleagues at Fordham University have helped shape in various ways the form and content of this book. I am especially grateful for conversations with Drs. J. Robert Starratt, Gloria Durka, Robert Siebert, Brian Kelty, and James Morgan.

I dedicate this book to my family, Eleanor Flanigan, Rachel Elias, and Rebecca Elias who give inspiration and support to all my endeavors. A Bishon Frise named Snowy has provided not only a helpful distraction from labors but also a philosophical model of searching puzzlement, deep thought, and ecstatic delight.

CHAPTER 1

PHILOSOPHY AND EDUCATION

INTRODUCTION

Philosophy of Education and Its Critics

Although philosophers of the past have written on education, philosophy of education in a formal sense has been in vogue for at least this century. However, in recent years the discipline has had difficulties establishing itself as an important part of teacher education, often included as only one part of courses labeled foundations of education. In general terms the application of philosophical ideas and analysis to education has suffered from critiques within and without the discipline.

Jacques Barzun complained about the deplorable books on education. He was especially disenchanted by a certain "Philosophy of Education for having said among other things judged foolish, that the problem of aims in education is a problem of values" (Barzun in Donohoe, 1973). Charles Silberman (1970) in his study of the schools was also critical of philosophy of education for not combatting adequately the mindlessness which he found in education.

Philosophy of education has had difficulty finding its proper role or voice in recent years. At times it has become too philosophical and consequently irrelevant to practicing educators. At other times when it attempts to be relevant, it fails to do justice to the task and methods of philosophy. For these reasons philosophy of education may be considered a discipline in decline. It has been attacked for being too removed from educational matters, irrelevant to teacher and administrator training, and fostering skepticism and radical ideas.

Notwithstanding these criticisms, some of which are valid, it is my contention in writing this book that educators need the type of training and discipline which comes from a study of philosophy of education, both from what philosophers have said and from their own efforts to philosophize. Philosophy is not a luxury for educators. It is a way to make educational leaders and teachers more rational and critical in their thinking and acting about education. Philosophy's emphasis on clarity, purpose, criticism, and justification are important values for educators. They are tools which educators need in order to accomplish their work effectively. Philosophy of education as applied by its best practioners remains a discipline that presents visions of what education and schools should be and details criticisms of current efforts to realize these visions. The strongest case for philosophy of education has been made by John Dewey (and repeated in our times by Paulo Freire) who saw it as a tool for the reconstruction of human experience, schools, and society.

Philosophy is one of many disciplines related to education, which in itself is not a discipline. Other disciplines include history, psychology, sociology, anthropology, economics, and biology. Philosophy in terms of education results primarily in practical theory or explanation as opposed to scientific theory (Scheffler, 1991, p. 118). Whereas scientific theory explains and predicts phenomena, practical theory is more likely to provide some guidance for enterprises such as education and law.

Brief History of Philosophy of Education

Just about every major philosopher in the West has written on education. While Plato viewed education as part of politics, Aristotle considered it as part of both politics and ethics. Augustine followed in the Platonic tradition and concerned himself with understanding how we learn and how teachers actually teach. Thomas Aquinas, who was actively involved in teacher education at the University of Paris, developed a theory of education which still bears his name: Thomism and neo-Thomism. Such Enlightenment and pre-Enlightenment thinkers as Rousseau and Locke wrote classic works on education. Rousseau wrote on the education of the young man and the young woman and criticized many of the educational practices of his time. Locke's ideas on education revolutionized our concept of child rearing and education. The premier German philosopher, Emmanual Kant, has left us his actual lectures to teachers on pedagogy. Other philosophers who wrote on education include George Hegel and Johann Herbart. In our country philosophers who have addressed educational issues include William James, John Dewey, Robert Hutchins, and Mortimer Adler.

Courses in philosophy of education were introduced into teacher education at the beginning of this century. These courses were mostly concerned with teachers' beliefs about life and schooling. Teachers were expected to have a philosophy of education. To aid them in this they often studied the formal theories of Plato, Comenius, Froebel, Herbart, and Rousseau. More often the courses included what was considered wise advice about the young and about teaching them in schools. (Broudy, 1981, p. 15).

The discipline of philosophy of education owes much of its origins to the work of John Dewey and his colleagues at the University of Chicago and Teachers College. His pragmatic approach encouraged other systems to develop in a formal manner: realism, idealism, and later existentialism. Dewey's work led to a strong reaction from liberal arts educators who saw him as the destroyer of the classical tradition and of education itself.

In the 1950s the analytic movement in philosophy began to dominate educational philosophy in the United States and Britain. Leaders in this movement in Britain were R. Peters, P. Hirst, and R. Dearden. Leaders in the United States were I. Scheffler, J. McClellan, P. Komisar, J. Soltis, and T. Green. This movement which shied away from systematic approaches that grounded themselves in metaphysics attempted to analyze the language used in ordinary discourse. This philosophy had its beginnings in logical positivism.

The work of Richard Peters, the foremost British philosopher of education, has been particularly significant in shaping contemporary thought on the subject. Philosophers of education were to bring to the field their own distinctive skills and achievements. It is not their task to formulate, discover and pass on practical educational principles. He also distinguished philosophy from a historical study of educational ideas and their use in illuminating present educational issues. Peters suggested four main areas of work for philosopher: (1) the analysis of concepts specific to education; (2) the application of ethics and social philosophy to assumptions about the content and procedures of education; (3) an examination of the conceptual schemes and assumptions used by educational psychologists; (4) an examination of the philosophical character of the content and organization of the curriculum and other questions about learning (Hirst, 1986).

The new analytic philosophy of education made the discipline more of a professional enterprise. Many philosophers of education were now trained in formal philosophy. They were philosophers interested in issues relating to schooling. However, the more rigorously philosophical they became the more they began to address their own colleagues and the less other educators and the general public.

In the 1960s philosophy of education courses, together with other foundation courses, were taught in different ways: by systems, issues, classics, and analysis of concepts. Often in these classes radical criticisms were leveled against education and American society. However, many influential books of this time were not works of professional philosophers: Paul Goodman, A. S. Neil, Jonathan Kozol, John Holt, George Dennison, and Edgar Friedenberg. Ivan Illich and Paulo Freire were exceptions because they had philosophical training. Many criticisms were made of these courses.

The turn to pragmatic goals in the 1970s also eroded the influence and prevalence of philosophy of education courses. The dominance of behaviorism at all levels of education, even state and federal, led an attack against what was happening in philosophy of education. Philosophers of education resisted valiantly the competency based teacher education movement and other behaviorally based practices.

Many educators became dissatisfied with courses in philosophy of education. Whereas schools and school administrators were interested in having a philosophy of education, a set of beliefs, most practitioners of the discipline preferred to do language analysis and criticize educational concepts. Philosophers in the main turned away from developing grand theories or comprehensive systems of education. Although some educators found the new approach challenging, many criticized it for fostering skepticism and radicalism.

The situation is mixed today. Analysts remain dominant in many schools of education. But in this era which some have called postanalytic and the era of the return of grand theory, there is room for philosophy to assume in a more modest manner the role which it previously played in education and in society. This is accomplished by many philosophers in their addressing issues of social and political importance.

The approach used in the NSSE (National Society for the Study of Education) yearbook of 1981 (Soltis, 1981) dedicated to philosophy of education avoids the systems approach by connecting philosophy of education with the subdisciplines of philosophy (ethics, metaphysics, epistemology, aesthetics, social philosophy, and logic). The two previous yearbooks devoted to philosophy of education had utilized the systems approach. The most recent yearbook was partially successful. Although some of the essays are highly technical, a number are inaccessible to educators without strong philosophical training. Broudy (1981) contends that educators expect more from philosophy of education than merely analytic essays. They can rightfully expect comprehensive visions from some philosophers of education.

Changes in philosophy of education can be expected because of the recent rise in interest among philosophers in issues of applied philosophy. Philosophers are again addressing issues of freedom and necessity, individuality and common good, personhood and mass society, mass and class, and truth and credibility (Broudy, 1981, p. 27). Philosophers also deal with many issues relating to the growth of science. Ethics has become especially relevant with its attention to medicine, law, business and communications. This rejuvenation of philosophy has begun to have some of its effects in education, as is seen in the increase in courses in ethics of teaching, counseling, and administration.

The analytic movement is still strong today but it is facing new challenges. The liberal education movement has reasserted itself in the writing of Allan Bloom, E. Hirsch and others. A phenomenological thrust is used by an increasing number of philosophers of education. Many philosophers still find Dewey's pragmatism a viable approach to education. But the greatest challenges come from social philosophers and theoretical sociologists of knowledge who have become critical of the social, political, and economic ideologies of education.

Kinds of Philosophy of Education

A distinction has been made between public and professional philosophy of education. *Public* philosophy of education is a genre which includes the broadest range of writings on education. It includes the writings of politicians, journalists, intellectuals, citizens, and educators who write about education. *Professional* philosophy of education is a discipline engaged in by those who have been trained specifically in philosophy. These find their sources in writings in philosophy, philosophy of education, and education (Soltis, 1981, p. 5).

A helpful classification of philosophies of education has been presented by Power (1982). Some philosophies of education can be termed *inspirational*. This form has as its purpose the expression of utopian ideals for the formal and informal education of persons: to lay down a plan for what is considered to be the best education. Examples of this genre include Plato's *Republic*, Bacon's *New Atlantis*, Rousseau's Emile, A. S. Neil's *Summerhill*, and B. F. Skinner's *Walden II*.

Other philosophies of education are termed *prescriptive* or normative. These philosophies give clear and precise directions for educational practice and urge a commitment to their implementation. This can be done with reference to either particular or general contexts. Examples include Johann Herbart's *The Science of Education*, Robert Hutchins's *The Higher Learning in America*, and Jacques Maritain's *Education at the Crossroads*. Frankena (1970) has analyzed such normative philosophies of education. They present the ideals or goals, justifications for these goals of a philosophical or religious nature, educational methodologies, and justifications for the methodologies.

A third approach to philosophy of education may be called *investigative*. This approach examines or inquires into policies and practices adopted in education with a view to either justification or reconstruction. Examples include Dewey's *Democracy and Education* and William Kilpatrick's *The Foundation of Method*.

The most recent approach to philosophy of education is termed *analytical*. It attempts to discover and interpret meaning in educational discourse and practice. Major examples include Richard Peter's *Ethics in Education*, Israel Scheffler's *The Language of Education*, and Thomas Green's *The Activities of Teaching*.

Another way of getting hold of philosophy of education is to examine the various tasks that it sets itself to do (Broudy 1981, pp. 33–35). Philosophy of education has an *educational function* in addressing from a philosophic or theoretical perspective issues arising in education: formulation of aims, curriculum, organization, teaching-learning, methodology of research, theoretical rationale of research, and ethical issues. Of course, not all educational problems are philosophical ones but philosophy can address an aspect of all issues. To do this philosophy should avoid as much as possible technical language; if it is used it should be carefully explained.

Philosophy of education in its *analytic function* can clarify the language and arguments used in educational discourse. It can also eliminate ambiguity in terms and give criteria for judging claims. Philosophers can be expected to encourage not fixed views and faiths but rational discourse, freedom of inquiry, and criticism.

Similar to this analytic function is philosophy of education's *critical function*, in which philosophers examine carefully proposals and policies, such as school desegregation and accountability. The philosopher can look at the policy within the social, moral, and ideological context in which it is presented.

Finally, some philosophers of education take on the *synthetic function* of providing "a synoptic, systematic, coherent set of beliefs and arguments about education that deals with the educational enterprise as a whole and that makes connection with a philosophy of life" (Broudy, 1981, p. 35).

The Teaching of Philosophy of Education

The traditional way of teaching philosophy of education has been to separate the field into schools of philosophy. There are many textbooks which use this approach. The schools are many depending on one's analysis of philosophical schools. There are several varieties of philosophical realism (classical, scientific, religious, neo-Thomism), idealism, pragmatism (experimentalism), existentialism (phenomenology), behaviorism, humanism, analytic, and reconstructionism.

What this approach amounted to was actually a study of the history of philosophy of education or the history of educational ideas. A strong argument such as Broudy's (1981) can be made for the importance of such a study. Since many students of education do not have a background in general philosophy, this approach gives the rich cultural heritage and world views which have predominated in Western history. The debate over the importance of cultural heritage is raging today because of the efforts of such neoconservatives as William Bennett, Allan Bloom, and E. Hirsch. These traditional systems can provide the background and the lens with which to think through today's educational problems. They contain the classical ideas necessary for philosophizing today.

Many (especially analysts) have criticized this approach because it tends to teach philosophy as a system or body of knowledge and does not involve students in actually doing philosophy, which is described as a set of activities of elucidation, argument, critique, clarification, analysis, synthesis, and so forth, aimed at reflecting on how we think about the world and our actions in it (Soltis, 1981, p. 4). Philosophy of education in this approach becomes critical thinking about important aspects of education.

It must be noted that philosophy is one of many academic enterprises involved in education, as well as in other practical enterprises. It devotes itself to particular types of inquiry. Many other factors (psychological, social, political, economic, and methodological) must be considered before educational policy and educational practice is agreed upon.

Argument of This Book

In this book I go back to older forms of philosophy of education. Experience has taught me that educators find value in what might be called a history of philosophical ideas in education. There is much to be learned from what the greatest minds have thought about education. Present issues and concerns in education often repeat past arguments. Present debates are often repetitions of past debates among philosophers. It is also valuable to view present debates in the light of these historic interchanges.

I also go back to another division of philosophy of education. I have organized the debates not explicitly around the various schools of philosophy of education but rather around the so called content areas of education. In this feature the book is similar to the treatises by Emmanual Kant and Herbert Spencer. Although recognizing that there are not clear cut distinctions among intellectual, moral, aesthetic, religious, physical, vocational, and political education, I believe that these are helpful frameworks through which to study the history of philosophical ideas in education.

In treating physical education, vocational education, and special education along with other forms of education, I compensate for a lack in most treatments of educational thought. Rarely have philosophers of education included these in their treatments. The inclusion of special education, though its treatment does not fit logically into the structure of the book's organization by reason of content, introduces students to a form of education that raises important issues about the nature of a good society and the right of all individuals in a society to an education to meet their needs.

Each chapter in the book is divided into two large sections. The first part treats the history of ideas in each area and in some cases the history of ideas as imbedded in practice. Where it was possible I have structured this section by counter-pointing a classical position with theories that re-state or oppose this position. This treatment provides the framework for understanding current discussions and debates in each content area of education. The presentation of these discussions and debates takes various forms. At times current debates are rehearsed. At other times clearly delineated theories are presented. At still other times significant issues are presented.

CHAPTER 2

INTELLECTUAL EDUCATION

As was mentioned in the first chapter, it is not easy to separate the different forms of education because there are close connections among the types considered in this book. Yet an attempt must be made if there is to be some clarity about educational aims, content, and methods. Thus there will be some intermingling of elements in each chapter.

This chapter is devoted to what might be called intellectual education. Many names can be given to this form of education. It is called *intellectual* because it develops the power of the intellect or mind; it is called *rational* or cognitive because it is both suited to rational persons and develops the reason or reasoning powers of individuals. This form is also called *general* education because it includes the most general areas of knowledge that persons are expected to possess. Though this may be identified as *liberal* education, it is not the same as liberal education since other philosophies also stress intellectual education. Also, there is a debate over just what should be included in liberal education. Many have argued against the overintellectualized theories which have been proposed.

Intellectual education of course applies to all forms of education. Varieties of education termed moral, political, aesthetic, etc. all have intellectual or cognitive components. Yet the cognitive element is so important that it is crucial to focus specifically on education which has as its direct end or goal knowing and understanding and does not necessarily intend any direct end beyond this.

In its most common usage education denotes the intellectual—the education of the mind. It is concerned with knowledge, comprehension, deliberation, and judgment. The term education is found among the first philosophers of education. For these philosophers and those who have come after them, an educated person is one who possesses the kinds knowledge esteemed by the society.

Before anything else education is a social concept. From a social perspective education initiates the new generation into the body of knowledge that is part of a culture. It introduces them to the common meanings and interpretations that society and culture have given to events and realities in the world. Education viewed socially thus attempts to help persons make sense of the world for new members of the community. An important debate is whether there are truths and values which transcend particular cultures since these are rooted in the nature of things and in a common understanding of human knowledge.

From an individual perspective education of the intellect is the acquisition of what is recognized as knowledge in general or in a particular culture. This knowledge is both general and particular.

HISTORICAL PERSPECTIVES ON INTELLECTUAL EDUCATION

The Classical Position

The first proponents of intellectual education were the Greek philosophers Socrates, Plato, and Aristotle. Their educational writings must be seen in the context of the struggle they had with the sophists. The Sophists proposed an education which was directed at the attainment the particular skills of the public speaker or lawyer. In the sophist tradition are found the Greeks Protagoras, Isocrates, and Hippias and the Romans Cicero and Quintilian (Broudy and Palmer, 1964, pp. 15–30). Although sophist education included a knowledge of facts, the psychology of audiences, and cultural information, all of these were subordinated to the acquirement of practical skills.

Socrates, an opponent of the Sophists, may be considered the father of intellectual education in the West. His chief contribution to education was a method of teaching disciples to question assumptions and to become knowledgeable. In his view persons who knew the good would do the good. Thus Socrates saw an intimate connection between intellectual education and moral education. Socrates believed that knowledge was the basis of virtues. Socrates proposed an education both by exhortation and by dialogue.

Socrates' ideas on education are incorporated in the writings of his disciple, Plato. Plato makes clearer what constitutes intellectual education. The teacher exhorts students to be more concerned with knowledge and truth than with making money and gaining knowledge. In these exhortations students were to be made to feel uncomfortable with their present state of knowledge. This discomfort was to lead to dialectical self-examination. It was this self-examination under the care of an expert teacher that should lead to a knowledge of what one knew in a previous existence. Plato illustrated this by giving the example of Socrates teaching the Pythagorean theorem to a slave boy through skillful questioning.

In the dialogues of Plato the conversations often revolve around attempts to arrive at the definition of concepts. For Plato to arrive at the definition of something is to get at the essence or nature of things. In his view the essences of things have separate existences outside the human mind and human reality.

Education for Plato was to take place in early years by conditioning through exposure to music, fables, and stories about the gods. In adolescence persons were to learn arithmetic, geometry, music, and astronomy. Of these, mathematics is the most important because it deals with abstractions and hypotheses. The highest level of knowledge was the dialectic, the knowledge of real concepts and real ideas. Plato's theory of education is presented in the Allegory of the Cave. Through the dialectic one contemplates what things really are and is then in a position to make judgments about what exists in this world. At the higher levels of knowledge we not only know that something is so, but we also know why it is so and why it could not be any other way. Plato describes arriving at final goal of education:

Then, when they are fifty, those who have come safely through and proved the best at all points in action and in study, must be brought at last to the goal. They must lift up the eye of the soul to gaze on that which sheds light on all things; and when they have seen the Good itself, take it as a pattern for the right ordering of the state and of the individual, themselves included. (In Broudy and Palmer, 1964, p. 42)

What the classical tradition presupposes is a particular view of the human mind and a relationship between our knowledge and the real order. The human mind by nature desires to know. Its power includes the capacity to know things the way they are. The mind goes through certain hierarchically ordered steps in the ascent to knowledge, a knowledge found in the seven liberal arts. In the classical view it is knowledge which makes a person both wise and happy. This fulfillment of the natural desires of the mind gives us an understanding of how we are to live. This education is called liberal or freeing not only because, as Dewey points out, it was the education of freedmen, but also because it accomplished the freeing of the mind from the illnesses of ignorance, illusion, and error. In the classical tradition this view of intellectual education has little to do with education for a specific vocation.

This classical view has had a dominant role in educational thought in the West. Educational leaders in the Christian churches accepted it in its basic form and added to the description of the workings of the mind a role for divine illumination. It also expanded the area of what is to be known by including knowledge about God and God's revelation. Renaissance humanists adhered to this tradition, but perhaps distorted it by placing undue emphasis on particular texts as the only way in which minds were to be developed and knowledge was to be found.

In the classical view an attempt was made to assert what knowledge is most worthwhile. The proponents contended that true values transcended particular cultures. Its contention was that the mind desired to gain knowledge of values which were immutable, absolute, and eternal. Most of the classical authors found these values rooted in the Good or in God. This metaphysical view has found favor in more recent times in the educational theories of Matthew Arnold, John Newman, and Alfred Whitehead. It also underlies the views of classical realists such as Jacques Maritain, Robert Hutchins, Mortimer Adler and others. The approach is often referred to as perennialism, humanism, rationalism, and neo-Thomism (after Thomas Aquinas).

This viewpoint also has had its critics. John Dewey (1916) and fellow pragmatists rejected this approach to education by attacking the metaphysics that underlies it and the elitist social condition that gave rise to it. Karl Popper (1962) sees this viewpoint as the basis for the closed society and totalitarianism. Sociologists of knowledge have rejected the absolutism and ahistoricism of this perspective (Young, 1971). Yet this position on intellectual education is still influential in discussions on education in our time.

Restatements of the Classical Position

The classical approach to intellectual education has received some contemporary restatements which take a number of forms. Some accept the metaphysical position of the relationship between mind and objective knowledge. Another restatement focuses on the activities of the mind. Still another restatement focuses on forms of knowledge.

General education

Some restatements of the classical position on intellectual education place emphasis on the qualities of the mind which should be developed through education and subordinate these to the forms of knowledge through which these qualities are to be developed.

The "Harvard Report" on *General Education in a Free Society* (1946) described academic areas such as natural sciences, humanities, and social sciences and distinguished these by reason of distinctive methods. Yet the report made it clear that what it intended was the development of certain intellectual abilities: to think effectively, to communicate thought, to make relevant judgments, and to discriminate among values. Effective thinking includes primarily logical thinking, the ability to arrive at universal truths from particular cases. It also entails the relational thinking of daily life and imaginative thinking. Communication involves skills of speaking, listening, writing, reading as well as the art of conversation. Making relevant judgments entails bringing one's ideas to the realm of one's experience. Finally, discrimination among values includes being aware of the character values of fair play, self-control, and intellectual values of love of truth and beauty.

In reviewing this report certain problems appear. Just how the three forms of knowledge develop the particular abilities is not made clear. Not enough attention is given to the forms of knowledge through which the mental abilities are developed. The four groups of mental abilities take different form in dealing with different forms of knowledge. There appears to be a claim of a transfer of learning across areas once the ability has been developed. This viewpoint is praiseworthy in that it considerably broadens the concept of intellectual education to include moral, emotional, and aesthetic education.

Forms of knowledge approaches

The classical tradition has received a restatement which avoids the epistemological and metaphysical positions that entailed a hierarchical organizing of subject matter into the liberal arts and dialectics. Paul Hirst (1974) has presented an approach to intellectual education which views forms of knowledge as distinct ways in which we structure our experience around the use of accepted public symbols. Hirst advocates the forms of knowledge approach as a contemporary restatement of liberal education, a statement which avoids the metaphysics of classical realism. Yet what he has presented is mainly intellectual education and not a full theory of liberal education since some significant elements are not present, as the discussion of his theory will bring out.

Forms of knowledge in Hirst's theory have the following characteristics. First, they involve central concepts which are peculiar to the form, and not reducible to any other form, for example, God and sin in religion; gravity and hydrogen in sciences. Second the form has a distinct logical structure. The concepts in the form denote certain aspects of experience and constitute a network in which experience can be understood. Third, the form has terms, structures, and expressions which are testable by experience. Fourth, the forms have techniques and skills for exploring experience and for testing their expressions of experience. For Hirst the forms are open to change and new forms can be created.

Hirst admits that while there are no clear dividing lines among the forms of knowledge they can be clearly distinguished from one another. Forms depend on other forms. The distinct forms of knowledge which he describes include mathematics, physical sciences, human sciences, history, religion, literature and the fine arts, and philosophy (1970). In his 1974 version he offers these seven forms: formal logic and mathematics, physical sciences, truths of a mental or personal kind, moral judgment and awareness, aesthetics (literature and fine arts), religion, and philosophy. Education for Hirst is the initiation of pupils into these forms of knowledge which are considered necessary and worthwhile for themselves (Hirst, 1974).

Education in these forms can be of two sorts: general or specialist. A general education includes a number of features. Persons must acquire through critical training not only a knowledge of significant facts but also of the conceptual schemes in each form and the types of reasoning and judgment used within them. Persons need to come to see things from the way that experts in the field see them and become aware of the major achievements in each form. An educated person must also perceive the relationships among the various forms of knowledge. The knowledge that is sought is the logic of the discipline as this is expressed in general and formal principles.

Specialist knowledge of the forms demands a knowledge of all pertinent facts and an ability to use all the techniques and skills of the form. The specialist not only knows science and history but also the philosophy of science and history.

Hirst sees no reason why intellectual education through the forms of knowledge must be taught through the accepted academic disciplines, though he considers this the most efficient way to organize a curriculum. He is open to the possibility that curriculum could be arranged around fields of study, both practical and theoretical. He suggests power as such a theme that might be approached from different areas.

Phenix (1964) has proposed a somewhat similar analysis of knowledge. From an existentialist perspective he suggests that human experience can be categorized into realms of meaning according to the ways in which we make sense of our existential experience in the world. For him education is the process of engendering essential meanings. The realms of meaning which he proposes are (1) symbolics: language mathematics, gestures and rituals; (2) empirics: descriptions of physical world and living things; (3) aesthetics: arts; (4) synnoetics: awareness of ourselves as persons in relation to others; (5) ethics: meanings that express obligation; (6) synoptics: meanings provided by history, philosophy and religion which attempt to construct a coherent pattern which includes all other realms of meaning.

Other philosophers and scholars have offered approaches to intellectual education which focus on the structure of knowledge or the structure of disciplines (Bruner, 1963). Yet it is Hirst's work which has been the paradigm controlling discussions among philosophers of education when it comes to examining intellectual education from the perspective of knowledge.

The power of the theory of forms of knowledge is shown in the many criticisms that have been made of it. Every aspect of the theory has been subjected to scrutiny: the inclusion of particular forms, the criteria for the forms, and the mutability of the forms. In recent years with the advent of ideological analysis from philosophers and sociologists of knowledge the theory has been judged by many to be elitist, narrow, and intolerant. Though Hirst made it clear that he was concerned with intellectual education, the theory has come to be viewed as embracing all worthwhile knowledge. If this is so, then the affective, emotional, physical, vocational, and political aspects of education are slighted. This way of using the theory has been criticized as a theory for ivory tower people (Martin, 1981).

A serious charge leveled against the theory concerns the apparent objectivity of the analysis by which Hirst arrives at his forms of knowledge and their function in establishing the curriculum of the schools. Hirst does not seem to be aware of the value judgments that are implicit in his analysis. His starting point is the classical tradition and the traditional liberal arts. While rejecting the metaphysics of antiquity, he is not equally aware of his own form of metaphysics. He has presented a rationale for a particular type of education which has been given the honor of being called liberal education. This happens to the education which is most esteemed in the best schools in his native Britain. He and his fellow British philosophers of education, R. S. Peters and R. Dearden, have identified education with liberal education and liberal education with intellectual education. What this does is denigrate any education which falls outside the parameters of intellectual liberal education. A similar argument has been offered by Martin (1981) who attempted to develop a concept of liberal education as the education of a person in all aspects: noncognitive, emotional, and vocational.

The more serious criticisms of Hirst's approach to intellectual education come from sociologists of knowledge. The force of their criticisms are apparent if the two theories of knowledge are contrasted. The rationalist tradition in which Hirst is situated holds a number of views about knowledge. It contends that certain facts, truths, and knowledge are universally valid. These facts, truths, and knowledge are valid independently of ourselves. For purposes of education these truths are expressed in forms of knowledge or disciplines which have a distinct logical structure, central concepts, truth criteria or forms of verification and modes of expression.

For sociologists of knowledge other assumptions operate. What is fact, truth, and knowledge results from agreements and transactions entered into by human beings. These agreements may vary from culture to culture and often do. The agreements about what constitutes fact, truth, and knowledge are a reflection of dominant cultural and ideological assumptions of a society, especially those of persons in power. Individuals begin to assimilate this knowledge at birth. The task of education from this perspective is to engage teachers and students in activities which bring about knowledge: questioning, verifying, valuing, observing, classifying, and deciding upon the criteria by which we decide what knowledge is.

In examining this alternative approach to intellectual education we move to what might more properly be called political education. A fuller treatment of this theory is found in the chapter on political education. This theory, identified most closely in our time with Paulo Freire, views all education as political. Rather than seeing education in the vision of Hirst as an initiation into what is necessary and worthwhile, it views education as dialogical and problem posing. Freire explains it best, though in a verbose fashion:

> Education is the problematization of the world of work, products, ideas, convictions, myths, arts, science: the world, in short, of culture and history which is the result of relations between human beings and the world. To present this human world as a problem for human beings is to propose that they enter it critically, taking the operations as a whole, their action and that of others on it. It means re-entering the world through the entering into of the previous understandings which may have been arrived at naively because reality is not examined as a whole. In entering their own world, people become aware of their manner of acquiring knowledge and then realize the need to know even more. (Freire, 1973, pp. 154-5)

From the perspective of sociology of knowledge the forms theory contains elitist values and ways of thinking into which students are socialized. This type of education is class oriented, does a disservice to the values of the working classes and ignores many aspects of education which are needed in society.

For the sociologist of knowledge it is not something intrinsic which makes particular knowledge worthwhile but something extrinsic, the value of function it assumes for individuals or societies. Less emphasis is placed by these theorists on the structure of knowledge.

This form of criticism attempts to make clear what are the ideological assumptions in all forms of education. More about this is presented in the chapter on political education.

The Pragmatic Tradition

Thus far the philosophical conversation and argument have been within the classical realist position. The major challenge to this position in the history of philosophy of education has come from the pragmatic tradition, particularly from the philosophy of John Dewey. In many writings spanning half of this century Dewey combatted classical realism and modern realist versions of liberal education. In doing so he proposed another form of intellectual education, which has been given various names. It is called *progressive* because it was the educational theory of progressive movements in United States history; it is called *pragmatism* because it is within the pragmatic tradition of American philosophy. It is also described as *experimentalism* because of the emphasis it places on experience and science. Finally, at times it is referred to as *instrumentalism* since it sees ideas as instruments of action.

Dewey's philosophy has been the most influential one in United States educational history. Some aspect of his thought will be addressed in almost every chapter of this book. In this chapter I will treat his criticisms of classical realism and liberal education. More importantly, his own approach to the education of the mind will be presented. In Dewey, however, it is even more difficult than in the case of other philosophers to separate the different forms of education: intellectual, moral, physical, and aesthetic, since his philosophy was developed precisely to break down the barriers which classical realism and liberal education had established. Notwithstanding this difficulty, it is still possible and indeed essential, to deal with the distinctive approach he takes to what we are calling intellectual education, education of the mind.

Dewey's criticism of classical realism

Dewey notes that classical realism was based on the premise that reason is superior to experience. In his analysis Greek philosophy arose in an attempt to arrive at a form of knowledge for guiding human behavior which was superior to custom and tradition. Its starting point was that rational intelligence was superior to habit, appetite, custom, impulse, and emotion in human affairs. Reason was considered a power or faculty of the person by which universal essences could be known. The Greeks thus introduced a distrust for empirical knowledge because this knowledge was not based on principles but rather on trial and error attempts to know. Reason enables us to know the immaterial, the ideal, and the spiritual; through empirical knowledge we know only what is sensual, carnal, material, and worldly. Dewey notes that for the Greeks the field of practice was identified with empirical knowledge since it includes dimensions of change, chance, and diversity. Dewey further adds that medieval philosophy both accepted this position and made an important addition to it. Medieval Christian philosophy contended that reason at its highest stages, called contemplation, could know God, the highest reality, and that this knowledge of God affords the greatest possible human knowledge in comparison to which all other knowledge is mundane, profane, and secular (Dewey 1916, ch. 20).

From this analysis of classical realism Dewey arrived at the conclusion that many of the educational ills of his time resulted from an adherence to this separation of rational knowledge from empirical knowledge. For him classical realism led to

The contempt for physical as compared with mathematical and logical science, for the senses and sense observation the feeling that knowledge is high and worthy in the degree in which it deals with ideal symbols instead of with the concrete; the scorn of particulars except as they are deductively brought under a universal; the disregard for the body; the depreciation of arts and crafts as intellectual instrumentalities. (1916, p. 266)

Critique of empiricism

Dewey contrasts his theory of experimentalism with the Enlightenment theory of empiricism which rejected the rational theory of knowledge presented in classical realism. For the empiricists appeals to reason and universal principles were considered obstacles to the development of thought and human progress. They contended that it was through sense observation and experience that we learned what was truly valuable. This appeal to experience could be used to challenge all authorities, intellectual and political. In empiricism experience became something intellectual and cognitive. Practice became something added on to our knowledge. Dewey criticizes the empirical theory of knowledge for leading to the view that the mind is essentially passive and receptive because the theory identified knowledge with the reception and association of sensory impressions. In its extreme form this theory reduced all powers of the mind to impressions from outside the person knowing. This radical empirical view is the intellectual sire of modern radical behaviorism as found in Skinner's operant conditioning. What Dewey rejected most in this theory was its lack of attention to active thinking on the part of the knower.

Dewey rejected this theory for offering merely destructive criticisms and not offering a constructive approach to knowledge. While he applauded empiricism's emphasis on immediate experience, he decried the limited range of the experiences included in the empiricist's purview. The theory in his view restricted knowledge to particulars and did not attend to the meaning and symbolic dimension of human knowing. For mind essentially meant responsiveness to meanings and experiences, activities persons engaged in, not impressions received from the outside.

For these reasons Dewey does not see how empiricism can function as the basis for a theory of learning and education. The theory did lead to more attention to direct experience of objects, use of pictures and graphic descriptions and thus decreased the utilization of a purely verbal education. Yet it did not go far enough to focus educational efforts on the active efforts of students.

Dewey's experimentalism

Dewey's theory of experimentalism is an attempt to find a middle way between the empirical explanation of knowledge as the reception of outside stimuli and the rationalist explanation of knowledge as either innate or abstracted from reality. It was only in finding this middle way could we arrive at a theory of knowing which did not lead to the dualisms between theory and practice, activity and passivity, learning as a body of knowledge and learning as an activity, and intellect and emotions.

Dewey's notion of experience as essentially an activity is the key to understanding his theory of knowing. Dewey uses two examples to explain his notion of experience. An observation of children learning brings out that they learn by doing. They react to outside stimuli by their own efforts to see what will happen to the objects they have perceived. Children learn what they might expect from things if they do such and such to them. Thus they learn the connections among things. If something happens, they are able to modify their behavior.

The other example that Dewey gives of experience, one that predominates in his writings, is the experience of the scientist. The experimental method of the scientist becomes for Dewey the way to understand human experience. Scientists learn not from reason above experience but from experience itself. Sense perceptions give rise to hypotheses or theories; the hypotheses are tested by gathering additional information from experience. In his view knowledge is best understood as the process of "instituting, conducting, and interpreting experimental inquiries and formulating their results" (Dewey 1916, p. 273).

The experimental theory of knowledge is thus based on a combination of empiricist and rational elements. Experience and rational processes are combined to form knowledge which is the product of the activity of the human mind upon the data of experience. Thus Dewey attempts to combine the best elements of rationalism and empiricism in forging his theory of knowledge.

Dewey's approach to intellectual education

Just as the theory of knowledge in classical realism led to a distinctive approach to intellectual education through the liberal arts, so Dewey's theory of knowledge has led to a distinctive approach to intellectual education and its curriculum. Intellectual education for Dewey, as all forms of education, consists in interaction between learner and environment. Education is not learning about other persons' ideas but it is rather developing one's own meanings from interacting with or experimenting with an environment. For Dewey education involves introducing students not into chance activities but into activities selected by teachers with a view to their potential for stimulating learning. By making experience an essential part of all learning Dewey is in a position to reject the dichotomy between intellectual pursuits and practical activities by arguing that "intellectual studies instead of being opposed to active pursuits represent an intellectualizing of practical pursuits" (1916, p. 274).

Dewey was opposed to the view that the education of the young entailed learning bodies of knowledge, called subject matter in educational settings. He argues against the view that subject matter has its own independent existence and that there is any value in itself in mastering subject matter (1916, p. 181). Dewey contends that a knowledge of subject matter has value for teachers because it provides them with standards by which to evaluate the knowledge of the young and enables them to interpret the activities of pupils. Teachers who have a knowledge of organized subject matter possess the valuable fruit of experience, not perfection or infallible wisdom, but a knowledge which can be surpassed in many ways. Committed as he was to an experimental view of knowledge, Dewey stressed that all bodies of knowledge are merely tentative and provisional hypotheses about the world of experience. All knowledge thus is relative and open to disconfirmation.

Subject matter in the education of the young is another matter. In the process of educating, teachers should not be occupied with subject matter but rather with the needs and capacities of children. Children are not to be introduced to preexistent knowledge through the use of textbooks but rather to be encouraged to learn and gain knowledge for themselves through their directed activities. Knowing, first of all, entails a knowing how to do something, learning by doing. Learning that or gathering information is a secondary form of knowledge which is always to be tested by personal activity. Bodies of knowledge are only the recorded learnings of others, which must be tested by our own learnings. Second hand knowledge, other persons' knowing, is only a means of moving us from doubt to discovery.

In adopting the method of science as the method of knowing Dewey committed himself to a specific form of intellectual education. His emphasis in education is more in providing students with the means and methods of learning than it is with initiating them into bodies of learning. Dewey and his followers gave considerable attention to problem solving, project, and activity methods.

My discussion of Dewey's approach to intellectual education thus far is based on his classic work, *Democracy and Education* (1916). By the time he published *Experience and Education* (1938), his short restatement of progressive education in the light of two decades of criticisms, distortions, and misunderstandings, he recognized that "the weakest point in progressive schools is in the matter of selection and organization of intellectual subject matter" (p. 78). Although he viewed this problem as an inevitable result of moving from a rigid curriculum to one based on student interests and needs, he still judged that progressive schools had failed in the matter of dealing with subject matter. Notwithstanding this observation, Dewey does not change his basic position in his contention that "the organized subject matter of the adult and the specialist cannot provide the starting point. . . . It represents the goal toward which education should continually move" (p. 83).

It is important to remember that in his writings on education Dewey almost exclusively addressed the situation of primary education. When Dewey addressed higher education, for example, the education of teachers, he stressed the importance of subject matter. Yet his theory of knowledge or subject matter is still one opposed to the rationalist's view and based ultimately on experience.

Criticism of Dewey's Approach to Intellectual Education

Experimentalism as a basis for philosophy has received considerable criticism for most of this century. Some liberal and rationalist educators have criticized Dewey's rejection of moral and intellectual absolutes. His naturalist philosophy has come under attack from religious philosophers for its rejection of distinctive spiritual realities. In his quest for unity and continuity he has blurred many important distinctions. The charge has been made that despite his attempt to offer a new theory of knowing, what he ends up with is a theory that is actually anti-intelligence and anti-intellectual.

Dewey can be faulted for basing his theory of knowledge merely on the scientific mode of knowing. Science is the paramount example he gives in discussing every major educational issue. This is understandable given the age of science in which he was writing. Although Dewey made valid criticisms of humanistic scholars in literature, philosophy, history, and religion, he neglected to treat adequately the distinctive methods and contributions of these disciplines. There is also truth in the complaint that Dewey has replaced the fixity of ideas, which he rejected in the traditional disciplines, with the fixity of problems which is found in the sciences.

No subject in the rationalist curriculum approaches the importance of history. Thus Dewey's approach to history is critical to understanding his theory and that of his opponents. For Dewey history is to be brought into the curriculum only if it could help solve present problems. For him history was history of the present, for historical inquiry is to be controlled by the problems and conceptions of the present culture. Dewey here confuses the role of the historian with that of the social reformer. Dewey himself selected the economic, industrial, and political aspects of history to support his views of the direction society should take.

While many historians have been sympathetic to this view, many others take issue with it and consider the past as worthwhile for studying in itself. Only by doing this, they contend, can we be sure that if we do want to learn lessons from history, we learn history's lessons and not those that we read into the histories of the past. Considered as subject matter, it is difficult to see how history can be brought into the curriculum in quite the experimental manner in which science is taught.

Dewey's concentration on science as the mode of knowing also led to his depreciation of the life of the spirit and contemplation. Even philosophy was justified in his view in so far as it was a tool of social diagnosis and social progress. He was even wary about the teaching of literature because it was a subject through which a literary, elite, and aristocratic class dominated American culture. He justified the subject in the curriculum only if it were connected with social studies and thus contributed to an understanding of contemporary problems. Dewey came to the point of seeing as futile all human endeavors which were not commonly shared activities directed at social betterment. The over-evaluation of social and political life left him unprepared to appreciate the intrinsic and even instrumental values of the life of the spirit and imagination. While in his artistic theory he recognized the value of what he calls consummatory experiences, his educational theory has little place for this view.

Dewey's theory of knowledge and his theory of education seem to be driven by the single-mindedness of the social reformer. While he was keen in showing the social origins of earlier theories of education in class systems, he seems somewhat unaware of the particular ideology or belief system which shaped his own thinking: an age in which there was an exaggerated belief in education's ability to bring about social reform and progress. When all knowledge and every theory of education is judged by this sole perspective, we have the distortions found in Dewey's philosophy of education.

CONTEMPORARY DEBATE ON INTELLECTUAL EDUCATION

Lest we think that the debate between Dewey and the proponents of a classical version of liberal education is long over, we need only review the debate over intellectual education in the curriculum in the past decade.

Today we are witnessing another debate over what form intellectual education should take, with classical realism or rationalism and Dewey's pragmatic experimentalism still centers of debate. Among the many criticisms of our schools today a predominant one decries the lack of rigorous intellectual education. These criticisms have been made of all levels of education in the United States. One proposal which has again been presented is a return to a rigorous intellectual and liberal education. This has been voiced by some scholars and educators as well as by political figures such as former Commissioner of Education William Bennett.

Though some attention has been paid to education in the schools in this debate, the colleges have come under the most criticisms. Critics such as Allan Bloom and E. Hirsch have decried the lack of cultural literacy among today's college students. Studies have detailed not only deficiencies in mathematics and science, which by now are largely accepted, but also lack of basic knowledge in the humanities.

The book which has received most attention and debate at this time is Allan Bloom's *The Closing of the American Mind: How Higher Education Has Failed Democracy and Impoverished the Souls of Today's Students* (1987). Bloom brings an important philosophical base to today's criticism. He argues for the reinstitution of a liberal education which he feels has been eroded by the liberalism of educators such as John Dewey. Bloom is one of the latest scholars to blame pragmatism and the liberalism to which it is connected for the ills of American education. His extensive use of Plato in his argument shows that the classical position is not dead, despite the many criticisms it has received over the years. The best seller status of the book and the widespread debate it engendered also support this position.

Bloom begins his tirade against progressive education by rejecting philosophical relativism, which is a central conclusion of pragmatism. He more strongly rejects the cultural relativism which is implied in this philosophy. He rejects the education of openness that does not accept natural rights which transcend class, race, religion, national origin, and culture. This philosophy of openness is open to all ideologies since it lacks shared goals and visions of the public good. Bloom traces this philosophy directly to the ideas of John Stuart Mill and John Dewey (p. 29). He contends that it was Dewey's pragmatism that undermined the American democracy established by the Founders (p. 56). The Founders were more indebted to the pre-Enlightenment thought of Locke and Hobbes. Bloom also puts a great deal of blame on American intellectuals who have subscribed to the value relativism of German scholars such as Nietszche, Weber, and Freud. Bloom is especially incensed that the pro-

gressives' fudging of the distinction between liberal and technical education has led to the fact that we consider a person educated who is a computer specialist even though he or she has no knowledge of morals, politics, and religion (p. 59).

Bloom pits the progressives' relativism and openness against the Founders' commitment to common visions, rights, and goals. He notes with
regret the fact that philosophy and religion are not required subjects in
many colleges while courses in non-Western cultures (which he deems all
ethnocentric) are increasingly required (p. 36). The universalism of
Greek philosophy, especially that of Plato, is deemed superior to non-
Western thought. He especially decries the disappearance of religion because of its influence in shaping the moral character of the nation (p. 56).

Bloom's commitment to academic rationalism is shown in his embracing the educational philosophy behind the Great Books program, one of
the main examples of intellectual liberal education in our time. He accepts its conviction that "nature is the only thing that counts in education, the the human desire to know is permanent, that all it really needs
is the proper nourishment, and that education is merely putting the feast
on the table" (p. 51). Bloom eloquently argues that

> A life based on the Book is closer to the truth, that it provides the material
> for deeper research in and access to the real nature of things. Without the
> great revelations, epics and philosophies as part of our natural vision, there
> is nothing to see out there, and eventually little left inside. The Bible is not
> the only means to furnish a mind, but without a book of similar gravity,
> read with the gravity of the potential believer, it will remain unfurnished.
> (p. 60)

Bloom is especially interested in the value of Books as intellectual
tools for promoting moral education and condemns such soft programs
as values clarification for their lack of substantial values. (A fuller discussion of moral education will take place in a later chapter.) Bloom is critical of softer forms of education (sentimental education) which focus on
relationships since these forms, together with contemporary music, ruin
the imagination of the young and "make it very difficult for them to have
a passionate relationship to the art and thought that are the substance of
liberal education" (p. 79).

The university is the institution that Bloom is most interested in reforming according to the philosophy of liberal education. For him the university

> Is the place where inquiry and philosophic openness come into their own. It is intended to encourage the noninstrumental use of reason for its own sake, to provide the atmosphere where the moral and physical superiority of the dominant will not intimidate philosophic doubt. And it preserves the treasury of great deeds, great men and great thoughts required to nourish that doubt. (p. 249)

Set within the American democracy, the university must remain critical of the present regime. It should avoid sycophancy toward those in power. It must avoid and keep distance from the democratic concentration on the useful. It is to be interested in things in themselves. The universities are to preserve the standards of the past but be open to new ideas if they meet those standards. For Bloom it appears that the ages of great spirituality are past and we are well served by them. He notes that

> The Bible and Homer exercised their influence for thousands of years, preserved in the mainstream or in backwaters, hardly ever being surpassed in power, without becoming irrelevant because they did not suit the temper of the times or the spirit of a regime. They provided the way out as well as the model of reform. (p. 252)

Having argued for the task of the university, Bloom details how it should go about carrying this out. It is to raise the permanent questions by keeping alive the works of those who addressed these questions. Bloom does not advocate blind following of past authorities for he places the essence of philosophy in the "abandonment of all authority in favor of individual human reason" (p. 253). The university might not know the answers but it does know the questions. The curriculum of the university is philosophy, theology, literary classics, and scientific classics written by Newton, Descartes and Leibnitz.

It is Bloom's contention that at the university level there is an unwillingness to think about the contents of a liberal education since a democracy of tasters and opinions has been permitted. He states that "there is no vision, nor is there a set of competing visions, of what an educated human being is" (p. 337). Not even the question is allowed. No claims of superiority of one discipline over the other are accepted. Even great universities cannot come up with a modest program of general education for its undergraduates. Bloom, as was mentioned earlier, argues for a Great Books approach in which classic texts are allowed to speak to us, ask us questions, involve us in their methods of inquiry. He decries the fact that the humanities, social sciences, and natural sciences do not take the Great Books approach. Without such an approach the university lacks first principles, coherence, a unified view of nature and our place in it.

Paideia Proposal

Before proceeding to the criticism of intellectual liberal education which has focused specifically around Bloom's book, I will describe a number of other approaches to intellectual and liberal education which have come to be associated with this revival of intellectual education through liberal education. These proposals focus on the first twelve years of schooling.

The *Paideia Proposal* (Adler, 1982), created by a nationally known groups of educators, has presented a plan for a strong intellectual education which incorporates the essentials of a liberal education. The proposal, however, does include a number of ideas from John Dewey, to whom, together with Horace Mann and Robert Hutchins, the book is dedicated. Similar to Bloom's treatise, this proposal takes as its starting point the need to strengthen American democracy. While it recognizes that education is lifelong, it focuses almost exclusively on the public school.

Public schooling, according to the proposal, has a threefold task: (1) personal growth or self-improvement through mental, moral, and spiritual growth; (2) preparation for the duties and responsibilities of citizens; (3) providing students with the basic skills common to all work (not training for a particular job). To accomplish this, education must be general and liberal as well as nonspecialized and nonvocational. The liberal approach dominates this work in its criticisms of vocationalism in public schooling, that is, training for particular jobs.

The proposal advocates one curriculum for all, a liberal and general one. All electives (except for the particular foreign language one wants to study) and specialized courses are to be eliminated. The proposal describes the three modes of teaching and learning which can be employed in school education.

The first mode, the acquisition of organized knowledge, is accomplished by means of didactic instruction, lectures, and responses. It makes use of textbooks and other aids and is appropriate in three areas of subject matter: language, literature and the fine arts; mathematics and natural science; history, geography and social sciences.

The second mode, the development of intellectual skills, takes place by means of coaching, exercises, and supervised practice. This mode operates in the teaching and learning of reading, writing, speaking, listening, calculating, problem solving, observing, measuring, estimating, and critical judgment.

The third mode, enlarged understanding of ideas and values, takes place by means of maieutic or Socratic questioning and active participation. It is used in the discussion of books (not textbooks) and other works of art and involvement in artistic activities, for example, music, drama, and visual arts.

A number of auxiliary subjects are also proposed for the curriculum: physical education, manual activities, and instruction in finding a career.

Cultural literacy

A call for an intellectual liberal education is at the heart of E. D. Hirsch's (1987) proposal for cultural literacy as the chief goal of education. What Hirsch, a professor of language, proposes is a form of literary humanism, one that does not directly depend on metaphysics. Rather than presenting a list of books, he presents a descriptive list of information actually possessed by literate Americans. He proposes an anthropological theory of education since it is based on the anthropological observation that all human communities are founded on specific shared information (p. xiv–xv). The basic goal of education in this perspective is "acculturation, the transmission to children of the specific information shared by adults of the group or polis" (p. xvi). This theory accepts the naturalness as well as the relativity of cultures. Thus it differs from the traditional liberal arts approach which focuses on truths that transcend cultures.

Cultural literacy is the network of information that all competent readers possess. It is the background information stored in the minds that enables them to read newspapers in an intelligent manner (p. 2). This knowledge lies "*above* the everyday levels of knowledge that everyone possesses and *below* the expert level known only to specialists" (p.

19). Hirsch argues that cultural literacy is necessary for social and economic life as well as for citizenship (p. 22). Basic cultural literacy should
be achieved by age thirteen (p. 30).

Hirsch indicts the schools for failing to transmit the cultural heritage
of the nation. He places the blame on the progressives who espoused philosophies of natural development (Rousseau) and pragmatism (Dewey).
While rejecting Dewey's contention than early education need not be
content specific, he recognizes that Dewey set forth the goal of cultural
literacy to be achieved through different methods. He rejects what he
considers the content neutral ideas of Dewey and Rousseau (p. 19).

Hirsch argues that the turning point in American education against a
content-centered education was the adoption of the *Cardinal Principles
of Education* in 1918. This document shifted from subject matter to social adjustment by adopting as the goals of education: health, command
of fundamental processes, worthy home membership, vocation, citizenship, worthy use of leisure time, and ethical character. The origins of
these ideas lie in the philosophies of Rousseau and Dewey. This document represented the triumph of progressive education. Thus practical
educational goals replaced the traditional emphasis on subject matter.

While Hirsch sides against the traditionalists who contended that the
wisdom of the West holds all there is to transmit, he also sides against
the pragmatists for their emphasis on the individual and their notion of
social utility. He is against the narrowness of the former and the excessive openness of the latter. He argues for a compromise, "a curriculum
that is traditional in content but diverse in emphases, that is pluralistic
in its materials and mode of teaching but nonetheless provides our children with a common core of cultural information" (pp. 126–127).
Hirsch is opposed both to the back to basics movement and the critical
thinking movement, the former because of its lack of depth and the latter
for its ignoring of specific content. He sees in these two movements a
polarization between those who stress facts and those who stress skills.

To these contemporary articulations of intellectual education through
liberal arts education can be added the proposals and writings of William
Bennett, former Commissioner of Education in the Reagan administration. A former philosophy professor, Bennett made clear what he thought
were the failings of American schools. The writings of these so called
cultural conservatives, together with writings of Diane Ravitch and
Chester Finn, have set the parameters of the educational debate in today's
America. An examination of the debate between these writers and critics

of liberal and radical persuasion goes a long way toward defining the intellectual grounding of intellectual or academic education.

Conclusion: The Current Debate

In debating educational issues Americans often raise questions which go far beyond education. The debate over liberal education today is a debate over the meaning of American democracy, the future direction of our economy, the values which we want to transmit to our children, and the emerging new pluralism which we are facing. It is also a debate about the United States' position in the world.

The hegemony of Western culture

The chief dimension of the debate is the issue of Western Culture. Cultural conservatives, to a greater or less degree, argue that the books and ideas of Western civilization should continue to form the intellectual basis of curriculum in schools and colleges. To be educated for life in this democratic society means to be familiar with these books and ideas. Bloom, the strongest proponent of this viewpoint, views the abandonment of this legacy as one of the main reasons for our failed American democracy. For him these ideas are given special status in the thought and writings of the founders of this country which form the basis of our political system. Bloom has been in the forefront of those who have resisted the introduction of non-Western books to a central place in American curriculum. Bloom and others decry the cultural relativism that finds a place in schools and colleges. The practical demonstrations of the debate are the bitter struggles on college campuses over what books are to be required reading, over the continuance of courses on Western Civilization, and to a neglect of the classics of Western thought.

Many scholars and educators have opposed the cultural conservatives on this fundamental issue. They argue against the concept of a Western canon. For them the existence of such a canon is a manifestation of the very ethnocentrism that Bloom charges as characteristics of Eastern thought systems. Furthermore, critics have noted that the classic writings of the West have usually excluded writings by women and persons of color. In the type of society which we are becoming and in the type of world that is emerging education needs to have an openness, they argue, to the thought and culture of all peoples. To do this the curriculum of the schools must include the emerging cultural realities of this world.

The problem with the cultural conservatives such as Bloom is that they tend to see things in terms of either/or. The problem with the critics is that they do not first affirm what is of value in the position of the cultural conservatives. There is a tension between the particular and the universal. The distinctive value of our particular Western tradition must be affirmed as well as the values of a more universal world culture. In education just as in politics, economics, and social life there will be tensions between these two tendencies. There seems to be little evidence to justify the strident tones of the cultural conservatives laments over the ignoring of Western thought.

Equity and equality

The cultural conservatives have raised again the issue of equity and equality in American education. Although this tension confronts every democratic society, in times of cultural crisis it becomes more pronounced. It is no accident that the conservative Reagan and Bush administrations fostered through their Department of Education views which are both economically and culturally conservative. The cultural conservatives are critical of the quality of American education. They have pointed to many national studies and reports which document the inferior status of American education. Their concern is to bring an element of excellence to this educational endeavor. This effort includes many reforms of a political, social and organizational nature. What concerns us in this chapter is the philosophical basis for these proposals.

The conservatives contend that a strong intellectual education through liberal studies is the best way of achieving excellence in the curriculum. Generally, they believe that all persons are capable of this education.

Their critics argue that the cultural conservatives in pursuing goals of excellence actually present what amounts to an elitist and aristocratic education which serves the needs of few persons in our society. While they admit that all persons should receive elements of a liberal education, they contend that the narrow way in which the conservatives describe this education makes much of it irrelevant to the needs of students in this world.

A democratic society will need to be concerned with both excellence and equity, even though limited resources often entail conflicts between these goals. The history of American education, even of the country in general, reveals this as a major issue in education as well as in public policy. Although the *Paideia Proposal* appears to strike the best balance in this matter, it too may not have faced up to the realities of educational abilities and needs in many parts of the country.

A democracy needs an educated citizenry and an educated leadership. It needs both managers and workers. In some ways the education of these groups will be similar. In other ways there will be substantial differences. No one approach to educational curriculum will meet the needs of both groups. Goals of excellence and equity must be balanced. Excellence as a goal recognizes the abilities of all and the needs of the country. The goal of equity forces us to focus on the injustices that continue to exist in even the best educational systems.

Education for its own sake or for social utility

The debate over the intellectual content of the curriculum raises the perennial issue of the ultimate goal of education. Those who argue for the liberal arts approach see education as its own goal in the sense that the educational processes are valuable for persons or that the content has intrinsic value. Though it is debatable whether such a purist position is realistic, it is clear that liberal intellectual advocates oppose any political, industrial, or social goal being considered as a primary purpose of education. They present certain truths or certain books as having intrinsic value and particular education processes as memorizing, discussing, and questioning, as valuable. Cultural conservatives argue that education should not be used to serve direct political purposes other than to educate a citizenry and should not be directly used to advance particular political causes. Certainly it should not be used to provide workers for the economy. Specialized forms of education can be used to promote these goals of education but the schools and the colleges should remain distant from them.

The critics contend that such neutral education is not possible, especially in the political area. They accept the basic axiom of Paulo Freire (1970) that neutrality in education is impossible, for education either liberates or domesticates. It is their contention that political values are included in the type of intellectual education which conservatives promote. This education provides a justification for the existing political arrangements and does not encourage the necessary criticism which this education should receive. They especially charge Bloom with presenting a specific political justification under the guise of neutrality.

Critics also do not accept the arguments of those who want to exclude vocational or manual education from serious consideration in the school curriculum. Educational systems do not exist in a vacuum; they serve social and public purposes. Society's large investment in the schools is directed not only at individual goals but also social goals and these include industrial goals. One of the points of genius in the American comprehensive school is that it has attempted to achieve a number of individual and social goals. While there is no doubt that there have been injustices in the way this vision has been realized, this does not mean that the vision is not worthwhile.

It is doubtful whether learning for the sake of learning can ever be a motivating goal for a large number of people, except for those in later years of life. The ideal of education for its own sake was not even a goal for Greek philosophers who made a connection between the life of the mind and the life of action. Greek philosophers connected education with the moral life of individuals and the political and moral life of the polis. Even Plato saw the formation of the philosopher-king as the ultimate goal of education. John Newman in his *Idea of a University* (1960) propounded the view of knowledge for the sake of knowledge as the proper goal of the university. Yet it is to be remembered that he was thinking of the education of gentlemen in the British Isles, a small part of the population. Although part of all persons' education should include studies pursued for their own sake, all knowledge has practical bearing and purposes.

The liberal position has value in that it points out the dangers of an excessive vocationalism in education which subordinates individual goals to the goals of industrial society. Yet a necessary process in education is to prepare persons for democratic and industrial life. Proponents of liberal education are often unrealistic in proclaiming the purely individualist goals of education at the expense of its social goals. We must never forget that the origins of liberal education lie in societies in which this education was made possible because of the existence of a laboring class. This education has prevailed in countries in which there exists a great distinction between those who rule and those who are ruled.

Notwithstanding this, there is great importance in the stress in such documents as the *Paideia Proposal* that a strong intellectual education through the traditional liberal studies be offered to all persons in society. What cannot be accepted is the view that this is the only education of importance to be presented in schools and colleges. A strong case can be made for other forms of education to be included as important dimensions of general and specialized education.

Cultural literacy or critical thinking

There are two different emphases in the present debate over intellectual education: cultural literacy and critical thinking. Though it is obvious that education should promote both of these goals, two different camps have emerged. The position of those who argue for a cultural literacy has been made. The centrality of cultural literacy is established by arguments asserting its importance in maintaining the values of Western civilization and of American democracy. Such a literacy is needed to function in this particular society and culture. Only such an education given to all citizens guarantees the type of people who can participate in democratic processes. The failure of many to achieve this literacy means that they will not be able to read intelligently and thus be prepared for social, political, and economic life.

Those who espouse cultural literacy as the overall goal of intellectual education contend that extensive focus on developing critical thinking will leave students without basic knowledge and information on which to think critically or to exercise their higher order skills.

Proponents of critical thinking as a primary focus in education draw their inspiration from Dewey's work on how we think. This movement represents an attempt to go beyond a knowledge of the basics and to foster such intellectual processes as observing, questioning, hypothesizing, analyzing, and synthesizing. What is foremost in this approach is not so much what is learned but how students approach facts and information. It is contended that if persons learn to think critically they will be better prepared for a future in which there is to be an increasing amount of information and in which new information will replace old information. The critical thinking literature also makes its argument on the basis of the value of a more participative methodology leading to a better and deeper grasp of principles.

Like the previous issues this debate has been rehearsed in educational circles for many years (Kliebard, 1987). One obvious solution to the issue is to say that we are to do both. The *Paideia Proposal* does this as do other proponents of intellectual education through liberal studies. Dewey also contended that the teacher had to engage children in processes which would lead to a knowledge of subject matter. But the main question may be the important one of the starting point and the ultimate goal in the educational process. For cultural conservatives the literate culture is the starting point and the central focus. For critical thinking advocates it is the engagement of students in certain mental processes that is the starting point and ultimate goal.

My view is that this debate continues because it can never be resolved. There is no one solution; there is not one educational theory in this area. One's major focus is determined in many cases by the stage of development of the students, what the subject is, and what the previous learning of students is in the particular area. I have found myself teaching from both perspectives depending on these and other factors. Also in the same course I have shifted from one perspective to the other. I see the value in both positions. In lecturing on history my tendency is to favor a cultural literacy orientation; in philosophy it is primarily to engage students in critical and analytic thinking. Though I recognize that the choice of starting point and ultimate goal is of importance, I believe that good educational practice (and theory) means making wise choices in particular situations.

When one moves to the theoretical level of arguing the merits of the one approach over the other the dominant issue might be an understanding of the present movement in educational history. Because both viewpoints have extreme expressions—process at all cost or product at all cost—what develops are curricular movements to counter or correct the extremes of past reforms. Dewey and his colleagues strongly opposed the classical and formalistic curriculum which had dominated the schools and colleges since the beginnings of education in this country. The excesses of progressivism were in turn subjected to the criticisms of liberal educators. At the present time both movements are reacting to the simplistic back to the basics movements which have dominated educational thinking for a number of years.

Conservatism, liberalism, radicalism

The arguments over intellectual liberal education in our time, as in previous eras, is not merely a debate over educational theory and practice. It is also a profound social, political, and economic debate. The debate began in the years of the Reagan administration and will no doubt continue throughout the nineties. This debate was prepared for by the events of previous decades. The 1960s saw the triumph of a neoprogressivism in education with alternative schools, open classrooms, elective system in colleges, introduction of special studies (Black, Women, Third World), integration efforts, and other educational reforms. This reform movement was followed by a period of retrenchment for economic reasons. Little by little in the 1970s the educational reforms of the 1960s were abandoned or modified. There was a movement back to the basics in the schools and efforts to establish core curricula at colleges and universities. By the 1980s there appeared a full scale critique of educational developments in the recent past and the full articulation of the liberal education position of cultural conservatives.

It is significant that the position of cultural conservatives is championed by one of the most vocal members of the Reagan Administration, Secretary of Education William Bennett. The educational reforms were intended to address social, political, and economic problems. The cultural conservatives felt that the American social system was challenged by education which focused on the values of particular groups within the nation. They proposed a liberal education that would teach common core values which transcended particular subcultures and which would bind the nation together. The American political system would be strengthened by a curriculum which stressed studies of history and politics. But the major concern of conservatives at this time is to use education as a way of dealing with perceived economic problems in the country. Many studies in the eighties documented the failure of the schools to prepare students for the very competitive market in which the United States now found itself, especially vis-a-vis Japan. What was called for was a stronger general intellectual education as a preparation for a specialized education. (It is interesting to note that two other educational reform movements in the United States were set off by negative comparisons of our achievements with Germany in late nineteenth century and Russia in mid-twentieth century.)

The critics of the position of cultural conservatives are fundamentally in opposition to the political, economic, and social agenda of Reagan-Bush administrations. These differences will be spelled out in latter chapters which treat explicitly the political, social, and economic aspects of education. As to educational policy, they argue that a curriculum which does not treat seriously the different cultures of the world does not serve national and international life well. They argue that the type of intellectual education proposed by conservatives will heighten class, racial, and cultural tensions. They further argue that education must not be tied too closely to the purposes of the national state, otherwise the country might lose an important source of social criticism. They also argue for more caution in connecting schools with the needs and demands of corporate America.

Because these matters will be treated in latter chapters no full assessment is presented at this time. I have entered into this argument to emphasize again the interconnectedness of all aspects of education. There is, as I have noted, something arbitrary in the divisions of this work.

It is easy to say that there is some truth on both sides of this argument but such is the case. We are at a particular juncture in history with major changes in many parts of the world. It is understandable that many in this time of great change would want to focus on stability in all areas, including education. But periods of change demand bold and risk-taking activities. Preferred approaches to education thus should be those which do not attempt to retreat to the past but which while recognizing past values attempt to meet present challenges and needs.

CHAPTER 3

MORAL EDUCATION

At the present time there is an increased interest in moral education in our country. This interest takes many different forms and has various motivations. There are calls for moral education or values education in public schools. Some states have developed curricula for introducing moral education into the schools. Professional schools such as business, law, medicine, engineering, and education have introduced courses in the ethics of the professions. Motivations range from a concern for the moral stability of our country, to inculcating a particular moral ethic, and to dealing seriously with moral issues in a pluralistic society.

Since antiquity the development of the moral or virtuous person has been a primary aim of education. It can be argued that this is even a prior purpose to intellectual or other forms of education. What a society wants to hand on, what it wants its young to learn are its ways of living, what it holds as most worthwhile and valuable. It wants the young to accept and live by the values which currently maintain society in existence. The maintenance of the life of a particular society demands the acceptance of moral values by a majority of its citizens and the guidance of one's actions by these values. If values are not accepted and ascribed to, chaos and lawlessness will result and the society will not be able to continue in existence.

All philosophers of education treat in one way or another the moral aim of education since all are interested in either analyzing or presenting a viewpoint on what makes good persons and a good society. Not all these viewpoints can be examined in this chapter. I plan to follow in general the strategy proposed in the first chapter. First, I will treat the classic position in this field, as well as its development, contemporary restatement, and challenges. The second section of the chapter will review current debates among philosophers of education and outline a number of approaches that are proposed.

HISTORICAL PERSPECTIVES ON MORAL EDUCATION

The Classical Position

The classical position, which was first enunciated by Greek philosophers, was further developed by early Christian educators, and has found adherents and advocates in every age. This position emphasizes the importance of rationality and virtue. It possesses a clear view of what the good person is and what constitutes the good society.

Greek Philosophy

The classical position centers around the question Socrates raised in the *Meno*: Can virtue be taught? In arguing with the Sophists, the rhetoricians of Greece, Socrates contended that they did not teach virtues but only the skills of public speaking and debate because their interest was in the training of politicians and statesmen. Socrates charged the Sophists with not even knowing how to define virtue, demonstrated by the fact that they could not properly respond to his questions.

For Socrates the common element in all virtues is knowledge. To be virtuous a person has to know more than the norms and standards of conduct. To be truly schooled in virtue persons have to act in such a way that the standards of the good, true, and beautiful become part of their decision-making conduct. These standards should be intellectually accepted and adhered to because persons recognize their rightness and not because of any social pressure.

In Plato's dialogues four methods are proposed for making persons moral or virtuous. First, students were to be given frequent and pointed *exhortations* to become virtuous. In the *Apology*, Socrates says:

Men of Athens . . . while I have life and strength I shall never cease from the practice and teaching of philosophy, exhorting any one whom I meet and saying to him after my manner: You, my friend . . . are you not ashamed of heaping up the greatest amount of money and honor and reputation, and caring so little about wisdom and truth and the greatest improvement of the soul, which you never regard at all. (In Broudy and Palmer, 1965, p. 33)

Socrates continuously exhorted his listeners to be concerned about the state of their souls or inner persons. He often used irony and enigmatic statements to do this, devices at which he was a master. He considered himself a gadfly to all those who were satisfied with themselves and who were unwilling to question the accepted norms of society.

Socrates' second method of moral education was engaging disciples in *dialectical self-examination*. He usually began by posing a question for which the disciple was certain to have an answer. Socrates, however, through extensive questioning convinced the disciple that he did not know the answer at all and in fact did not even know the definition of the essential terms of the question. Once the disciple admitted ignorance, he was deemed by Socrates ready for a positive examination of the concept and what it entailed in everyday practice.

Third, Socrates contended that through *self-discipline* and self-mastery pupils were to build up a system of value principles and priorities that constituted the healthy soul. In the schema presented in the *Republic* the power of reason, which constitutes wisdom, is to rule in all choices. Desire for gratification is to be subordinated to reason through the virtue of temperance. The function of reason is to enable a person to have courage, the virtue which is to be manifested in how persons act in the face of danger. The harmonious functioning of the various parts of the person (emotions, intellect, and will) and the harmonious functioning of the various parts of the state (rulers, military, slaves, etc.) constitute justice for the individual and for the state.

In Platonic moral theory the young are to be conditioned or trained through these disciplines in such a way that when they are older they will see the intellectual justification for such conditioning and constant reinforcement, including the use of punishment when they fail to be virtuous. This conditioning is to be carried out by all components of the culture: nurses, teachers, music, and stories. Because educators possessed correct standards of right and wrong, they were in Plato's view justified in imposing standards on the young. These absolute norms were innate within persons, perhaps learned in a former existence, and were to be recalled through a process of careful questioning at the hands of skilled teachers.

Fourth, moral education is to reach its completion with intellectual training that ended in a study of dialectics. The main method for this training is the *dialectical conversation* or exploration. This conversation is directed at achieving a knowledge of the true essences or definitions of things. For Plato the mind can apprehend the essences or natures of things through a dialectical process. Mathematics is important in this process because it prepares persons to deal with abstractions. Dialectics gives a knowledge of the way things are and not just of appearances. Plato's famous Allegory of the Cave describes the painful process by which a person is freed from the bondage of false and doubtful opinions and arrives at a true knowledge of reality.

Plato saw moral significance in many educational activities which we tend to view as separate from the moral sphere. He saw moral significance in sports, especially when a competitive spirit was avoided. Sport for him was connected with hygiene. Early education for Plato was made up of gymnastics for the body and music for the soul. Dancing as controlled movement was also viewed as promoting moral discipline. Plato, however, was critical of some sports and music for their harmful effects on many people, especially the young. He also condemned poets for their many lies and false statements about the gods. Understandably, for Plato mathematics and philosophy had more value than poetry. In a bit of irony, in the process of condemning the arts Plato reveals how he himself had been thoroughly educated in the poetry and traditions of his people (Marrou, 1956, p. 110). In latter chapters the educational significance of sports and the arts will be explored.

Plato's disciple Aristotle added significantly to the classical tradition. While his *Ethics* describes the form and style of life which are necessary for happiness, his *Politics* details the kinds of institutions which make this life possible. The goal of the ethical life proposed by Aristotle is the achievement of happiness through the careful exercise of rational activities. This exercise of rational activities should result in the acquisition of virtues which Aristotle divides into intellectual virtues (e.g., wisdom, intelligence, and prudence) and moral virtues (e.g., liberality and temperance). While intellectual virtues come from explicit instruction, moral virtues result from habit, or more specifically from moral apprenticeship. In the course of time we become just persons by performing just actions and, if we perform just actions consistently, we are properly called just persons.

Aristotle recognized that there is a paradox involved in these statements: we must perform just actions before we can be called just, but we must be just in order to perform just actions. He resolved this paradox by arguing:

> But the moral virtues we do acquire by first exercising them. . . . We become just by performing just actions, temperate by performing temperate actions, brave by performing brave actions. . . . A difficulty, however, may be raised as to what we mean when we say that we must perform just actions if we are to become just, and temperate actions if we are to become temperate. It may be argued that, if I do what is just and temperate, I am just and temperate already. . . . (In Peters, 1974, p. 36)

Aristotle attempts to resolve the paradox by contending that we become virtuous by performing actions which are virtuous, without, however, having full knowledge of the acts and a deliberate choice of them. Once we form the good disposition then virtuous actions flow from the good disposition which has been created. Aristotle, however, does not deal with the development of moral virtues through the influence of social environments, parental training, and instruction by teachers.

For Aristotle virtue is not inborn but rather a consequence of training. Also, virtues cannot be emotions or capacities because virtues involve making choices, an achievement that is not within the power of emotions or mere capabilities. The Philosopher also distinguishes between voluntary and involuntary actions and contends that we are called virtuous by reason of our voluntary actions. Virtue for Aristotle fundamentally consists in achieving the mean or middle place between two vices. Courage is the mean between the excess or rashness and the deficiency of cowardice. This doctrine has engendered many disputes. It works in some cases but not in all (MacIntyre, 1966, p. 66).

For Aristotle prudence is the keystone of all virtues. It is the virtue of practical intelligence which enables us to apply general principles in particular situations. Without prudence a person cannot be virtuous for prudence enables us to decide how a given principle applies in particular situations. Prudence is connected with the process of deliberation.

Aristotle also gives detailed explanations of the virtues of great-soulness and justice. Furthermore, he distinguishes among the various kinds of justice that have become well known among Western philosophers.

While Plato tended to reduce all virtues to justice, Aristotle sees the moral life as constituted by a number of virtues.

Aristotle was a strong advocate for the development of habits in the moral education of children, though he also recognized that as persons grow older, they must see for themselves the reasons for their actions. Of habit he writes

> But the virtues we get by first exercising them, as also happens in the case of the arts as well. For the things we have to learn before we can do them, we learn by doing them, e.g., men become builders by building . . . ; so do we become just by doing just acts, temperate by doing temperate acts, brave by doing brave acts. This is confirmed by what happens in the State; for legislators make the citizens good by forming habits in them. . . . It makes no small difference then whether we form habits of one kind or another from our very youth; it makes a great difference or rather all the difference. . . . (In Peters, 1974, p. 80)

Aristotle made a number of other important points about habit. He maintained that the power given to us by nature to be virtuous is brought to maturity by habit and that we acquire habits by continual practice. Children are to encouraged to perform virtuous actions and then later in life they will come to understand fully the meaning and reasons for their actions. In later life they will come to understand the why of things.

In summary, the classical position in moral education as presented by the Greeks involves a number of principles. Moral truth like all truth is absolute. There are unchanging moral values, and moral absolutes. Habit is important in the early stages of moral education. Later on in life persons can arrive at a more rational or intellectual approach to the moral life. The moral life consists of developing habits of virtue. In the classical approach a great emphasis is placed on the values of the intellectual life. In reading the treatises of these moral philosophers we recognize how their language and thoughts still shape many of our basic considerations on the moral life.

The Development of the classical tradition

The classical tradition in moral philosophy and moral education has found powerful expression in the work of religious humanists. Christian writers on morality and moral education drew first of all on their religious traditions. Both the Jewish and Christian tradition included a large number of moral exhortations and advice on raising children in a moral fashion. The Jewish scriptures placed a great stress on the law but also focused on the values of love and justice. The Christian scriptures continued these emphases and presented Jesus as the embodiment of the moral and holy life.

As the Christian church came into contact with Greek and Roman thought some Christian teachers and writers attempted to correlate religious faith with secular learning and culture. As Christianity spread into the Greek world and came into contact with Greek philosophy, it attempted to relate its teachings to this thought in order to appeal to the more educated of those who expressed an interest in Christianity. The philosophies of Plato and of the Stoics were utilized by Christian writers to explain Christian teachings and ethics in a rational manner. Although there was no doubt that they regarded religious knowledge as superior to secular wisdom, Christian authors found it useful in their teaching and writings to apply Greek philosophy.

Although Christian writers in the early years made use of Greek and Roman philosophy in developing moral teaching, the high point of the Church's relationship with the classical tradition came in the medieval syntheses of the scholastics. The greatest scholastic philosopher and theologian, Thomas Aquinas, utilized the classic tradition to expound Christian teaching, including the ethical teaching of the Church. In a number of significant ways he transformed the thought of Aristotle. The *theoria* or contemplation of Aristotle became for Aquinas the vision of God which is the final goal and satisfaction for all human desires. Aquinas modified the list of Aristotelian virtues by supplementing them with the religious virtues of faith, hope, charity, religion, and humility. He used Stoic and Hebrew concepts as a framework within which to discuss both the human goals and virtues. Aquinas also contended that the law of nature found in Greek philosophy is completed and perfected by the supernatural law found in revelation. Believing as he did in the basic sinfulness of all persons, he declared that revelation and the special help of God were necessary for living a truly moral life.

Challenges to the classical tradition

The classical approach to moral education, especially as modified and supplemented by religious teachings, went essentially unchallenged by philosophers and educators until the Enlightenment when educators began to place less emphasis on tradition and authority and stressed more the development of the natural capacities of individuals. The appeal to absolute moral standards was considerably muted among Enlightenment thinkers who turned to reason, feeling, and natural intuition to ground moral education.

Jean Jacques Rousseau is representative of Enlightenment philosophers who took issue with the classical approach to moral education. He proposed a radical individualism according to which persons grew morally, as well as in other ways, by natural development, by encounter with things and by encounter with nature rather than by direct attempts to inculcate virtues or absolute truths. According to Rousseau's *Emile* (1956 edition) children will develop morally only if they are free to be themselves, and free to be both creative and spontaneous. Since children are born good, the blame for any evil that they do comes from a corrupt society and not from any innate depravity that religious educators utilized to explain moral wrongdoing. The task of the moral educator is to inculcate moral actions by controlling the environment of children. Although Rousseau's approach begins with natural development, it ends with the controlled environment of modern day behaviorists. His appeal, however, to the power of the example of parents' and teachers' moral guidance resonates with the modeling proposed by behavioristically oriented social learning theorists. Rousseau gave special attention to the moral education of adolescents, favoring an education through a study of history and society.

Moral philosophy since the Enlightenment has developed a number of competing positions and alternatives to the classical position. Utilitarians such as Jeremy Bentham have placed emphasis on the consequences of actions in the determination of moral worth. Deontologists such as Emmanuel Kant have, on the other hand, stressed the importance of the motives of individual actors. In more recent times logical positivists such as A. J. Ayer have reduced ethical statements to emotive or noncognitive statements. All three of these ethical theories have tended to place little or no emphasis on universal and absolute truths in the moral area. The contemporary restatement of the classical position (to be treated next) as well as the pragmatic alternative offered by John Dewey (to be treated later) are all attempts to deal with these attacks on the classical position.

Contemporary restatement of the classical position

The classical position in moral philosophy and education has received a powerful restatement in the work of Alasdair MacIntyre and a group of philosophers and theologians influenced by him. In his magisterial *Af-*

ter Virtue (1984) MacIntyre argued against contemporary theories of moral philosophy by presenting an ethic of virtue and character. His goal is to provide a basis for a shared public justification for morality. This restatement is presented as a way to give intelligibility and rationality to morality.

MacIntyre sets his argument for an ethic of virtue within the context of the moral confusion and debate which characterizes contemporary society and education. His main argument is against emotivist moral theories which reduce moral judgments to personal and thus subjective preference and which deny absolute moral principles. While MacIntyre refuses to find the basis for morality in religious beliefs, Stanley Hauerwas (1981) attempts to utilize MacIntyre's thesis in developing a restatement of the classical tradition which also makes use of religious beliefs.

MacIntyre rejects the Enlightenment attempt to base morality and moral education on a purely rational basis. What all Enlightenment philosophers reject is any view of humans that considers them to have an essence that defines their true end. Where these thinkers failed, according to MacIntyre, was in their attempt to eliminate the notion of what the goal of persons was, a concern which is at the heart of the classical position. In more technical language he charges these modern thinkers with rejecting the theological ethics of classical and Christian ethics. Enlightenment theories gave us merely individual moral persons, that is, persons not considered in their relationship to history, tradition, and culture. What resulted, according to MacIntyre, was an ethics based either on what was useful (utilitarian ethics) or what was dutiful (deontological ethics).

In constructing his own approach to ethics MacIntyre contends that something like Aristotle's ethic of virtue needs to be vindicated. The central aspect of Aristotle's theory which he elucidates is his conception of the virtues that MacIntyre considers to be the basis for a whole tradition of thinking and acting.

MacIntyre argues for the superiority of the Aristotelian approach on the basis of its ability to prevail over other views and for its flexibility in modifying itself to incorporate the important emphases of other viewpoints. From a knowledge of the history of this tradition we can have confidence that it is based on sound principles that have a good chance to endure (1984, p. 270). MacIntyre terms this tradition the "best example we possess of a tradition whose adherents are rationally entitled to a high measure of confidence in its epistemological and moral resources" 1984, p. 277).

MacIntyre's sophisticated restatement of the classical tradition proceeds through three stages. Virtues are presented as qualities which are
necessary to achieve the goods internal to practice. Second, he presents
an argument that qualities contribute to the common good of a whole
life and society. Third, he proposes that virtues are related to the pursuit
of what is good for human beings within a particular social tradition
(1984, p. 273).

MacIntyre's preferred treatment of the moral life as the virtuous life
is that found in Aristotle. Virtues are what enable persons to achieve
their goal of blessedness, happiness or prosperity. In this viewpoint,
moral education entails fostering acting virtuously, that is, acting from
inclinations formed by the cultivation of certain virtues. Aristotle's ethic
is also based on the fact that certain actions are absolutely prohibited or
positively enjoined.

Though grounded in Aristotle's theory of morality, MacIntyre's approach to morality also contains some criticisms of this position. He rejects the strictly biological basis upon which Aristotle builds his theory
of virtues. In his view Aristotle's theory must also be disconnected from
the social context of the Greek city states, which was hierarchically organized according to classes. Third, Aristotle's rejection of the value of
conflicts is to be replaced by a view that it is "through conflict and some-
times only through conflict that we learn what our ends and purposes
are" (1984, p. 164). Thus the very dealing with moral conflicts becomes
for MacIntyre a powerful form of moral education. MacIntyre also finds
a place in his theory of virtues for the distinctively religious virtues of
forgiveness, charity, and humility.

For MacIntyre the arena within which virtues are exercised is called
practice. He gives his own particular meaning to this important term in
his moral philosophy:

> Any coherent and complex form of socially established cooperative human
> activity through which goods internal to that form of activity are realized
> in the course of trying to achieve those standards of excellence which are
> appropriate to, and partially definitive of, that form of activity, with the
> result that human powers to achieve excellence, and human conceptions of
> the ends and goods involved are systematically involved. (1984, p. 187)

Examples of practices are football, chess, farming, architecture and inquiries in history, physics, music. Practices thus embrace arts, sciences,
games, politics. To do well in a practice one must accept and achieve

standards of excellence and obedience to rules. When we are able to accomplish this we are virtuous. Thus we are virtuous in our relationships to others when we achieve standards of truthfulness, trust, justice, and courage. There are also practices which are clearly evil, such as torture.

Contemporary practices are always related to a tradition of accepted rules and standards which are preserved in the institutions of society. Of the many moral traditions which are present in society, MacIntyre judges that it is only the Aristotelian tradition that "restores intelligibility and rationality to our moral and social attitudes and commitments" (1984, p. 258).

MacIntyre's effort to restate and reconstruct the classical position in moral philosophy and education has received a great deal of attention and criticism. While many have praised the book for its rejection of emotivist and relativist approaches to moral philosophy, others have objected to the argumentation and the conclusion. The book has been criticized for using historical arguments to establish what is fundamentally a philosophical position. Some have also argued that the position is fundamentally an argument for moral relativism.

Education for virtuous character through narrative

MacIntyre's restatement of Aristotle's position on virtues has led moral philosophers to enunciate an approach to moral education that looks to the development of the virtuous character. These philosophers develop the basic insight of MacIntyre that in the cultures of Greece, the Medieval World, and the Renaissance the chief means of moral education was the telling of stories of heroes and saints provided the historical memory and moral background for these societies (MacIntyre, 1984, p. 121). These stories are considered educative because they present human life as a struggle between defeat and victory. It is the moral tradition from heroic societies that MacIntyre wants to reconstruct since "the telling of stories has a key part in educating us into the virtues" (p. 216). For MacIntyre

Deprive children of stories and you leave them unscripted, anxious stutterers in their actions as in their words. Hence there is no way to give us an understanding of any society, including our own, except through the stock of stories which constitute its initial dramatic resources. Mythology, in its original sense, is at the heart of things. (p. 216)

Moral life in this perspective is viewed as the development of those virtues necessary for people to successfully progress through the physical and moral dangers of life. In this viewpoint

> Each human life will then embody a story whose shape and form will depend upon what is counted as harm and danger and upon how success and failure, progress and its opposite, are understood and evaluated. (p. 144)

The virtues individuals need in life are to be defined in terms of the conflicts that individuals face. For example, the virtues of feudal societies turn out to be the virtues of loyalty and justice, the military and chivalric virtues and the virtues of purity and patience (p. 171).

The philosopher-theologian Stanley Hauerwas has attempted to show how moral growth depends on the development of character through narrative. Extending MacIntyre's ideas he contends that the development of moral character comes about not through an adherence to principles but through acquiring a "narrative that gives us the skill to fit what we do and do not do into a coherent account sufficient to claim our life as our owns" (1981, p. 151).

The Pragmatic Tradition

The classical tradition has endured many criticisms over the years. Utilitarians, emotivists, deontologists, and others have attempted to base moral philosophy on grounds other than a rational understanding of natural and absolute moral principles. The one tradition which incorporates many of these criticisms and viewpoints and deals extensively with the educational implications of these challenges, is the pragmatic tradition of John Dewey. Dewey often addressed himself to the role of education in forming moral character.

John Dewey's moral theory

Once Dewey abandoned the idealist metaphysics of his earlier days he began to reject some key elements of the classical tradition in philosophy. His main criticism of this tradition was its failure to deal with practical matters. He rejected the Greek notion that knowledge of practical matters was an inferior form of knowledge, wisdom, judgment, and technical expertise. In his view Greek philosophy translated into rational form the doctrine of escape from the vicissitudes of existence by means of measures which do not demand an active coping with conditions. For deliverance by means of rites and cults, it substituted deliverance through reason. This deliverance was an intellectual, a theoretical affair, constituted by a knowledge to be attained apart from practical activity. (1929, pp. 13–14)

Dewey thus charges Greek philosophy for the traditional philosophical bias against practice in favor of the universal, invariant, and eternal.

Dewey accused Christian theologians of adopting the main tenets of Greek philosophy and using them for their own purposes. He accused them of glorifying a life of knowing apart from and above a life of doing. In his view in medieval Christians thought:

the perfect and ultimate reality was God; to know him was eternal bliss. The world in which man lived and acted was a world of trials and troubles to test and prepare him for a higher destiny. Through thousands of ways, including histories and rites, with symbols that engaged the emotions and imagination, the essentials of the doctrine of classic philosophy filtered its way into the popular mind. (1929, pp. 233–234)

Rather early in his career Dewey began to develop an ethical theory free of the absolutism of metaphysics. The task of ethical theory was not to determine absolute norms but rather to offer "a general statement of the reality involved in every moral situation. It must be action stated in its more generic terms, terms so generic that every individual action will fall within the outlines it sets forth" (Dewey, 1892, in *Early Works* 3, 155–158). Dewey did not want an ethical theory that offered a rigid body of rules or one that was too abstract for providing help in determining concrete actions.

Dewey's most thorough discussion of moral theory is found in his *Ethics* (1908; *Middle Works* 5:6). In this work he argued against the utilitarians who focused on consequences in determining the morality of actions and Kantians who stressed the motives of individuals. In attempting to make use of the valuable elements in both theories as well as the insights of functional psychology, Dewey espoused an ethics of self-realization in which both happiness and the dictates of practical reason called for the cultivation of democratic character (Westbrook, 1991, p. 153). Moral theory should be concerned with the development of character, that is, the main tendencies and dispositions of persons. For Dewey the good character was the person who cultivated the social good, the

welfare of those affected by one's actions. An action is thus bad if it does
not allow the social interests and tendencies of persons to develop. While
Dewey found a place within his moral theories for the Aristotelian tradition of virtue ethics, he was more concerned with how these were united
in a social self, or more properly a democratic self, and were developed
by self chosen actions in particular situations.

Dewey's second major attempt to deal with moral theory is found in
his *Theory of Valuation* (1939). In this work Dewey rejected any hierarchical ordering of values. He contended that the task of the moral life
was to develop intelligent methods of judgment. Against the emotivist
theories of logical positivists like A. J. Ayer who reduced moral valua-
tions to emotive or noncognitive expressions, Dewey argued strenuously
for the role of intelligent judgment in moral life. Moral judgments are
made in problematic situations where it is difficult to determine what is
the correct path to follow. Moral judgments are concerned with determining the best means to desired ends. Dewey continued to argue that
there were no ends in themselves or absolute goods but did allow the
importance of general values such as health, justice, happiness, or freedom. He hastened to add that these were not transcendent absolutes but
generalizations which came from common experience.

Many criticized Dewey's theory of ethics for failing to state standards
by which cultures or experiences might be judged and for reducing values
to facts. Dewey's standard for moral judgment, as stated earlier, was the
good social character, possessing many virtues, working for the good and
happiness of others. In this person self-interest and social interest were
united. For Dewey this standard for moral judgment

> does say that we should desire those objects and find our satisfaction in
> things which also bring good to those with whom we are associated in
> friendship, comradeship, citizenship, the pursuit of science, art, and so on.
> (1908, pp. 247–248)

By the time he revised his moral theory in the thirties, with the rise of
fascism in Europe, his views appear a bit less optimistic, with even some
notes of the tragic. He recognized even more the uncertainty and conflict
that permeate the moral sphere in the face of which individuals will have
to make choices among rather contradictory options. By now he realized
the limitations of both science and philosophy in the moral sphere. To
inquiry and adjudication must be added the work of the imagination. He

even found room for a common faith that he termed religious. Dewey recognized the importance of religious faith (a nontheistic religious humanism in Dewey's philosophy) for turning moral convictions into an intellectual assent. Religious imagination was for Dewey a more broadened form of the aesthetic imagination. He even found it within himself to see a role for the churches in the moral sphere when he asserted that

> The fund of human values that are prized and that need to be cherished, values that are satisfied and rectified by *all* human concerns and arrangements, could be celebrated and reinforced, in different ways and with differing symbols, by the churches. In that way the churches would indeed become catholic. (1934, pp. 55–55)

Dewey's theory of moral education

Throughout Dewey's writings on education one finds the recurrent theme, education is to build moral and democratic character. Education is to promote in children the habits and virtues that would enable children to realize themselves in a democratic society. He expressed this moral purpose of schooling in his pedagogic creed (1897), written in his early years:

> An interest in the community welfare, an interest which is intellectual and practical, as well as emotional—an interest, that is to say, in perceiving whatever makes for social order and progress, and for carrying these principles into execution—is the ultimate ethical habit to which all the special school habits must be related if they are to be animated by the breath of moral life. (Dewey, 1964 (1897), p. 115)

Dewey gave attention to the teacher's role in shaping moral character. The teacher was to direct by indirection, for Dewey believed character to be truly moral had to develop freely from within the child. The teacher's task was to both hand on the values of a particular society and, more important, to aid children to participate in the growth of society. Dewey contended that the moral life is lived only as individuals appreciate for themselves the goals for which they were laboring, and do their work in a personal spirit of interest in these goals. Teachers had the task of establishing the conditions that would enable children to use their natural moral powers. Dewey was confident that through this process children would forge the connection between self-realization and social service that he saw as the basis of the moral life. Dewey recognized that doing this required a great deal of teachers. Dewey in this area as in others tried to maintain a balance between allowing the natural growth of the child and suggesting a positive role for teachers.

Dewey's concern with moral education was thus connected with his view that the school was an important agency for progress and reform in society. Dewey's main criticism of schools in his time was that they tended to reproduce societies rather than transform them. At times he seemed to believe that if the schools did their task adequately, there might not be need for other social agencies. In later life he was less optimistic about the role of schools, viewing them as only one of many agencies for the reform of society. By then he realized the power of the competitive spirit in society and the ills that accompanied it.

The distinctive contribution that Dewey made to methodology in moral education was his proposal that the scientific method should be used in cultivating children's capacity for exercising moral judgments. The scientific method was to be used, however, in the context of a democratic community. The schools were not only communities of inquiry but democratic communities of inquiry (Westbrook, 1991, p. 172). Dewey encouraged teachers to teach science not as a body of knowledge but as a way of enhancing moral reasoning. He also advocated the study of history as an effective tool for moral instruction. For him the particular value of history was that it enabled

> the child to appreciate the values of social life, to see in imagination the forces which favor men's effective cooperation with one another, to understand the sorts of character that help and that hold back. (1908, *Middle Works* 4:192)

Dewey recommended the scientific method for moral education because of his view of the role of reason in morality. For him moral reasoning was no different from other forms of reasoning, the only distinction being in the topics treated and not in the procedures of thought. Because reason for Dewey had a practical dimension, he gave it particular relevance in the moral sphere which essentially deals with practical moral problems. Moral reasoning concerns problems of value, developing alternative solutions, gathering the facts, and making determinations. While other philosophers have tended to give emotion and habit a greater influence in the moral sphere, Dewey also saw a connection among reason, habit, and emotion.

It is clear then what Dewey considers to be the goals of moral education. It is to engage students in reflecting on moral issues according to the processes of the scientific method: problem setting, hypotheses, examining alternatives, gathering evidence, and arriving at conclusions. These moral problems should be addressed with both affect and passion; they should be problems about which one is deeply concerned. All moral education is to take place within the context of a community of persons who are seeking to address the same moral problems with a sense of moral responsibility. Education is to aid persons in developing habits, virtues, and dispositions that guide action in everyday life. A further goal is to attempt to have persons unite these habits in a consistent pattern, that is, to develop moral character.

Critique of Dewey's theory of moral education

Because Dewey's theory of moral education is at the center of many contemporary debates, no extended criticism is given at this time. The main criticisms proposed to the theory are his rejection of the distinction between fact and value, between what is and what ought to be. The term value appears to include more than the term fact: it has an implied prescription that this is what one should do. Others question his rejection of a hierarchy of values. Many moral arguments are precisely about what is more valuable, for example, property rights or life rights. Finally, Dewey has often been faulted for his handling of the relationship between the individual and society. While some have criticized him for an excessive individualism, others find in him a subordination of the individual to the collectivity. It appears that in his effort to avoid this dualism he has only succeeded in leaving an unclear synthesis.

CONTEMPORARY PHILOSOPHICAL DISCUSSIONS ON MORAL EDUCATION

The past twenty years have witnessed a great deal of writing in the area of moral education from a philosophical perspective. In the United States this is in large part due to the work of the philosopher-psychologist

Lawrence Kohlberg. Today it is possible to differentiate a number of different philosophical positions on moral education. There are proponents of the classical position such as Mortimer Adler and William Bennett who advocate an ethic of moral virtue. The classical position is also found in certain forms of natural law ethic. Kohlberg is responsible for an approach to moral education which might be termed an ethic of justice. In reaction to his work feminist scholars such as Carol Gilligan and Nel Noddings have formulated an ethic of care which they cast as a feminist voice. One can also distinguish in the work of analytic philosophers Richard Peters and John Wilson what might be called an ethic of reason. Finally, there has also emerged an ethic of social criticism in the writings of such radical thinkers as Paulo Freire and Henry Giroux.

It is obvious that each of these dimensions of reality—virtue, justice, care, reason, and criticism—are the components of any comprehensive theory of moral education. What is at issue is the special emphasis to be placed on one value and the ability of that value to adequately sustain a comprehensive theory of moral education. While each of these approaches has a particular strong point relating to its principal concern, each has deficiencies in other areas.

The Ethic of Virtue

The *Paideia Proposal* which reflects the thinking of Mortimer Adler recognizes that a primary educational objective is "personal growth or self improvement—mental, moral, and spiritual" (Adler, 1982, p. 16).

Those who propose an ethic of virtue reject the value relativism that is prominent in American education today. As in the area of intellectual education, Allan Bloom (1987) has led the charge against the relativism of values that permeates American society, and especially its educational system. His advocacy of the Great Books in education comes from his view that such an education "feeds the student's love of truth and passion to live a good life" (p. 345). Bloom is a classical scholar, steeped in the philosophy of Plato and Aristotle, who also maintains much of the elitism of their world view. He charges Dewey's pragmatism with failing to find adequate value in the past and with over-committing to the values and methods of science. It is significant that for Bloom Plato's *Republic* is the one book on education because it really explains to him his experiences as a man and a teacher, and he uses it "to point out what we should not hope for, as a teaching of moderation and resignation" (p. 381).

Education for Bloom is clearly about virtue. Every educational system has the goal of producing virtuous human beings. This education proceeds by "recognizing and accepting man's natural rights . . . a fundamental basis of unity and sameness" (p. 37). In Bloom's view the goals of present day education go counter to this democratic education because of its commitment to relativism of truths and values, excessive openness to all ideas and life-styles, and exaggerated equality.

Bloom is highly critical of educational procedures such as values clarification in which students talk about their value preferences. Terming such education propaganda he contends that it will not provide the experience and the passion that are the bases of moral reasoning. The goal of moral education is to generate a moral instinct, a second nature, which is necessary not only for the building of character but also for the development of thought. What he proposes for moral education is the classical approach of presenting

> To the imagination of the young a vision of a moral cosmos and of the rewards and punishments for good and evil, sublime speeches that accompany and interpret deeds, protagonists and antagonists in the drama of moral choice, a sense of the stakes involved in such a choice, and the despair that results when the world is "disenchanted." (p. 60)

Bloom is deeply concerned that parents no longer have control over the moral education of their children. This is so, because he believes that the mass media, especially music and television, are very influential in shaping the morals of the young. Like Plato he takes music not as entertainment but as serious education, contending that "music is at the center of education, both for giving the passions their due and for preparing the soul for the unhampered use of reason" (p. 72).

Bloom gives some attention to how moral education should take place. He states that "education is not sermonizing to children against their instincts and pleasures, but providing a natural continuity between what they feel and what they can and should be" (p. 80). The Great Books of the liberal arts tradition and exposure to great works of art are the chief methods that he proposes. Although concerned mainly with educational efforts in colleges and universities, Bloom does address moral education in such general terms that his ideas are useful to educators at many levels.

Many have found Bloom's diagnosis of the ills of American culture somewhat exaggerated and his proposed remedy woefully inadequate. It is hard to see how the classical education he proposes could cure all the ills that he details. Bloom does not seem to want to accept the changing nature of American society which gives increasing attention to the needs and aspirations of many groups. A purely literary and aesthetic moral education leaves untapped much of what we have learned in the past one hundred years about human persons and their development.

Ethic of Reason

While the ethic of virtue proposed by Bloom, Adler, and others places strong emphasis on exposure to the Great Books, another group of philosophers in the rationalist tradition focus on the development of the rational powers of persons. These analytic philosophers, notably Richard Peters, Israel Scheffler, and John Wilson, have offered a sustained effort to develop a cognitively oriented approach to moral education.

The notion of morality presented in this approach focuses not on a set of moral rules but on a rational procedure for confronting moral issues, the development of individual inquiry, and deliberation. In this view there is a concentration on the centrality of the autonomous character or individual. Peters thus describes the purpose of moral education:

> My concern is for the development of an autonomous type of character who follows rules in a rational discriminating manner, and who also has character. To do this a man must ascribe to some higher-order principles which will enable him both to apply rules intelligently in the light of relevant differences in circumstances and to revise rules from time to time in the light of changes in circumstances and in empirical knowledge about the consequences of their application. (1981, p. 33)

The rules which Peters proposes, impartiality and consideration of interests, provide the criteria for justifying rules and exceptions to rules.

Moral principles are important in the ethic of reason. John Wilson has enumerated such key principles as concern for others, sympathy, a sense of fair play, a sense of feeling for others or one's own interests, a commitment to other peoples' interests, and a willingness to regard others as equals. Thus it is clear that while Wilson has proposed to present a merely formal or procedural ethic, he does make much use of general normative principles. He does, however, avoid proposing specific content.

Also, other principles might also be proposed such as truthfulness, generosity, and honesty (Wilson, 1969).

The role of reason in moral education is clearly defined by Wilson. The ethic of reason in moral education includes acting for a reason which is related to other people's interests. It also entails being logically consistent in one's reason, knowing the facts and facing them, and applying all these skills in action. Wilson contrasts this approach to other approaches such as accepting an outside authority, imitating ideal persons, accepting on faith how we should live, viewing moral choices as personal preferences, doing what we were taught or experienced, or accepting what other people say or do.

The almost exclusive concentration on reason by Wilson and others tends to obscure other important elements in moral development and education. Also, the consideration of other persons' interests would appear to be rather reductive of the whole sphere of moral principles and considerations. What distinguishes Wilson's approach from others is his concern to move away from the teaching of specific moral values or behaviors towards an emphasis on our general ability to reason in a moral manner.

Wilson does not appear to have sufficiently attended to the paradox in moral education that we want to form habits but also to educate people to question received opinions and their own habits. His theory does not adequately account for the decisive importance of the influence of others and of earlier habits on a person's moral stance and behavior. Does the formation of habits prevent any relevant moral education? This is where a moral philosophy based on reason, and perhaps any philosophical approach to moral education, falters: the failure to examine the psychological constraints and social influences on a person's moral development.

The form of moral education proposed for the ethic of reason has been described by Wilson and others. It entails a systematic teaching about the moral sphere and about moral thinking. Teachers are to be moral philosophers and not moralizers. Moral problems to be probed by students can come from history and literature. The importance of a dialectical approach in discussing issues is stressed.

Wilson has given attention to the preconditions for moral education which include such things as the ability to have a sense of person, a sense of self-esteem, the experiencing of meaningful personal relationships, and the skill of confronting one's feelings. Many educators would view these as essential components of moral education. If persons already possess these qualities, the task of moral education would appear to be assured.

Ethic of Justice

Lawrence Kohlberg has also mined the classical tradition, but with somewhat different conclusions than Allan Bloom and other classicists. Opposing what he terms the bag of virtues approach to moral education, he chose to focus on the one virtue which he views as critical for moral development and education, the virtue of justice.

Kohlberg began his work with psychological research on the development of human reasoning that intended to refine the work that Jean Piaget (1922; 1966) had done on moral reasoning in children. From a study of male adolescents he came to the conclusion that there are definite stages of moral development through which persons pass. In general terms, people pass from preconventional understandings of morality where emphasis is placed on such extrinsic factors as punishment and approbation to conventional understandings where stress is placed on conventions and laws. Some persons rise to a post conventional stage where decisions are made on the basis of inherent rights or universal principles (Kohlberg, 1981; 1984).

It is not easy to situate the moral theory that undergirds Kohlberg's ethic of justice. He considers his moral philosophy to be influenced by Socrates in its methodology, John Rawls for its concept of justice, Kant for its view of the moral agent, and Dewey for its interactionist view of the educational process.

There is a universalist element in the Kohlberg approach to moral education in that justice is viewed as a reality which is independent of specific cultures and societies. Morality is rooted in a body of statements which can be generalized to all situations. Justice for Kohlberg refers to a concern for the welfare of others as well as a concern for the fair and equal treatment of others. By asserting the value of universal moral principles Kohlberg places himself against cultural relativists, though his concept of justice and moral principles are expressed in general and ambiguous terms.

Kohlberg clearly sees a place for reason in moral development and education. Reason for him is an interactive process in which general principles are applied to concrete problems and dilemmas. Reason to be properly applied must be impartial, that is, unaffected by personal and group pressures. What reason arrives at is prescriptive for persons and universally valid. The goal of moral reasoning is to lead not to the development of virtues and habits but to the accomplishment of actions. Critics contend that in neglecting the development of virtues and habits Kohlberg has ignored an important component of moral education. Kohlberg has in more recent writings added a greater emphasis on value content, school settings, and real problems.

Kohlberg has attended to the pedagogy that flows from his moral theory to a greater degree than has any other moral philosopher. He proposed a method of moral education which he believed respects the integrity of persons and their natural development. In this role the teachers can do some direct teaching but only in a anti-indoctrinative manner, though he does admit that some teaching of moral doctrines is necessary, especially for the young.

The role of the teacher is to be a facilitator for cognitive moral growth. The teacher's task is to help students focus on real moral problems and reflect critically on the alternative ways in which these problems could be resolved. When this is done students are guided in thinking reflectively and critically about the adequacy of their own thinking about moral alternatives. The final task is to suggest to students a mode of thinking and acting that is more efficient than their present method. In his later writings Kohlberg has come to realize that the teacher also functions as an agent in moral socialization by teaching moral content and behavior in a direct manner. While in earlier writings he saw the role of the teacher in terms of proposing moral dilemmas and leading students in a discussion of them, Kohlberg came to recognize a more directive role for teachers as citizens and members of a just community.

Developments in Kohlberg's theory came about when he attempted to apply his theory to curriculum, the building of just schools, and teacher training. Involvement in schools made him realize that some direct teaching had to take place in the form of civic education. This experience also sensitized him to the existence of a hidden curriculum along side the overt curriculum of the school. In his efforts to influence teacher education programs, Kohlberg attended more than previously to the practical aspects of moral education.

Kohlberg at the end of his life began to accept some of the positions which he seriously challenged in his early work. He came closer to the classic view in many ways with his acceptance of direct teaching, universal truths, and practical experience. From a psychological perspective the

Kohlberg theory remains the ruling paradigm for understanding moral development. His pedagogy has also received wide acceptance. What has been challenged is the adequacy of his moral theory which reduces the moral sphere to justice and rights. The main challenges have come from feminist philosophers and psychologists who have added an ethic of care and concern to Kohlberg's ethic of justice and rights.

Ethic of Care

Carol Gilligan (1982) is the foremost scholar who has proposed an ethic of care as an alternative or supplement to the ethic of justice expounded by Kohlberg and others. While this position has been elaborated at a philosophical level by Nel Noddings (1984), it has received psychological validation from Gilligan and others. Gilligan has significantly advanced this debate with her contention that the ethic of care is the preferred ethic of women while the ethic of justice is the preferred ethic of men. She further charges Kohlberg with sexist bias because he placed the ethic of justice higher than the ethic of care on his scale of moral reasoning.

It is relevant to note that long before Gilligan's work moral philosophers described an ethic of care in terms of an ethic of love. Traditionally, moral philosophers and psychologists have not been satisfied with reducing morality to a morality of justice. The classic studies of Hartshorne and May (1928–30) defined morality in terms of justice (honesty and altruism) and care (service). Peters (1981) and Frankena (1973) recognized at least two virtues or moral principles: the principle of justice and the principle of benevolence.

There are various forms of the ethic of love. Some philosophers such as John Stuart Mill equated this ethic with utilitarianism which makes the greatest benefit to others the criterion of morality. John Fletcher's situation ethics also makes this identification. Butler and Clarke held to the principle of benevolence along with the principles of justice and veracity. Thomists maintain this position in arguing for principles of the natural law not derived from the law of love (Frankena, 1973, p. 56).

Frankena (1973, p. 57) makes a distinction between act agapism and rule agapism. The former applies the rule of love directly to each particular case. It becomes a form of antinominianism or situationalism. A modified act-agapist gives a place to rules of thumb drawn from past experience. The rule agapist determines what rules of action are most love-embodying and follows them in each particular situation. Frankena does not see any clear value to the position of agapism unless it is connected with principles of beneficence, utility, or divine revelation. Asking whether all our duties can be derived from the instruction to love, he responds that the principle of love at least needs the principle that we should love all equally, which is a principle of justice.

Gilligan is clearly situated in this tradition of agapist ethic. She has concluded from her research that many persons view moral problems in terms of conflicting responsibilities to care rather than in terms of competing rights. This form of moral reasoning, a care orientation, centers around responsibility and relationships, just as the morality of justice focuses on reasoning about rights and rules (Gilligan, 1982, p. 19). She and her colleagues also contend that 75 percent of females use a care orientation and only 25 percent a rights orientation. The case for men is different: 79 percent with a rights orientation with 14 percent using a care orientation (In Kohlberg, 1984, p. 341). Gilligan contends that she has described a morality which is complementary to the morality of justice rather than sequential or opposed.

Gilligan argues that the morality of rights is premised on persons defining themselves as separate from others rather than in connection with them. In her view women's outlook and reasoning is thus more connective than separative. To many women, she asserts, the morality of rights and rules appears to be one of indifference and unconcern (Gilligan, 1982, p. 22).

Gilligan has also offered a developmental sequence parallel to Kohlberg's stages of moral reasoning. The first stage is one of care for self in which central issues are self-survival. In a period of transition one begins to question the selfishness manifested at this stage. A second stage is marked by a care for others in which one does not want to hurt others and expresses a willingness to sacrifice self. In a period of transition this ethic of self-sacrifice is questioned. In a final stage persons live the tension inherent in balancing care for self with care for others.

Gilligan's theory has not gone without criticism, even from feminist scholars. Some have pointed out that the theory comes close to idealizing women's morality and neglecting the historical and social contexts within which it develops. Others contend that Gilligan has revived an essentialist, ahistorical understanding of women. (Auerbach, 1985; Lloyd, 1983; Nicholson, 1983)

Kohlberg in defending his own theory has offered a number of criticisms of the ethic of care enunciated by Gilligan. He believes that the kinds of problems offered by Gilligan could be answered by using his universalistic justice ethic or respect of persons and rules and with the concept of reciprocity and contract. Yet he admits that they can also be handled by a morality of particularist relationships which separates these special relationships from universalist relationships governed by justice. Such particular relations include relations to family, friends, and groups of which we are members. This ethic deals with such ideas and attitudes as caring, love, loyalty, and responsibility.

Kohlberg contends that he and Gilligan are using the term "moral" in two different senses. He uses it to refer to the moral point of view which he describes as impartial, universal, and consensual. The ethic of care is in his view more suited to the real world of personal moral choices, for example, divorce or abortion, while he attempts to deal with moral choices in nonpersonal spheres. Thus it may be that the different kinds of moral dilemmas call forth the invoking of different types of moral considerations.

While Kohlberg does accept some differentiation between the ethic of care and the ethic of justice, he does not believe that Gilligan has established a structural difference between the two. He states that he does

> Accept Gilligan's differentiation of two orientations in moral judgment which may vary in emphasis from person to person and from situation to situation. We do not believe, however, that the growth of justice and the ethic of care represent two distinct tracks of moral stage (i.e., structural development) (1984, p. 358)

Just as Kohlberg has proposed an education for justice that he believes will foster an ethic of justice, so feminist educators, especially Nel Noddings (1984) have advocated an education for care. Moral education for care is viewed as a community-wide task for enhancing the moral life of persons in their relationships with others. To act ethically is primarily meeting others in genuine encounters of caring and being cared for. This form of education rests on a basis of affective relationships. This feminine approach in which all persons can participate utilizes thinking at the service of the affective dimension. Intelligence must have as its aim the promotion of a caring atmosphere in all institutions of society.

The teacher is described as one who cares. To care for others is to receive them completely and nonselectively. It means to place oneself at the service of the other. In language reminiscent of Martin Buber's description of the I-Thou relationship, teachers are to be present to others and place their power at the service of others to inform, guide, and assist others in their ethical development. Though not equal with students, educators must seek to include others by receiving and accepting their feelings and to work cooperatively with them.

Teachers are urged to enhance the ethical ideal in others through a number of different methods. They do this through dialogue with students about issues of importance: God, sex, killing, fear, hope, and hate. Schools have the freedom to examine all questions while home and church promote particular value systems. The dialogue should take the form of a dialectic between feeling and thinking with the goal of bringing all into contact with one another and with significant ideas. Teachers should also present themselves as ethical models in their caring for others.

Teachers must also engage in cooperative practices with students, being available to them in a relationship of friendship. These practices have the purpose of developing skills and competence in caring. They include helping in tasks of cleaning and fixing, caring for persons and animals. Caring apprenticeships might be fostered by caring for the elderly or animals. Attention is to be paid to the development of a caring atmosphere in schools and classrooms. The feminine approach to moral education views what happens in the classroom more as a matter of relationships than of objective subject matter and objective relationships.

The educational pedagogy of the ethic of care has much in common with the educational philosophy of Carl Rogers and Martin Buber. Although critics might object that it does not prepare people for the hard ethical realities of the "real" world, its proponents argue that it is precisely the lack of caring in institutions of society that needs to be challenged through educational practices. Some educators go even further in their rejection of the ills of American schools and society by arguing that moral education needs an even more radical ethic, an ethic of social criticism.

Ethic of Social Criticism

In more recent years a distinctive ethic of social criticism has emerged within the field of education that focuses on raising ethical questions about schooling in so far as this relates to serious social, political, and economic illnesses in society. This ethic emerges from the critical social theory which is rooted in the philosophical analyses of the Frankfurt school. Though a full treatment of critical theory will be presented in the chapter on political education, I think it is important to highlight this form of educational criticism as an ethic of social criticism. If this is not done, there is a danger of viewing ethics merely as a form of personal or private behavior.

Criticism in critical social theory has been defined as

> That intellectual, and eventually practical, effort, which is not satisfied to accept the prevailing ideas, actions, and social conditions unthinkingly and from mere habit; effort which aims to coordinate the individual sides of social life with each other and with the general ideas and aims of the epoch, to deduce them genetically, to distinguish the appearance from the essence, to examine the foundations of things, in short to really know them. (Horkheimer, 1972, p. 270)

This definition indicates that criticism is intended to be both an intellectual and a practical endeavor. One of the weak points of the theory is, however, its failure to address the mechanisms of social change.

Over the years the ethic of criticism has focused on a number of themes. It is concerned with pointing out the role that schools play in fostering the domination that is found in many societies. It shows how knowledge has become an instrument of power and domination. It deals with how people are socialized into cultures and uncritically assume the values of a dominant culture. (Apple, 1979)

The common themes of critical social theory have been described by Henri Giroux (1981, pp. 18–19). It stresses the essentially dialectical nature of social reality and the importance of persons in establishing that reality. It rejects as reductionist the view that reality is adequately understood in economic terms. Liberation thus is understood not only in economic terms but in terms of all human needs (psychological, aesthetic, sexual, etc.). Focus in investigations is placed on persons and relevance is found in everyday life. Finally, class is considered an important element in the analysis of any society.

A prominent critical theorist on whom educators have depended for developing an ethic of criticism is Jurgen Habermas (1979). One of his major concerns is that persons critically analyze the ideologies of the societies in which they live. Ideologies in his viewpoint function to repress certain actions. Repression entails a distortion of communication and interaction in society.

Inspired by the analyses of Habermas and others, critical social theorists examine the conflicts in society between competing groups whose interests are in competition. These theorists examine social customs, laws, social systems, and power structures, especially focusing on the language of those who are in control. Areas where critical theorists have concentrated include sexist language, sexual bias in the workplace, racial biases, the power of the media in shaping opinions. These critics extend their criticisms to examine all situations where the potential for oppression exists: schools, prisons, armies, industries, and the very political system itself.

Applied to education and schooling the ethic of social criticism raises a number of issues. It calls into question how the dominant ideology of society is inscribed in the form and content of classroom material, the organization of the school, the principles that structure the selection and organization of the curriculum, the attitudes of the school staff, and the discourse and practice of those within the school (Giroux, 1981, p. 22). This ethic in a special way examines how the dominant classes in society exercise hegemony or control over all other classes.

As formulated by Michael Apple (1979) critical social theory is clearly an attack on the values of the capitalist system which in his view controls media, production, consumption, and the distribution of goods. Schooling in his view helps to reproduce and sustain an unjust, inequitable, and inhumane maldistribution of power. It does this by teaching a selective version of knowledge. For example, history glorifies the leaders of the capitalist state and science is taught in the interests of capitalist expansion. History and social studies emphasize consensus and do not do justice to the existence of conflicts in the past and present. Knowledge thus is reduced to a cultural capital.

Critical social theorists have examined in a special way the culture of the school and how this reflects the values of the dominant culture. Schools are viewed as excellent places for studying the many cultures of a society. Schools are places where various cultures compete for language, styles, aesthetics, and skills. They are places to study the many contradictions of society. Practices which have been called into question include homogeneous tracking, grading practices, and absence of certain topics in the curriculum.

A critical social ethic is insistent on exposing how the hidden curriculum of the school fosters moral values. David Purpel and Kevin Ryan (1976) insightfully point out the power of this curriculum:

The schools cannot avoid being involved in the moral life of students. It is inconceivable for schools to take the child for six or seven hours a day, for 180 days a year, from the time he is six to the time he is eighteen, and not affect the way he thinks about moral issues and the way he behaves. Nor can we divorce the intellectual from the moral realm. One can suppress discussion about moral issues and values and the formation of morals. Moral education goes on all over school buildings—in the classrooms, in the disciplinarian's office, in assemblies, in the gym. It permeates the very fabric of teacher-student relationship. The school, then, cannot help but be a force for growth or retardation—for good or evil—in the moral life of the student. Moral education is an inevitable role of the school. For the educator, it goes with the territory. (1976, p. 9)

Critical theorists go further than this to point out precisely when the hidden curriculum of the school teaches in imposing the values of the dominant class on all students in the school.

The aims of the critical theorist in education are fundamentally political and social reform to be accomplished by engaging administrators, teachers and students in a mode of criticism of society and the schools. These theorists have presented critical analyses and research toward this end. Their work has not yet attended to educational methodology to foster critical attitudes in students except in general terms to make them aware of what the unjust structures of society are and what are the reasons for the maintenance of these structures.

What the radical social critics in education have presented are a number of important educational principles which should govern practice. One of their main contentions is that education should not be neutral but should take an advocacy position on such issues as student rights, teacher rights, and the rights of the oppressed. In their opinion educators need to take more seriously their moral obligation to question the ethics and the justice of educational systems and societies of which they are a part.

CHAPTER 4

AESTHETIC EDUCATION

All persons in a society would agree that one of the purposes of education is to expose students to art, to give them an understanding of it, give them an appreciation of it, and to foster artistic creativity. The beautiful in nature and in works of art is considered by many a critical concern of education along with the true and the good.

When it comes to actual practice, however, aesthetic education appears to be rather low on the contemporary scale of priorities. Maxine Greene (1981) contends that the arts are generally neglected in educational institutions. Arts, with the exception of literature, tend to be relegated to creative domains, where rather few students are engaged in them. She contends that few

> Think about introducing students to the modes of attending that a particular performance requires, to the qualities that distinguish the work of art they are about to hear or see, to matters having to do with expressiveness and style. (p. 117)

Though few do this, many expect young people to have basic aesthetic understanding.

Education in the arts has often been considered an extra, a refinement, or a completion. This attitude is demonstrated by a study of educational history. Aesthetic education is not usually presented as something essential to one's education. Also, when budgets are cut, it is often art education that receives attention first. As the curriculum has expanded to include many practical and socially relevant subjects, the time allotted to the arts has diminished in many schools. To counter this trend philosophers have redefined aesthetic as part of basic education (Broudy, 1991).

Philosophers of education have devoted attention to this dimension, not, however, to the extent that they have concerned themselves with intellectual and moral education, reflecting no doubt, that less importance is generally accorded to the arts. Yet the work which has appeared in this area is significant in its reflection upon the principles and aims of aesthetic education. In this chapter my purpose is to trace the evolution of philosophical ideas on aesthetic education, present theories of art, examine the justification for this form of education, discuss the various aims of aesthetic education, and reflect on teaching and learning for aesthetic literacy.

It must be stated again that the treatment in this book is an analytic one. The distinctions used in this book to divide up the educational enterprise break up the unity of education. These divisions are merely for analysis and understanding. All subjects in the curriculum can serve intellectual, moral, aesthetic, and political purposes. Furthermore, though there are distinctions among intellectual, moral, and aesthetic education, there are also similarities and relationships.

Aesthetic education is the preferred term in this treatment. Another term that appears among educators is education in or through the arts or art education. Recently educators have begun to speak more often about the education of the imagination. Maxine Greene has used the term aesthetic literacy as the goal of aesthetic education.

HISTORY OF IDEAS ON AESTHETIC EDUCATION

My review of historical perspectives on art and aesthetic education is intended to show where our contemporary language and issues have come from. This rather selective treatment points out the major shifts that have taken place over the century in theories of art and in approaches to aesthetic education. I make no attempt at being comprehensive.

The Classical Tradition

It has long been recognized that the classical or realist tradition that places emphasis on art as imitation or representation is a controversial one. Plato in the *Republic* made a strong case that education in the arts may be frivolous at best and dangerous to true knowledge and morality at the worst. For these reasons Plato argued that the major Greek artists must generally be excluded from the educational system of Greece. He allowed that the poets may be taught at the lower levels of education, provided, however, that objectionable passages are purged. They are certainly to be eliminated from higher forms of education. Although many efforts have been made over the years to explain away Plato's attacks on the poets and dramatists, it is clear that Plato had serious doubts about the value of poetic and dramatic experience.

The arts are attacked by Plato because in appearing to sanction immoral activity they do not lead the young to correct moral behavior. They are also attacked because they present a distorted view of reality. Even though Plato considered art to be a natural instinct of expression, in point fact he treated it as an imitation of an imitation (things in the world). This is so because Plato considered things in this world as copies of ideal forms in the world beyond. Plato was really only interested in knowledge of these pure ideas and forms, a knowledge given only by mathematics and philosophy. Thus for Plato the arts offered only imitations, illusions, and confusions.

Plato in attacking the arts in reality criticized the educational system of Greece which gave a predominant role to Homer and the artists. Eric Havelock, a renowned Platonic scholar comments

It is clear . . . that the poets in general and Homer in particular were not only considered as the source of instruction in ethics and administrative skills but also enjoyed a sort of institutional status in Greek society. This status received, as it were, state support, because they supplied a training which the social and political mechanism relied on for its efficient working. (1971, p. 27)

In a sense, the arts in ancient Greek society included all there was to know. They were "an encyclopedia of ethics, politics, history, and technology which the effective citizen was required to learn as the core of his educational equipment" (Havelock, 1971, p. 26). Seen in this context, Plato's actual argument is for the superiority of intellectual education and the subordination of aesthetic education to moral education. Seen as a reaction to what he viewed as an extreme position, his theory does present some cautions on aesthetic education. If he were writing today he might argue for more of Homer and the poets, while reserving his strong-est condemnation for the arts of the mass media.

Plato's discussion of art introduced the idea of art as *mimesis*, a term which has often been used to explain the nature of art. Plato gave this term a number of meanings. It refers, first of all, to a certain manner of composition, a dramatic style in contrast to a purely descriptive one. It also refers to the performance of an actor who impersonates another, that is, a dramatic imitation or impersonification as contrasted with sim-ple rehearsals. Furthermore, *mimesis* refers to the process by which the young apprentice repeats what he has been told by a master, thus giving the term an educational dimension. Finally, the term comes to refer to the very act of engaging in art, the imitation of the world of Pure Ideas, the total act of artistic representation, as well as the process by which an audience becomes identified with that vision.

No matter what other descriptions of art have been given, it must be recognized that much of art has this imitative or representative nature. This imitation or representation should not be seen as purely mechanical. The artist in a way is asked to improve on nature, to present it differently, and to select some aspects for our attention.

While Plato's intellectual arguments against the arts have been gener-ally rejected, along with his idealist metaphysics, his moral arguments are often heard in the words of those who propose censorship of the arts on moral grounds. He argued that the young should not be exposed on moral grounds to certain music, literature, sculpture, and paintings. Given the exposure that the young have in most cultures to all forms of human life in art, music, and literature, there seems to be little justifica-tion for moral censorship in schools. A stronger case can be made for teaching about well-established forms of art so as to promote a discrimi-nating approach to art and life. It should also be noted that Plato paid the arts a backhanded compliment in his exaggeration of the value of the arts in intellectual and moral education.

The social origin of Aristotle's views on aesthetic education are also important. Aristotle's theory of art is connected to the social situation where practical activities were done by slaves, thus servile arts. Aristotle made a distinction between the liberal arts and the servile or menial arts, the former being actions of the mind and the latter actions of the hands. For this reason the fine arts of music, painting, and sculpture were clas-sified by Aristotle with the menial arts. Engaging in these arts involved physical agencies, careful practice, and external results. For Aristotle the young should learn music but only to the point of appreciating it when it is played by slaves and professionals because playing music belongs not to the liberal arts but to professional practice. For Aristotle, one might as well teach children cooking. Thus in Aristotle's way of thinking the more mental an activity the higher it is on the scale of human activities. It is only through mental activity that persons are made independent and self-sufficient whereas manual or practical activity keeps people servile or subservient. As will been seen below, John Dewey pointed out the social and philosophical biases in these views of Aristotle.

For Aristotle, as for Plato, the fine arts aim at imitating nature. However, not accepting Plato's view of art as a copy of a copy, Aristotle believed that the artist penetrates to the ideal or universal element in things and then imitates or portrays this in some concrete form. Furthermore, for Aristotle poetry is of more value than history since it deals with universals while history deals with particulars. The educational value of poetry lies in the fact that poets deal not with concrete persons or behaviors but with types of persons and behaviors. Thus in attending to a concrete work of art we come into contact with the universal type or form. Aristotle also contends that it is natural for us to imitate nature and to delight in works of imitation. Thus the enjoyment and imitation of Homer actually make us better persons.

Aristotle argued that there was an educational and a moral value in the arts. He advised that the young learn to draw in order to acquire a more correct judgment of the works of artists. He also contended that music should be introduced into the education of the young because it has the power to form character. However, Aristotle does not stress the educational value of art to the point of ignoring its recreative aspect.

Aristotle's theory of art included the important concept of *catharsis*, which many consider to have profound educational implications. Although much has been written about this concept, the common opinion is that *catharsis* refers to a temporary elimination of the emotions of pity and fear (Copleston, 1953, p. 367). Works of tragedy aim to evoke pity for the sufferings of the hero in order to relieve the soul of these emotions through a harmless and pleasurable outlet. Aristotle presumed that these emotions are dangerous, at least when they are present in excess. For Aristotle music, as other arts, can be for education, for purification, or for intellectual enjoyment as well as for relaxation and recreation after exertion.

In conclusion, the classical tradition on aesthetic education is a mixed one. It attests to the powerful effects of the arts in education and in culture. Various justifications are given to the life of the arts: recreational, intellectual, and moral. Arts recreate the human spirit. They teach us some things about this world. Both Plato and Aristotle were concerned that the arts be taught in such a way that they foster moral education. The arts provide an education for the emotions and passions. The case made by Plato for censorship of the arts in the education of the young attests to a belief in their power to shape both individuals and cultures.

Plato and Aristotle in establishing the foundations of art proposed a realist theory of art. Art is an imitation or representation of reality. While for Plato art is an imitation of the ideal forms, for Aristotle it is an imitation of the essences of concrete things. Their theories do not entail a mechanical reproduction of reality since they allow for some creativity in the artist. The task of the artist, at least for Aristotle, was to improve on reality without disfiguring it.

Though the classical tradition in art has generally been supplanted by other traditions in succeeding generations, classicism in arts has found a place in each modern century. Classicism has been strong especially in Europe. What marks this classicism is attention to forms, to ideas imbedded in forms, and to the representational aspect of much of modern art. Classical traditions do not favor the free play of the imagination. They also contend that works of art have to be judged by fixed rules or according to classical models.

Challenges to the Classical Tradition

The realist or representational theory of art was the dominant theory at least until the beginning of the eighteenth century. For a long time, however, it had been recognized that the art of lyric poetry could not easily be explained as imitative. In the writings of Rousseau one finds the first real challenge to the classical tradition. Art was viewed by him not as a description of the world but as an overflow of emotions and passions. Thus realistic art gave way to "characteristic art" or expressive art. Beauty as imitative became in the romantic view of art a secondary and derivative aim of art. This view of art as expressive was also proposed by the Germans Herder and Goethe. The romantic view of art tended to reject standards and models. Art is viewed not as a matter of imitation but of inspiration. Beauty is both unique and incomparable, the work of a genius.

Although some artists at this time were interested only in the expressive element in art to the rejection of the notion of art as imitative, others stressed that expressive art also needs a material or a formative element for its realization. The intuition of the artist has to be embodied in a particular material (Cassirir, 1944, p. 156). Thus came about the view that art is both expressive and representative.

The philosopher who attempted to combine both the subjective and the objective, the form and the matter, and imitation and expression was Emmanuel Kant, who in so doing established art as an autonomous sphere. Cassirer explains that

> Up to the time of Kant a philosophy of beauty always meant an attempt to reduce art to an alien jurisdiction. Kant in his *Critique on Judgment* was the first to give a clear and convincing proof of the autonomy of art. All former systems had looked for a principle of art within the sphere either of practical knowledge or of the moral life. (Cassirir, 1945, p. 152)

The effort of Kant and other Enlightenment thinkers was to point out that persons are creators of themselves through the means of the power of mind on material things. The view that individuals make their own knowledge, control their own feelings, and make their own history carried over into the aesthetic area in the theory that art is a creative act which expresses the very nature of the self.

This new view of art also received attention for its cultural educational potential. The German artist and philosopher Frederich Schiller, writing *Letters on Aesthetic Education* during the years of the French Revolution, addressed the role of art in human life and culture. Schiller saw in art the power of synthesizing the impulses of human nature with the demands of free reason, of establishing a balance between sensuous drives and moral imperatives. Wondering what forces in society would help lead to human rights and freedom and not to violence and terror, he proposed art as a power that could unify various human impulses into a synthesis of conflicting beliefs that could sustain a nation in the face of social and cultural crisis. Art, in his view, was able to do this because through the development of the play impulse it held before people immortal examples. Play has this potentiality because it enables people to rise above purely physical and material existence. Thus art in his idealistic view was a vital factor in forging a political revolution.

One question often raised about Schiller's theory is whether or not he puts the aesthetic above the moral in education. Is the moral law to be subordinated to the demands of beauty and the arts? Walter Grossman argues that Schiller did not place the aesthetic over the moral. In his view, for Schiller

> Aesthetic education prepares man to be a human being, embracing life in its fullness without overstepping the measure set up by the imperative of reason. It is an education necessary in order to make man a free individual who has assimilated the demands of this imperative in such a way that they have become his second nature. (1971, p. 40)

In contrast to the exalted role that Schiller ascribed to aesthetics, Herbert Spencer, the nineteenth-century British educator, in *Education: Intellectual, Moral, and Physical* placed the arts at the bottom of the five areas of the school curriculum: education for human preservation, education for securing necessities of human life, education for rearing and disciplining of children, education for maintaining social and political relations, education for leisure life. While recognizing the importance of arts as part of human leisure, he argued that they should occupy only a leisure part of education.

> Accomplishments, the fine arts, *belles lettres*, and as all those things which, as we say, constitute the efflorescence of civilization, should be wholly subordinate to that knowledge and discipline in which civilization rests. *As they occupy the leisure part of life, so should they occupy the leisure part of education.* (1903, pp. 74–75)

Given Spencer's belief that science alone provided the most worthwhile knowledge, it is easy to understand how he relegated the arts to the leisure part of human life. His views have been shared by some people in every age.

Aesthetic Education and John Dewey

Just as John Dewey challenged the classic traditions on the nature of intellectual and moral education, so he brought critical and fresh ideas to the role of the arts in education. At the beginning of his educational career the manual and fine arts played an important role in the laboratory school which he established in Chicago. This school provided a wide range of materials and experiences in the arts: the visual arts, both fine and practical, music, drama, and literature. His stated ideal was that the arts should "represent the culmination, the idealization, the highest point of refinement of all the work carried on" (Mayhew and Edwards in Bernstein, 1967, p. 361).

Dewey's fullest philosophical treatment of art is found in *Art and Experience* (1934). This work begins with Dewey's usual critique of the classical Greek tradition. Dewey charged the Greeks with making too sharp a distinction between the theoretical and the practical and for devaluing anything which they viewed as practical in nature. In Dewey's view, the Greeks, in depreciating the practical, thereby underestimated the value of all human experience. Although Plato judged all art as inferior to the contemplation of ideal forms, Aristotle judged the practical arts as inferior to contemplation. For the Greeks the highest form of knowledge was contemplation; for Dewey it was practical and aesthetic activity which is controlled by thought. Dewey saw a close connection between the intellectual, the aesthetic, and the practical. Against the classical view he argued that

> The enemies of the aesthetic are neither the practical nor the intellectual. They are the humdrum; slackness of loose ends; submission to convention in practice and intellectual procedure. Rigid abstinence, coerced submission, tightness on one side and dissipation, incoherence and aimless indulgence on the other, are deviations in opposite directions from the unity of experience. (1934, p. 40)

In *Art and Experience* Dewey proposed two definitions of art. In his broad definition art is almost equated with human experience because of Dewey's contention that the aesthetic quality is not limited to a special experience but can pervade all experiences. In this view art refers to the quality of production, fulfillment, and consummation in all experiences. The goal for persons is to make all experiences artistic and aesthetic. The aesthetic experience differs only in degree and not in kind from other human experiences. What makes an experience distinctively aesthetic was the interest and purpose that controlled the experience in that an artist intended to produce an experience that would be enjoyed for its aesthetic beauty. Art for Dewey is both a natural event and the completion of nature.

In keeping with this broad definition of art Dewey expanded the meaning of appreciation in education. The imagination is to be engaged not only in the fine arts but in all human activities. He decried the exaggerated use of fairy tales, myths, fanciful symbols, and verse in education of the imagination at the expense of serious involvement in a full range of activities. On the other hand, he valued the education of imagination through manual activities and laboratory exercises.

Within the context of this broad definition of art, Dewey made no clear cut distinction between the useful or industrial arts and the fine arts. Both of these forms of art engage the emotions and imagination, demand a method or skill, contain the adaptation of tools to materials with increasing perfection, and involve technique. Dewey gave his explanation of appreciation when he described it as the enhancement of the qualities which make our experiences appealing, appropriate, and enjoyable. Exposure to works of art gives us high standards by which to make judgments in everyday life. The experience of works of art makes us discontent with the conditions of our existence as well as urges us to seek what is more noble. The arts

> reveal a depth and range of meaning in experiences which otherwise might be mediocre and trivial. They supply, that is, organs of vision. Moreover, in their fullness they represent the concentration and consummation of elements of good which are otherwise scattered and incomplete. They select and focus the elements of enjoyable worth which make any experience directly enjoyable. They are not the luxuries of education, but emphatic expressions of that which makes any education worthwhile. (1916, p. 238)

Dewey also recognized that there was a more specialized meaning to the aesthetic which emphasized works of art as end products. He was, however, insistent on viewing the activity of the artist in continuity with the activity of every person. Thus for him a work of art is not merely the physical statue, painting, or composition but also the experience of this physical work of art in such a way that a work of art is recreated each time it is aesthetically experienced. The meanings and values expressed through a work of art can be experienced many times. This view of art stresses the power of a work of art to both express and communicate. Dewey wrote

In the end, works of art are the only media of complete and unhindered communication between man and man that can occur in a world full of gulfs and walls that limit community of experience. (1934, p. 105)

This power to communicate underlies the great power of art in the development of human civilization. Like Schiller, Dewey saw art as playing an important moral function by its imaginative projection and presentation of ideals. He could say, as Plato could never say, that "the moral prophets of humanity have always been the poets even though they spoke in free verse or by parable" (1934, p. 348). The arts keep alive the sense of purpose in a society and often supply the power of overcoming existing structures.

Dewey gave great praise to artists when he put their role as social critics above the philosophers. He pointed out that while philosophers made criticism of society self-consciously and directly, artists were more powerful critics because they taught

Not directly, but by disclosure, through imaginative vision addressed to imaginative experience (not to set judgment) of possibilities that contrast with actual conditions. A sense of possibilities that can unrealized and that might be realized are, when they are put in contrast with actual conditions, the most penetrating "criticisms" of the latter that can be made. . . . Only imaginative vision elicits the possibilities that are interwoven within the texture of the actual. (1934, p. 348, 349)

Dewey exercised his own critical role as philosopher when he decried the effects of capitalism on the relationship between art and common life. In his view capitalism was responsible for the emergence of the museum culture in which art was associated with wealth and superior culture. Museums take art away from their natural communities and common experience. The debilitating effects of capitalism, he believed, were also seen in the workplace which he found devoid of the beauty befitting human existence. Not only must art be accessible to all but it must also permeate all human social relationships and institutions.

Aesthetic education

Dewey had already discussed the relationship between art and education in *Democracy and Education* (1916) He argued that one of the purposes of art was to bring about changes in the world. True artistic activities are not mere sentiments nor fancies to stimulate eccentric fancy or emotional indulgences. They are concerned with the transformation of things. Dewey decries in education the separation and mutual contempt of the practical man and the man of theory or culture, the divorce of fine and industrial arts (p. 135–136).

Dewey also recognized the value of the recreative role of art. Art provides an outlet for human instincts. Dewey concluded that

> Education has no more serious responsibility than making adequate provision for enjoyment of recreative leisure; not only for the sake of immediate health, but still more if possible for the sake of its lasting effects upon habits of mind. Art is again the answer to this demand. (1916, p. 205)

In Dewey's view even work can become art if it is suffused with the play qualities of art.

Dewey did not propose the arts as a separate part of the curriculum but rather as a dimension of everything done in school. He recognized that students could achieve better works of art if art were taught separately but he felt that the integrated approach used in his schools favored greater emotional and personal fulfillment. Thus for Dewey aesthetic education is primarily for the enjoyment, expression, and refinement of human experiences.

Dewey's theory of art has received careful criticism from C. M. Smith (1971) who contends that his theory cannot form an adequate basis for aesthetic education. She argued that because the aesthetic experience is reduced by Dewey to ordinary human experience, there is no distinct subject matter for art instruction. Also, Dewey's more specialized description of art as a work of art appears to end in a private and subjective experience that is not pedagogically useful. She also did not see how his views on art can be reconciled with the major emphases in his social and educational thought, namely, intelligence and its instrumental nature, the growth and continuity of experience, and the acquisition of shared meanings through deliberate and intelligent social interaction.

In assessing Dewey's opinions on art and experience one must see them within the context of his time. His main concern was to show in a culture that valued only theoretical intelligence, the basic continuity of all human experience and intelligence, the role of the imagination in an integrated view of intelligence, and the social dimensions of intelligence. He also wrote in a time when the fine arts were a part of education. In developing a Deweyan approach to aesthetic education today, a different case might have to be made in which Dewey's insights on aesthetic education would be relevant. It must be admitted, however, that Dewey's presentation of art as primarily a good in itself and only secondarily an instrumental good, goes counter to one of the basic premises of his pragmatic philosophy which places the highest value on utility.

Education through Art: Herbert Read

The British philosopher Herbert Read was responsible for increased attention to art in the first part of this century. In his *Education Through Art* (1958, 3rd ed.) he protested the tendencies in modern society and education that stifle spontaneity, freedom, and artistic expression. He argued that

> The secret of our collective ills is to be traced to the suppression of spontaneous creative ability in the individual. The lack of spontaneity, in education and social organization, is due to that disintegration of the personality which has been the fatal result of economic, industrial, and cultural developments since the Renaissance. (1958, p. 201)

To counteract these developments he argued that art should be a major school concern in all subjects, that the arts help persons to know deeply, and that art can aid in the development of a true moral sense.

Read applied the theory of art as expressive form to education. Like Dewey he argued for a view of art which affected all school subjects. He commented

> ... the integral education which I conceive is relatively indifferent to the fate of individual subjects, since its underlying assumption is that the purpose of education is to develop generic qualities of insight and sensibility, which qualities are fundamental even in mathematics and geography. (1958, p. 221)

Thus art is, in Read's opinion, something like a general method whereby all subjects may be taught.

Art for Read applied not primarily to works of art but to the activity of the mind which produces them and appreciates them. This activity is the emotional intuition of the forms or essences of things; through this intuition one becomes aware of things as if for the first time. For Read, since art is also a means for exploring the self, it fosters one of the aims of education which is to help persons clarify their emotions and discover themselves.

Because Read regarded art as essentially play activity, he ascribed great value to the art expressions of children and cautioned against imposing adult realistic models on them. His ideas were influential in stressing children's imaginative art in schools.

A number of criticisms have been made of Read's proposals (Parsons, 1971). Read claimed too much for the intellectual and moral intuition of children. Some systematic intellectual knowledge and some knowledge of moral rules would appear to be necessary for intuitions to be effective. Read appeared to slight the public character of knowledge and morality, and seemed to have a great faith in the child to arrive easily at correct knowledge and moral behavior. Although no doubt Read proposed a rather romantic view of persons, his proposals for the value of art as protest against the constraints within modern society are still valuable.

This brief historical perspective on art, with special attention on writers who focused on education in art, provides a background for contemporary discussions on aesthetic education.

CONTEMPORARY DISCUSSIONS ON AESTHETIC EDUCATION

Theories of Art

The search for a theory to explain the nature of art continues to our time. Some, however, have despaired of developing a single theory that will explain the many forms of art that fill our world: classical, romantic, impressionistic, modern, postmodern, pop art, and many other forms. Can there be a theory of art that explains the many forms of art: music, painting, sculpture, architecture, and drama? Like in other areas, each theory explains some aspects of reality but leaves others poorly explained. Perhaps it is valuable to look systematically at the various theories that have been offered. A knowledge of these theories affords the educator ways of dealing with the different arts. The value of each theory is that it emphasizes an important perspective in which to understand

and present art. Each of these theories can be related to a general philo-sophical position.

Enough has been said above about the *imitation and representational* theories of classicism and neoclassicism, which are also called artistic re-alism. This theory is connected with philosophical realism found in the neo-Thomism of Jacques Maritain or the metaphysical theories of Alfred Whitehead. Classic plays and classical sculpture can be explained as imi-tating or representing cosmic and human rhythms, forces, and realities. In attending to these works we are often moved to feel that we are in the presence of the really real. These theories have the value of focusing on the work as such. While such theories do have a place for understanding the power of the imagination, they do not emphasize the free play of the imagination. This imagination is to be guided by rules of reason, space, and time.

A second theory of art has been covered in the preceding section, the *romantic or expressive theory* of art which places emphasis on the inspi-ration and imagination of the artist and sees art as the expression of the artist's feelings and emotions. This theory best explains lyric poetry and much of modern art. A number of philosophical explanations have been given for the expressive theory of art.

The philosophical theory of logical positivism interprets statements about art in an emotive manner. Ayer (1946, ch. 6) espoused an *emotive theory of art* according to which the statement, "The painting is good," expresses feelings of approval evoked in a person. The emotive theory is also used to explain moral and religious statements. This theory helps to account for the wide variation in aesthetic standards across ages, cul-tures, and individuals. The theory pays no attention to such objective standards as formal harmony or expressive power. The theory also does not distinguish between aesthetic and moral experience. While this ap-proach does help clarify some of our language about aesthetic experi-ences, it in no way penetrates to the essence of the artistic experience to probe what role it plays in the life of individuals and cultures.

Another philosophical approach to explain art from a basically ex-pressive perspective is *phenomenology and existentialism*. Although this theory focuses essentially on the subjective experience, it also takes into account some elements in objects as they are perceived. The basis for un-derstanding the aesthetic experience is found in Heidegger's explanation of knowing as comprising three activities: affectivity, understanding, and expression. Persons must be open to experience that comes through feelings. To do such is to be open to moods, understandings, and expressions. We then come to an understanding of the object of our feelings. Finally we express what we have understood. These activities may occur simultaneously (Kaelin, 1971, pp. 151–152; Kaelin, 1991).

Two fallacies must be avoided in understanding human knowing, of which aesthetic knowing is a part. The intentional fallacy says that something means what we intend it to mean. The affective fallacy says that our response to works of art is purely a subjective phenomenon caused by our own inner workings (Kaelin, 1974, in Denton, p. 59). In Kaelin's view the significance of a work of art is determined by its felt expressiveness which is based on actual ordering of perceived qualities (1974, p. 59).

Kaelin also wrote of the teacher as artist. As an artist the teacher is concerned with the world of the student, with understanding the expression of the student, and with offering students opportunities to express themselves. The task of the teacher-artist is described in these terms:

His is the task of ordering the qualities of the learning experience by controlling the communication between the openness of the student—who must express his own universe—and his own as the first critical appreciator. (1974, p. 50)

There is also a role for the teacher as critic who possesses certain questions to raise about artistic expressions.

Maxine Greene (1981) also favors a phenomenological interpretation of aesthetic experience, although she insists that other perspectives are also necessary such as the imitative and the expressive. For her the artistic-aesthetic is an identifiable province or domain in which to interpret the world. Drawing on the work of Schutz for her analysis, Greene states that "art works select out certain dimensions of experience, frame them, set them apart; and, by so doing, they make available new possibilities of perception and cognition" (p. 126).

Aesthetic experience depends on the attending consciousness of the perceiver to see things differently from the conventional and the routine. By paying attention to a work one can sense the feelings in the work. The task of art education is to foster this alternative awareness and perception in students. (Later in this section Greene's suggestions for aesthetic literacy will be explored.)

The aesthetic theory of Emmanuel Kant has given rise to a *theory of expressive form or symbolic theory* developed by such philosophers as Susanne Langer and Ernest Cassirir. This theory emphasizes the function of art to give understanding and knowledge. What art conveys are feelings which have been objectified. This theory describes art as a "cognitive experience distinguished by the dominance of certain symbolic characteristics and judged by standards of cognitive efficacy" (Nelson Goodman in Greene, 1981, p. 124). Art is to give persons a knowledge of something they did not know; it may or may not bring pleasure or enjoyment to persons. The value of a work of art depends on the power with which it forms and makes accessible an emotional content. In this theory of art

> The artist . . . wants first of all merely to give form and substance to what he has divined of the emotional content of the world; that is the goal of his labor and his life. The works, however, which he thus creates, leave his studio and go out among people, to whom they publish what he felt. What they want now is to be understood. This means they want to be comprehended in rhythmic-formal terms, and thus communicate their emotional content correctly. (Otto Baensch, 1961, p. 35–36)

The purpose of art then is to give revelations. All art is not immediately understood. Preparation and attention can bring us to the point where the work opens up and speaks to us.

In Cassirir's neo-Kantian analysis art is described in terms of matter and form, the terms used by Kant in his attempt to explain all thought. Cassirir tried to balance matter and form, objective and subjective, representation and expression. He did this by arguing that art is not an imitation but a discovery of reality. It is a discovery of the forms of nature. For example, the painter and the sculptor teach about the realm of visible world, its pure and visual shape and structure. The great dramatists reveal to us the true forms of our inner life. Thus Cassirir explained that great works of art are

> Neither merely representative nor merely expressive. They are symbolic in a new and deeper sense. . . . They are not simply a momentary outburst of passionate feeling; they reveal a deep unity and continuity. (1944, p. 162)

Susanne Langer has also presented a theory of art which focuses on art as a symbol that expresses meaning through form. Art in her view creates perceptible forms expressive of human feeling. Art expresses feelings in a way that discursive language cannot. In fact, it is only through art that the life of feeling can be formulated and conveyed since art objectifies feeling so that we and others can contemplate them. This contemplation leads to self-knowledge and knowledge of other aspects of life (Langer, 1953). Langer's theory of art will also be treated below as it affords a powerful intellectual justification for aesthetic education.

In this century another prominent philosophical approach to art has come from the *Frankfort school of social theory*, a school which takes much of its inspiration from the critical approach of Kant, the ideological critique of Karl Marx, and the psychoanalysis of Freud. Members of this school take a basically cognitive approach to art. The criticisms of art offered by members of this school were anticipated by the work of John Dewey in his critique of art in capitalist societies. In their criticism of advanced capitalist society critical theorists have focused on how culture, including the arts, serves the interests of the dominant classes and adds to the oppression of lower classes in society. This school began to have influence in the United States in the 1960s through the work of Theodor Adorno and Herbert Marcuse.

Art is viewed by members of this school as a form of human self-creation in the process of endowing things with use and meaning, a view of art which stresses both a subjective and an objective element. This self-creation, however, takes place in a specific social and political context. Art says something not only about the individual's feelings but also about his or her feelings about the world.

Members of this school also see art as social and political statements about what the world is or about what the world should become. Thus art can be used by a state to support particular programs. Critical theorists have pointed out how totalitarian regimes have attempted to use art to foster their policies. In our own time we have witnessed the political power of the artistic imagination which combats forms of totalitarianism. Artists who played an important part in the dissident movement against Communism have also been active in building a new Europe.

Some critical theorists openly called for the politicization of art to meet the fascist challenge. Art was to serve the purpose of aiding the struggle of the worker's movement for self-consciousness. They contended that fascist leaders used the arts for their political purposes. Other theorists question this direct connection of art with politics feeling that art will thus be liable to corruption.

Many members of this school have expressed a strong antipathy towards the works of high culture because such works often entailed the exploitation of workers. In Walter Benjamin's view many of the great works of art

> Owe their existence not merely to the effort of the great geniuses that created them, but also to the unnamed drudgeries of their contemporaries. There is no document of culture which is not at the same time a document of barbarism. (In Arato and Gebhardt, 1978, p. 187)

For this reason members of the school were ambiguous towards art, both participating in culture and rejecting many cultural achievements. Marcuse's position is a radical one for in his *Essay on Liberation* (1969) he called for the integration of life and culture through the abolition of art and the aestheticization of daily work and life. Others saw in some forms of art, rooted in community life and work, a utopian character that challenged present oppression and gave hope and shape for a better world.

Critical theorists direct much criticism at the role of the arts in the mass media and point out how they serve to defuse many criticisms of society. Art has become an important instrument in a capitalist culture to entice consumers. The mass media, in their view, have cheapened artistic experience and subordinated it to meaningless entertainment and consumption.

This critical perspective is one that can be relevant in aesthetic education. Works of art can be attended to by students not only as the expressions of individuals but also as a reflection of particular social and political contexts. The aesthetic experience, as all human experiences, is thus socially conditioned. On the other hand, much art can be seen as attempting to critique present social realities and pointing to possibilities beyond those that now exist.

I have not attempted to treat all theories of art in this section, but have rather focused on such theories that appear to have relevance to aesthetic education. Some notions from these theories will be developed in the next section in an attempt to review the various philosophical justifications offered for aesthetic education.

Philosophical Justification of Aesthetic Education

Most subjects in the school curriculum do not need philosophical justification. This is not true, however, for education in the arts. With the exception of literature, the place of the arts in the curriculum often needs justification, especially when there is a desire to cut school budgets. It is not enough to state that the enjoyment of aesthetic experience is an end in itself and that works of art have intrinsic value. Reasons must be adduced which are considered educationally sound.

Imagination has generally been neglected in education, especially at higher levels. Charlton (1964) gives a number of reasons for this omission. The scientific method of thinking has dominated in education. An older faculty psychology which put special focus on imagination as a separate function of the mind has been discredited. A Social Realist School argued that education should entail moving children away from dreaming and illusion to the world of reality. The use of fairy tales and imaginative works is thought to lead to false expectations about the world and to the failure to prepare children for the real world. Furthermore, many have thought of imagination in terms of a sick mind or a leisurely or useless relaxation. Even Shakespeare has been quoted against imagination:

> The lunatic, the lover, and the poet
> Are of imagination all compact.
> The poet's eye, in a fine frenzy rolling,
> Doth glance from heaven to earth, from earth to heaven;
> And as imagination bodies forth
> The form of things unknown, the poet's pen
> Turns them to shapes, and gives to airy nothing
> A local habitation and a name.
> Such tricks hath strong imagination
> That, if it would but apprehend some joy,
> It comprehends some bringer of that joy;
> Or in the night, imagining some fear,
> How easy is a bush suppos'd a bear.
> (A Midsummer Night's Dream, V.i.7–23)

A common form of justification of aesthetic education appeals to *psychological grounds*. People need the recreative values which art enjoyment and production can afford. Given the burdens of modern life and the obstacles and frustrations that people encounter, aesthetic experiences are needed for enjoyment. Also, educating the young in the arts affords opportunities for sublimation of desires and energies. Psychological forms of justification often stress the play element in all artistic endeavor and enjoyment. Artistic play enables one to be free to transcend the toil, frustration, and fatigue of life. By expanding our consciousness of the world art holds out to us larger realms for enjoyment and achievement. As explained above, Read has offered a detailed justification for art on psychological grounds.

Psychological justifications for aesthetic education are also based on developmental psychology. Psychologists see in the arts a means of aiding persons to develop to maturity and to deal with inner conflicts. The arts, which deal with symbols, aid children in developing thinking power, a rich affective life, and psycho-motor skills. Art can also be helpful for adolescents and adults by enabling them to face and express internal conflicts and frustrations. Furthermore, the aesthetic pleasure which comes from experiencing or creating a work of art can give energy and satisfaction.

Many have offered an *intellectual argument* to justify aesthetic education, viewing art as a form of knowing. The imagination can be seen to be a way of both apprehending reality and of increasing our awareness of reality. This justification seems to be based on a philosophy of realism. Through the imagination we can rearrange previously experienced elements into new groupings. Works of art contain in a concrete form the fundamental ideas of human civilization and culture; exposure to and appreciation of them increases our knowledge of these ideas. A reading of William Styron's *Sophie's Choice* or viewing the film made from the book brings a knowledge of the Holocaust and how it impinged on human lives. It does so in a more vivid and powerful manner than purely historical and psychological studies.

A well argued and widely accepted justification for aesthetic education on intellectual grounds can be found in the theory of Susanne Langer (1967), who contended that through art we become conscious of the elements of our feelings and are enabled to articulate these feelings in a concrete form. Thus the work of art is an objectification of feelings, a symbol capable of representing or standing for a particular feeling. Furthermore, art can foster social and cultural education and understanding because it can reveal

> The fact that the basic forms of feeling are common to most people at least within a culture, and often far beyond it, since a great many works do seem expressive and important to almost everyone who judges them by artistic standards. (1967, p. 64)

Langer believed that art education is important for the education of feelings. She argued that education of the feelings is at the very heart of personal education. She contended that

The arts objectify subjective reality and subjectify outward experience of
nature. Art education is the education of feeling, and a society that ne-
glects it gives itself up to formless emotion. Bad art is corruption of feeling.
This is a large factor in the irrationalism which dictators and demagogues
exploit. (Langer, 1971, p. 94)

Another justification offered is that aesthetic education promotes *moral
development*. Many argue that education of the imagination leads to
moral development because it can increase the capacity for sympathy,
concern, justice, and other moral virtues. Art has an effect on the moral
life because people are influenced by things which they experience deeply
and vividly. Good art has the potential of facilitating the good character
and inhibiting bad character. What we encounter in good art enhances
our sensitivity to moral situations. Art does a great deal to define the
ways in which we both understand and relate to the world. Iredell Jenkins
made this point:

How and what we see and hear; our settled views of different types,
classes, and races of men; our opinions of social customs and institutions;
the expectations and purposes with which we face the future; what we
think to be desirable, right, and permissible –all of this comes to us quite
largely through artistic presentation. (1971, p. 225)

Art can foster the moral sense in an important way. What art appeals
to is feeling. Great art gives us a feeling of what good is and what evil is.
The case can be made that the moral person must not only have a knowledge of good and evil but also a feeling for good of evil. To *know* that
something is right or wrong generally is knowledge that most often
comes from others. To *feel* that it is so is more often a knowledge that
comes from within. It is the arts that deal in a special way with this inner
sense of morality.

A *cultural or social* justification of aesthetic education is based on the
realization that education includes handing on a culture. For persons to
be considered educated in a particular society they need a knowledge of
the values of a society, many of which are found in the works of art of
that society. Another cultural argument is that aesthetic education must
include the encouragement of students to use the culture in order to sur-
pass it. Among the students of today are the great artists of the future,
as well as those who will make contributions to culture. The human
community will be enriched by the artistic expressions of all its members,

not only those of the past. Another form of cultural justification is found in the arguments of those who see as an important part of aesthetic education the producing of both critics of art and of the cultures within which the arts arose.

Aims of Aesthetic Education

In a general sense aesthetic education has as its aim the fostering of aesthetic experiences. In the broad sense aesthetic experiences refer to the enjoyment element in any human experience. Thus all forms of education can be considered aspects of aesthetic education. In a stricter sense, aesthetic experiences are those which are connected with what are generally considered works of art. Aesthetics as a field of study is thus concerned with a number of activities. It refers to activities concerned with the skills necessary to create works of art. Second, it focuses on the ways and means of contemplating works of art. Third, it entails the appreciation of works of art. Aesthetic education is thus concerned with imparting skills, providing for contemplation, and fostering appreciation of works of art (Clark, 1964). With regard to the aims of aesthetic education, a national study on the teaching of the arts in the United States gave these as the aims of art education: (1) more discriminating consumers of art; (2) better art producers or performers; (3) better learners; (4) more integrated human beings or better persons; (5) a better community or society (Rockefeller, 1977, p. 279). The fourth aim was discussed earlier in this chapter in establishing the psychological grounds for aesthetic education. The fifth aim was also discussed earlier in the discussion about the cultural and social values of the arts.

Aesthetic education is involved with the *education of artists* by helping students to create works of art or to perform artistically. This is the education of artists where the emphasis is on doing. There is a general opinion that artists are born and not made. It may be preferable to call this art education and not aesthetic education. All educational institutions should encourage those who have these special talents. In our society this form of education has become a rather specialized area of training with initial instruction taking place with private tutors and schools, and more advanced training in specialized schools and institutions.

The best thing that educational institutions can do to produce future artists is to foster artistic creativity in the production and performance of art. While creativity is often spoken of in education with reference to discovery methods in science and mathematics, the term appropriately refers to the ability to produce something original or to do something in an original manner. To decide that something is creative or a person is creative we must make a value judgment about them or about a work. The term to be rightly used demands reference to some criteria.

A discussion on creativity centers around children's art. While many place great emphasis in the education of children on getting them to draw and produce art, the value of such drawing is disputed among educators. The philosophical question concerns whether or not the term creative can be applied to such art. White (1971) reviewed arguments in this area. He thinks that the term creative is used too loosely, though he does not deny the value of creative drawing and writing. These efforts can be valuable as enjoyable and possibly therapeutic activities. He remains somewhat skeptical of the educational value of such activities and questions the appropriateness of terming them creative.

Aesthetic education attempts to produce *choosers of good art* who are discriminating in their tastes. This is an important task, given the impact of the mass media on the young. The task of the school vis a vis the arts becomes one of exposing the young to the classical and accepted works of art. It does this by helping students to know about the history and forms of art. This type of education must face the issue of criteria for good art, which was discussed above.

Aesthetic education aims at producing *appreciators of good art*. Appreciation refers to internal states or to knowing works of art and not merely knowing about or of them. Putting persons in the presence of works of art is not automatically to produce the aesthetic experience. Teachers must prepare students for these experiences through instruction, readings, and discussions.

Maxine Greene makes a distinction between aesthetic education and art appreciation. For her, art appreciation entails "diverse efforts to acquaint students with the structures of particular art forms, their language, their history, their studies" (1981, p. 120). Art appreciation takes a number of forms from introductory to art criticism. Aesthetic literacy demands art appreciation.

For Greene aesthetic education demands that aesthetic experiences be given a central role in education. These experiences entail a certain type of literacy. The task of aesthetic education is to enable students to be literate in this way. Literacy entails certain interpretive skills such as discrimination, sensitivity, and responsiveness. Aesthetic education is to enhance a person's ability to perceive works of art.

The most thorough treatment of the practical objectives of aesthetic education has been presented by the British philosopher, F. E. Sparshott (1971), who analyzes twelve aims which he groups according to whether they foster the perceptual awareness, the cognitive awareness, or the creation of works of art. The objectives relating to *perceptual awareness* are the following: first, to enhance a person's appreciation of any work of art, a goal sought in art and music appreciation courses; second, to make persons more sensitive to beauty in general, in nature as well as art; third, to increase responsiveness not to beauty but to the perceptible environment in general.

Objectives relating to *cognitive awareness* are the following: fourth, to make people media conscious, which includes a study of the ways in which information reaches us from our whole environment; fifth, to make people more knowledgeable about the arts, by stressing art history; sixth, to impart a critical vocabulary which will enable persons to articulate their responses to works of art; seventh, to acquaint persons with the world's great masterpieces; eighth, to improve persons' discrimination between good and bad art; ninth, to open persons to new and unfamiliar styles of art.

Objectives relating to the *practical sphere* are the following: tenth, to make persons more creative or at least to encourage persons not to become less creative than they are; eleventh, to instill the practice of artistic production in one or more fields; twelfth, to impart skills that may or may not be used. Sparshott in treating these objectives recognizes that there may be tensions and conflicts among them. He also recognizes that aims without a discussion of ways to achieve them is not a complete treatment of aesthetic education.

Education of the imagination

For many writers today aesthetic education entails the education of the imagination. Since the word has many usages, some clarification of the meaning of imagination is necessary. The word imagination has a number of uses (Charlton, 1964). In its descriptive usage it refers to the process of making images. Thus I can say that I imagine what the picture or statue will look like when it is finished. We also use the word imagine to express the idea that we once believed such and such but do not now.

We say, I imagined that I would pass the test. The benefit of hindsight is present here. Also, the word is used to refer to conjuring up of images in one's imagination. We tell people to imagine that they are in Berlin. This usage implies that people must have some experience to conjure up images in their imagination. They do not arise spontaneously. The imagination has been prepared by experiences. In this usage we see *in imagination*.

Another usage of imaging refers to the activity of *supposing, postulating, or assuming*. It is the act of playing with an idea. Imagination in this usage is involved in hypothesis forming. This type of imagination may not involve imagery for it may be scientific or mathematical.

A common use of the word, one which bears more directly on aesthetic education, is designated thinking imaginatively, doing something *with imagination*. This involves creativity and entails a certain degree of originality. Charlton (1964) noted that in this usage

> The essence of imagination here is the seeing of relations which previously have gone unobserved, and this is characterized, particularly, in the poet's use of words and especially in the metaphorical use of words. (p. 143)

The use of metaphor is essential in this form of the imagination. The use of metaphor enables us to use imagination in which, in Koestler's (1964) words we engage in

> An act of wrenching away an object or a concept from its habitual associative context, and seeing it in a new context. It is an act both of destruction and of creation, for it demands the breaking up of a mental habit, the melting down with the blow lamp of Cartesian doubt, of the frozen structures of accepted theory to enable a new fusion to take place. (p. 519)

In Charlton's analysis imagination is not a nuclear faculty but a distinctive kind of thinking. In his view we feel, think, and act imaginatively. Imagination is a certain quality that can be present in all human activities. He sees room for many kinds of imagination: mathematical, poetical, historical, and pictorial.

Imagination comes into play in many academic areas. The work of many historians is one of imaginative reconstruction and not really an account of what actually happened. Historians are selective in painting their pictures of a person or event. They attempt to enter into minds, places, and times not our own. This can be exaggerated at times, in the story about Agnellus, the ninth-century Bishop of Ravenna, who wrote a book about his predecessors and said this:

> Where I have not found any history of any of these bishops, and where I have not been able by conversation with aged men, or by inspection of the monuments which remain, or from any other authentic source, to obtain information concerning them, in such a case in order that there might not be a break in the series I have composed the life myself, with the help of God and the prayers of the brethren. (In Muller 1954, p. 232)

Aesthetic Education: Teaching and Learning

In this final section I will present some of the suggestions that philosophers have made for teaching and learning in the arts. Some attempt will be made to offer suggestion in the various forms of art.

Education in attention and perception

Maxine Greene (1981) has given special treatment to education in attention and perception as a major task of aesthetic education. For her, one should not think of aesthetic education in terms of discrete competencies in teachers or learners. Emphasis should rather be on releasing students to attend and to move deeper into works of art. The key concept is that of attending and qualitative perceiving. Works of art are to be perceived as a whole, as privileged objects of perception. Teachers should provide a wide range of experiences in perceiving and noticing. The capacity to perceive and attend can be learned and the capacity for imagining is essential for education. Imagination can transform what is perceived. Perception is a work that one takes on personally.

Education in art criticism

Aesthetic education should include education in criticism. Criticism involves ratings of works, reasons for the ratings, and rules and norms of judgment (Ashner 1971, p. 431). Criticism entails expressing favorable or unfavorable judgments about a work of art. What criticism does is make standards of judgments explicit. Criticism helps persons not only to appraise but also to understand. Often we do not know what a work of art is until we express some judgment about it. A good way to foster criticism is to encourage taking a positive and then a negative viewpoint before arriving at a final judgment. Any education in art criticism should entail a discussion of standards for judgment. The question of objective and subjective standards also needs discussion. Even criticism itself should be subjected to critical judgment (Smith, 1991).

Philosophers of art have offered some basic criteria for judging a work of art (Beardsley 1971, p. 438). Does the work possess *unity*, such as Haydn's *Creation*? Does it possess a well defined meaning? Does the work have adequate *complexity*, such as a Pasolini or Bergman film? Does the work have an *intensity* of quality, as in a Shakespeare romantic sonnet? Other criteria advanced by educators include originality, honesty, boldness, social value, and ability to please. The critic can also raise questions about the intentions or sincerity of the artist as well as the effects of the work on individuals and groups.

Education in literature

Maxine Greene advocates the imaginative teaching of literature. Literature enables persons to break with the stereotyped, the mundane, and the conventional to explore inner horizons and feelings. Literature education is directed at providing heightened knowledge of the world, by equipping students to make enlightened value judgments, and by enabling them to learn more about themselves and the human condition. Commenting on learning through literature, Greene writes

> Informed encounters, then, with literature perceived as art cannot be expected to add to the store of verifiable knowledge; nor can they be expected to redeem those who experience them, to make readers better, wiser, more humane. They may, however, enable individuals to break through the conventional mental and emotional sets that stifle inquiry and hinder growth. Releasing imaginative activity, they may stimulate self-reflectiveness, and with it, self-creation. They may, by communicating an awareness of the momentousness of being human and responsible, arouse those who try to form their own experience, to pursue meaning—in fact, to learn. (1971, p. 211)

What Greene says about learning through literature is also true with learning through other arts.

Students should be given opportunities to disclose to others the meaning of what they read. They should be encouraged to take their own positions as well as to learn what the teachers and critics think. The ultimate purpose of the literature is the self and world understanding of the student. Greene advises that "the teacher's object can only be to launch the student on his own journey, to goad him to his own action and his own choice, to confront him with possibles" (1974, p. 84).

Teaching as art

While this chapter has focused primarily on the arts and literature as the subject matter of aesthetic education, a case can be made that teaching and learning in all subjects should attend to aesthetic standards. Teaching can be viewed as an artistic performance and schooling as a drama (Starratt, 1990). Many teachers regard their classes as artistic creations in attention to the ways in which presentations, interactions, and responses will take place. Teaching must be adapted to the group and changing circumstances. The moods and attitudes of students are to be heeded. Aesthetic devices and techniques can be used with profit in teaching.

The analogy between teachers and artists, though a good one, must be applied carefully. In an effort to counter a technology of teaching with an aesthetic of teaching, we must not romanticize the artist. As Greene notes

> There have been artists who conceived themselves as seers and poet-priests, who—like Emerson and Whitman—created in wonder and joy. But there have also been artists—like Baudelaire, Dostoevsky, Wagner, Nietzsche— who were tortured individuals, given to melancholia, deadly fits of boredom, contempt for the middle class and the masses, various sorts of depravity. (In Smith, 1971, pp. 557-8)

It is clear from the lives of many artists that aesthetic perception, appreciation, and creation do not of themselves ennoble a person. The analogy often oversimplifies the complexity of the aesthetic experience.

Learning also has its aesthetic dimensions. Students must be personally involved to the point of commitment. Learning includes the use of all powers of the person: imagination, memory, and mind. Philosophers have often spoken of the beauty involved in learning even abstract subjects. John Hospers speaks of this beauty:

When we enjoy or appreciate the elegance of a mathematical proof, it would surely seem that our enjoyment is aesthetic, although the object of that enjoyment is not perceptual at all: it is the complex relation among abstract ideas or propositions, not the marks on paper or the blackboard, that we are apprehending aesthetically. (In Smith, 1971, p. 542)

A number of mathematicians have written about the aesthetic experiences that mathematics have afforded them, though generations of students may object to such expressions of ecstasy.

The educational significance of this discussion is that all teachers and all subjects, in fact, all activities in the school, can increase the aesthetic experience and appreciation of students. Those who plan curriculum might set aesthetic or expressive objectives as concomitant goals in learning. School administrators can be sensitive to the the aesthetic in planning school events and in promoting an appreciation of the arts.

CHAPTER 5

RELIGIOUS EDUCATION

Closely connected with moral and aesthetic education in the curriculum of the schools is religious education or education in religion. The formal study of religion is not found in public schools in the United States though it is a school subject in many countries of the world. The teaching of religion in public schools in this country takes place in a rather indirect way through the various subjects of the humanities. Of course, religion is part of the curriculum in private schools run by religious groups and in church educational programs for children and adults. Interestingly, religious studies thrive in many colleges and universities, even in state colleges and universities that do not have religious affiliation. There also exists in the United States a small association of scholars and educators who advocate the teaching of religion in public schools. The absence of religion in the public schools has led to the founding of schools sponsored by religious groups, in the past mainly Roman Catholic and at present evangelical and fundamentalist Protestant. The number of Islamic schools in this country has increased recently.

This chapter will present some historical perspectives on the changing role of religion in education. It will trace the movement from the religious school where religion dominated the curriculum to the secular school where religion is virtually excluded. The second section of the chapter will review the continuing discussions on the role of religion in schools by presenting the various justifications that are offered for its inclusion.

HISTORICAL PERSPECTIVES ON
RELIGION IN EDUCATION

Historically religious groups have been faced with two choices with regard to the education of the young. They have encouraged their members to attend the secular schools or they have established their own schools. When they have used secular schools, they have at times worked to have religion included as part of the curriculum.

This historical perspective will deal particularly with teaching religion in schools of the West, especially the teaching of Christianity. The philosophical discussion in this historical perspective will be indirect rather than a treatment of the ideas of particular individuals. The philosophical ideas are imbedded in the various types of schools which have been established and the role of religion in them.

In the early years of Christian history the church encouraged its members to attend the state schools and did not establish its own schools. For the next thousand years the Christian Church controlled education in the West and used the classical education of Greece and Rome as the basis for its educational philosophy, institutions, and pedagogy, supplementing it in appropriate ways with religious teachings. In the past two hundred years the state controlled education in the West has either subordinated the influence of the Church or legislated it out of existence. In some countries provision is made for the teaching of the majority religion in public schools.

Christians and the Classical School

All religions are keenly interested in education through both formal and informal institutions. In the early years of Christian history the learning of the truths of the faith and the laws of Christian behavior were primarily a family responsibility to such a degree that parents were warned that they did not fulfill their obligation by simply handing over their children to religious teachers or institutions.

Christians in antiquity made extensive use of the schools of the state, since they recognized that the learning of the Christian religion demanded a minimum knowledge of reading and writing. While one might have expected Christians in the early centuries to have established their own schools, they did not do this in Greco-Roman times (Marrou, 1956, p. 422). In not doing so they did not follow the example of the Jews who organized schools around the study of the Bible, the Mishna, and the Talmud. Except in a few special cases, Christians in this period

> Simply added their own specifically religious kind of training—which . . . came from the Church and the family—on to the classical teaching that they received along with their non-Christian fellows in established schools. (Marrou, 1956, p. 424)

Christians were content with the schools of the time since they had not worked out their own view of education. They took it for granted that the general education of persons preceded the education of the religious person.

Although Christians accepted the classical school, there was opposition to many aspects of classical culture which were viewed as inimical to the Christian way of life. For some more rigorist Christians, the Bible and the teachings of the Church contained all that a person needed to know to live and achieve salvation. Those who advocated using the schools often issued guidelines for dealing with the objectionable aspects of classical culture. Some parts of this literature were ignored while others were interpreted in accordance with Christian teachings.

Paradoxically, Christian schools first began to emerge in the fourth century when Christians were forbidden by the Emperor Julian to teach in the state schools. When Julian introduced a decidedly anti-Christian spirit into classical education, Christians reacted by establishing their own schools and by reproducing their sacred writings in the various literary forms of classical literature.

While Christians did not establish their own lower schools, they did establish some schools, called catechetical schools, where their members studied the Bible and the theology of the church. These schools, though not numerous, produced a great body of literature that has been read and studied by Christians for centuries. The most notable of these schools were established at Alexandria and Caesarea.

A specifically Christian school, the monastic school, which had few of the features of the classical school, began to appear in the fourth century. In these schools the monks offered to young members of the community and children an education which was spiritual and ascetical rather than intellectual. Education in the basics was certainly part of this system because members of monasteries were required to read the sacred books. However, only a small number of parents sent their children to these schools of perfection. Accordingly, the religious education of children remained a family responsibility. Gradually the monastic schools, especially in the Western part of the Empire, began to broaden their curriculum to include grammar, Virgil, the poets, and the historians. At the same time monasteries in the East remained committed to ascetical education and did not enroll students who planned to return to secular life. The monasteries of the West became places where the Scriptures were studied and where monks and nuns learned to read and write. Monastic rules written at this time include laws on the admission and education of children.

The early Middle Ages also saw the establishment of some nonmonastic schools, primarily for the education of young men who were considering entering the priesthood. The episcopal or bishop's school enrolled future priests and provided elementary education under the direction of a magister or teacher. This school later developed into the medieval university. The presbyteral school, or priest's school, was organized in rural parishes. The legal canons of the church provided that all parish priests were to establish such schools for future priests. These schools mark "the birth of the modern school, the ordinary village school—which not even antiquity had known in any general, systematic form" (Marrou, 1956, 447).

When the classical schools disappeared in the early Middle Ages as a result of the Germanic invasions, the only remaining schools were the church schools. Gradually these church-sponsored schools admitted young men of aristocratic status who did not desire to become priests or clerics. The education given in these schools was not sympathetic to the classical culture, focusing rather on the basics of reading and memorizing the Scriptures. These schools were similar to the earlier rabbinical schools and to the Muslim schools which developed in later years. In these early Christian schools the role of the teacher became highly exalted because he was the person who knew the secrets of writing, especially the secrets the Holy Writings. This attitude was in contrast to the low regard in which teachers in the classical schools were regarded. In these schools which taught letters and morals there developed the essence of the Christian school and medieval education, a feature that distinguished it from the classical school, namely, the "synthesis of teacher and spiritual father in the person of the school teacher" (Marrou, 1956, p. 451).

The classical or humanist tradition in education did not totally disappear in the early medieval period. This tradition was maintained in such places as the University of Constantinople, the patriarchal schools in the Eastern part of the Empire, and the schools in North Africa and Italy. These schools attempted to combine classical learning with Christian teachings. This ideal of Christian humanism came to full fruition during the reign of Charlemagne.

The Schools of Christendom

In the Middle Ages the Church dominated education in the West. Beginning with the reign of Charles the Great the Christian Church provided the unifying force for education in all areas that now comprise Europe. Until the modern period

> Education . . . was a single process: it had an unquestioned Christian ideology; an agreed curriculum in Latin based upon the study of classical literature, both pagan and Christian; a single pedagogy, that of the master instructing *ex cathedra*; and one pervasive support system, involving progression from elementary through grammar school, to university, all under the aegis of Holy Church. (Bowen, 1975, p. xxi)

Education thus was primarily directed to the propagation and advancement of Christianity.

The very foundations of European education lie in the Christian schools established in the Carolingian Era (768–840). Under the direction of Alcuin, the English schoolmaster, the palace school was expanded. The curriculum of the school included grammar, classics and the Bible. Charlemagne set out the principles of the schools he established:

> And let schools be established in which boys may learn to read. Correct carefully the Psalms, the signs in writing, the songs, the calendar, the grammar, in each monastery or bishopric, and the Catholic books; because often men desire to pray to God properly, but they pray badly because of incorrect books. And do not permit mere boys to corrupt them in reading

or writing. If the Gospel, Psalter and Missal have to be copied let men of
mature age do the copying, with the greatest care. (In Bowen, 1975, p. 13)

This period also witnessed the emergence of schools that were connected
to the cathedrals of the empire and in which classical learning was joined
with religious learning.

Developments in higher education during the Middle Ages paved the
way for an education that depended less on faith sources and more on
the powers of human reason and knowledge. This debate among theologians presaged the beginning of the modern period. The dispute was over
the power of dialectic or reason in the sphere of religious knowledge.
Peter Abelard, a teacher within the cathedral schools, invested human
reason with great power to deal with the mysteries of faith, while Bernard of Clairvaux, a teacher within the monastic tradition, gave little
place to reason and emphasized the principle that reason should be used
not to demonstrate the truth of religion but to explain that truth. Abelard introduced an important educational principle in the face of much
opposition: tradition and habit must be continually examined lest they
lead a society into stagnation. By testing the limits of belief he brought
into theology and education the principles of criticism and creativity that
could check the dangers inherent in conservation and tradition. These
issues were also raised among Jewish and Islamic scholars through the
influential writings of Averroës and Moses Maimonides.

Medieval universities developed out of the cathedral schools and took
on important intellectual functions in many areas of Europe. While these
universities included arts, medicine, and law in their curriculum, theology was still the most prestigious area of study. Teachers for the lower
schools were prepared at the universities, the University of Paris being
the dominant school for theological studies. The study of theology included lectures and debates or disputations.

Scholasticism, a specific approach to the study of theology developed
within these universities. Scholastics, or school teachers, attempted to
make a synthesis between the philosophy of Aristotle and the teachings
of the Church. Although for centuries church scholars had used the more
idealistic philosophy of Plato to explain Christian teachings, now they
turned to the more earthly philosophy of Aristotle. Thomas Aquinas, the
greatest of the scholastics, even developed a theory of education which
emphasized the active role of the student and teacher in the learning process in contrast with the long standing theory of the Platonist Augustine

which interpreted education as the process of bringing out of learners the innate knowledge which they already possessed. Although these radical views were condemned at the time, eventually the Thomistic view of theology and education developed into a Roman Catholic orthodoxy.

The movement to the modern period was further advanced by the revival of classical learning in the various humanisms of the Renaissance period. While Italian Renaissance writers like Petrarch focused on the power of the classics to foster moral discipline, humanist scholars in England added a more explicit religious dimension to education. Also, theological studies were foremost in the curricula of Oxford and Cambridge. English grammar schools remained linked to the church. England's greatest humanists—Colet and Moré together with Erasmus of Rotterdam applied humanism to the support of Christianity. These humanists moved away from the aridities of scholasticism and promoted a simpler religious piety.

Erasmus has given to the West a detailed theory of humanist and Christian education. In his *Handbook of the Militant Christian* he explained how the classics can serve Christian purposes:

> If you but dedicate yourself entirely to the study of the Scriptures, if you meditate day and night on the divine law, nothing will ever terrorize you and you will be prepared against any attack of the enemy.
> I might also add that a sensible reading of the pagan poets and philosophers is a good preparation for the Christian life. We have the example of St. Basil, who recommends the ancient poets for their natural goodness. Both St. Augustine and St. Jerome followed this method. St. Cyprian has worked wonders in adorning the Scriptures with the literary beauty of the ancients. Of course it is not my intention that you imbibe the bad morals of the pagans along with their literary excellence. I am sure that you will nonetheless find many examples in the classics that are conducive to right living. Many of these writers were, of course, very good teachers of ethics. (Erasmus, 1964, p. 14)

For Erasmus Christianity was a way to both intellectual and spiritual development. He placed emphasis not on attendance at religious events but on the inner spirit of learners. In his treatise on education he anticipated later views on the need to adapt material to the developing young person and to be attentive to the individuality of each child.

Of the leaders of the Protestant Reformation Martin Luther was the most deeply involved in promoting schools wherein Christianity was taught. Luther advocated the establishment of schools throughout Germany. Such schools were to give instruction in both secular learning and the Scriptures and to use the German language in accomplishing this, though he wanted students also conversant in the Latin, Greek, and Hebrew. Luther stated that

> Even women and children can learn from German books and sermons more about God and Christ—I am telling the truth!—than all the universities, foundations, monasteries, the whole papacy, and all the world used to know. (In Bowen, 1974, p. 369)

Besides utilitarian arguments for schooling Luther stressed that attendence at schools would enable students to fulfill their service to God and their fellow citizens through the inculcation of a learned piety. Thus the basic premise of schooling was that it was the way to promote the maintenance of God's law in the world. Luther advocated that schools be established by civil authorities.

As for the actual study of theology Luther stressed the value of the direct study of the Scriptures and less dependence on the philosophy of scholasticism used in the Catholic Church. Although he considered philosophy of little value in religious education, he did see some humanistic value in its study:

> Philosophy understands naught of divine matters. I don't say that man may not teach and learn philosophy; I approve thereof, so that it be within reason and moderation. Let philosophy remain within her bounds as God has taught. (In Bowen, p. 371)

Education for Luther then was closely connected to religion and to the reformation of the church. He goes so far as to say that "when schools flourish things go well and the church is secure. . . . God has preserved the church through the schools" (In Bowen, 1974, p. 373).

Within the Catholic Church the educational leadership was taken by the Jesuits or Society of Jesus who developed a systematic rationale or plan for education. The Jesuit *Ratio studiorum* presented details for grammar schools and universities. The author of the *Ratio*, Ignatius Loyola, brought systematization but not originality to this plan. The Jesuits spread this system of education throughout the world, including the Americas. The education promoted by the Jesuits was classical humanism and the philosophy of Aristotle as interpreted by Thomas Aquinas. Jesuits gave greater weight to the powers of philosophy and human reason in religious education than did the Protestant Reformers. The ultimate aim of this education was religious, that is, to aid individuals to attain the final end for which they were created, life with God. Thus Jesuits took on the obligation to set

> A good moral example, [and, since] learning and methods of presenting it are necessary for the attaining of this end, therefore, after it seems that a fitting foundation for self-denial and for the necessary progress has been laid for those who have been admitted to probation, the education in letters and of the manner of utilizing them, so that they can add to a better knowledge and service of God, our Creator and Lord, will be treated. (Fitzpatrick, 1933, p. 49)

The Jesuit system has influenced all forms of Catholic education in the modern period.

In conclusion, the schools of Christendom were set up to achieve primarily religious purposes, even though secular and utilitarian ends were also pursued. Their primary purpose was to hand on a Christian culture and to initiate students into a religious way of life. At the same time the growing independence of these schools and the value placed on secular culture and worldly aims prepared the way for the secular school, that is, the school freed from church authority and placed solely under state control. The teaching of religion, however, was not totally eliminated from the modern secular schools. Many different arrangements are in place to deal with religious culture. Also, in the modern period religious schools continue to exist, offering various rationales and justifications for their existence.

The Secular School

In seventeenth- and eighteenth-century Europe a movement began which ultimately led to the secularization of the institutions of society, including the schools. Philosophers at that time began to challenge the reliance on authority and tradition that had marked the age of faith. These philosophers appealed to reason, feeling, and experience as legitimate sources of knowledge along with faith. Gradually the state assumed greater and greater control over education in many countries, as the influence of the church diminished. In education a movement of secularization was set in motion that would ultimately end in the secular school in which the study of religion would have at best a minor role. The evolution of the secular school will be traced in the historical developments of education in the United States.

In colonial America schools and universities were established primarily for religious purposes, as instruments for handing on a Protestant culture. The colonies passed laws to see to it that children became literate so that they might better seek their salvation through the reading of the Bible. The prominence of New England in education resulted from the strong Puritan legislation on religious instruction. This legislation first enjoined parents and then schools to catechetize children in the Puritan faith. Similar legislation was found in other colonies where various religious groups such as Dutch Reformed, Quakers, Baptists, Moravians, and Anglicans set up schools for their young members. Fewer schools existed in the South, partly because the more liturgical Anglican Church did not place as much emphasis on biblical literacy (Welter, 1962, p. 18). Outside of New England, communities and their schools showed more respect for religious differences.

The content and flavor of religious instruction in these schools can be seen in the *New England Primer*. The primer includes the Lord's Prayer, the Creed, the Ten Commandments, and a list of books in the Old and New Testaments. The primer also includes a short catechism on the basic tenets of the Protestant faith. The answers in the catechism were to be committed to memory. Noah Webster's spelling book had many of the religious and moral characteristics of this primer. The primer described the good child (Spring, 1986, p. 25) as follows:

Good Children Must

Fear God all Day   Love Christ Always
Parents Obey,   In Secret Pray,
No False thing Say   Mind Little Play
By no Sin Stray   Make no Delay

In doing Good.

Grammar schools were also established in the colonies for the needs of the ministry and the future ruling class. The typical grammar school included in its curriculum both classical and religious studies. Languages studied were Latin, Greek, and Hebrew. The curriculum included the study of the catechism and various religious exercises.

The small colonial colleges were for the most part religious establishments for the training of clergy. Harvard was established in 1636 in order to prevent an illiterate ministry from developing in the Churches. In its earlier years over half of its alumni were clergymen.

A case can be made that the secularization of education in the United States was rooted in the establishment of academies where practical studies were introduced into the curriculum. Academies in England had started as dissenting institutions against the control of education by the state and the Anglican Church. Robert Molesworth and Joseph Priestly were leaders in the movement to foster freedom of thought and speech in education, which entailed some degree of separation from church and state control (Spring, 1986, pp. 15–18). While the academies in the colonies may not have had the same vigorous elements of religious dissent that academies had in England, their emergence and their stress on education in useful subjects did pave the way for a more secular school.

At the beginning of the national period one prominent voice was raised against the common practice of religious instruction in schools. Thomas Jefferson contended that children were too immature for religious inquiries. He stated that

> Instead, therefore, of putting the Bible and Testament into the hands of children at an age when their judgments are not sufficiently matured for religious inquiries, their memories may be stored with the most useful facts from Grecian, Roman, European, and American History. (In Spring, 1986, p. 41)

Jefferson also felt that majority rule should have no place in religion. His goals for primary school included moral education but not religious education. The moral education that he proposed, however, was to be carried out through reading and not through direct teaching. Jefferson did not even include religion among the subjects for higher education although he invited Christian denominations to set up seminaries on the border of the University of Virginia. Jefferson's Bill for Religious Freedom became the model for states seeking to disestablish the Christian religion (Cremin, 1980, p. 114).

Despite the views of Jefferson and others and even though there was a decline in religious fervor at this time, early eighteenth-century education was still largely influenced by religious bodies in the United States. Although religious instruction was an essential part of the curriculum in the academies and charity schools, many decried that moral and religious education was neglected. Before the movement for the common school could succeed, it was essential to determine the role of religion in these publicly financed and controlled schools. Horace Mann, the father of the public school, worked out a compromise in Massachusetts according to which the various Protestant bodies would support the common schools provided that a nondenominational Protestantism was still taught within the schools. Mann proposed that the common core of Christian religious beliefs, which he felt were demonstrated as true in human history, be taught in schools; thus the schools were to be nonsectarian. The common core which Mann proposed was similar to the tenets of the Unitarian faith which he professed. Mann's argument for religious education was connected with religious freedom:

> The religious education which a child receives at school, is not imparted to him, for the purpose of making him join this or that denomination, when he arrives at years of discretion, but for the purpose of enabling him to judge for himself, according to the dictates of his own reason and conscience, what his religious obligations are, and whither they lead. (Mann, 1957, p. 104)

For a period of time Mann struggled to convince members of churches to accept his proposed form of religious instruction for common schools. What turned the tide in favor of this approach was the efforts of Roman Catholics to secure public funds for their own schools. In response to this request Protestant churches rallied around the nondenominational common school. Many state legislatures enacted legislation prohibiting state aid to religious schools (Welter, 1962, p. 107).

Another strongly motivating factor for including religious instruction in the common schools was the belief that the nation needed students who had strong moral character. Since it was widely believed that morality was based on religion and the Bible, religion was a necessity in the schools. Though the majority accepted that the schools were to be nonsectarian, they did not accept that they should be without religion.

The main opposition to the continuation of religion in the public schools came from Roman Catholics. Catholics expressed a number of objections to the common schools. They were opposed to the Protestant King James version of the Bible used in these schools and to the pro-Protestant and anti-Catholic bias expressed in many of the textbooks. Rebuffed by state legislatures Catholics established schools and colleges where the Catholic faith could be handed on. Even after establishing these schools Catholics joined other groups in the community in legal suits directed at eliminating Bible reading, prayers, hymns and other sectarian practices from public schools. Furthermore, the increasing number of Catholics who could not be accommodated within Catholics schools found their way into public schools. Also, in some parts of the country and among certain ethnic groups the Catholic community favored the public schools over religious schools. (McCluskey, 1964)

Although the common school movement spread because of economic, political, and social reasons, it can be seen fundamentally as a nineteenth-century effort to preserve Protestant orthodoxy in the United States (Kaestle, 1983). This religious effort was partially successful in that it united the various Protestant groups in support of the common schools.

Though for the most part Protestant churches were united in favor of some religion in the school, in the form of Bible reading and prayers, opposition to these practices came from a number of influential educators. The United States Commissioner of Education, William T. Harris, made clear his objection to Bible reading, prayers, and the teaching of the catechism, considering them forms of Protestantism. While Harris affirmed his high regard for these practices, he felt that they belonged in churches and homes and not in schools. In 1863 he warned

> that the prerogative of religious instruction is in the church, that it must remain in the church, and that in the nature of things, it cannot be farmed out to the secular school without degenerating into mere deism bereft of a living Providence. . . . The church management must not rest in security on the belief that the time is coming when it may safely rely on an unsectarian instruction in the elementary schools for the spread of true religion. (In Tyack, 1970, p. 226)

Another influential educator, John Dewey, also raised his voice against religious practices in schools. In a 1908 paper, "Religion and Our Schools," he called for an end to religious instruction in public schools. His complaint was not against religion as such but against the supernatural and dogmatic religions of his time. By this time in his life Dewey had abandoned traditional religious beliefs in favor of a more naturalistic understanding of religion, which he considered more consonant with science and democracy. He concluded that

until the non-supernatural view is more completely elaborated in all its implications and is more completely in possession of the machinery of education. the schools shall keep hands off and shall do as little as possible. (In
Westbrook, 1991, p. 418)

In Dewey's fuller treatment of religion he made no case for the inclusion
of religion in the schools. Dewey also opposed the introduction of the
practice of released time for religious instruction on grounds that it
would harm the social unity of the school and promote divisions and
antagonisms among students (Dykuizen, 1973, pp. 275–277).

It is interesting to note that Dewey was a charter member of the Religious Education Association and addressed its first convention in 1903
on the topic of "Religious Education as Conditioned by Modern Psychology and Pedagogy." In the talk he explained how the principles of the
new psychology of child development might he utilized by religious educators. He concluded the talk in this manner:

If methods of teaching, principles of selecting and using subject-matter, in
all supposedly secular branches of education, are being subjected to careful
and systematic scientific study, how can those interested in religion—and
who is not?—justify neglect of the most fundamental of all educational
questions, the moral and religious? (Dewey, 1974; 1908)

Religious instruction through Bible reading continued in the public
schools well into the twentieth century despite the opposition of these
prominent educators. Catholic protests against the King James version of
the Bible usually lost in the courts, with the courts maintaining the rights
of schools boards to limit the rights of minorities. The courts asserted the
principle of majority rule and argued that the Bible was being read not
for sectarian purposes but to instill virtues in students. In some states
laws were even passed requiring the reading of the Bible in public
schools, while in others it left it to local option. Most laws required
teachers to read passages of the Bible aloud each day. When challenged,
the state courts upheld these laws until the 1950s when the Supreme
Court of the United States ruled against these practices. After the First
World War the battle over religion in the public schools was waged over
the issue of the teaching of evolution, which fundamentalists considered
contrary to the clear teachings of the Bible (Tyack, James, and Benavot
1987).

A number of factors finally led to the complete secularization of public schools in the United States. Protestant control over education at local levels was weakened with the growth in numbers of Catholics, Jews, and secular humanists. Many people began to accept that moral and civic education was not dependent upon the teaching of religion. The teaching profession drew into it many persons who did not profess the Protestant religion. The Supreme Court of the United States finally asserted in *Engle v. Vitale*, a case from New York, and in *Abington v. Schempp*, a case from Pennsylvania, and *Murray v. Curlett*, a case from Maryland, that in matters pertaining to religious freedom majority rule should not prevail. While most vestiges of Protestant dominance had long been removed from the curriculum what was left was the reading of the Bible and the recitation of prayers. These were finally declared unconstitutional. With religious instruction and prayer now removed from the schools, the attention of educators could now focus on what role religion might play in the education of the young.

Conservative Protestants have reacted to these developments by either establishing Christian schools or lobbying for the reintroduction of prayer in public schools. An analysis of the prayer-in-schools movement reveals a number of critical factors. The issue is ideological for many in that it symbolizes the effort to maintain Christian control over the schools. Advocates are motivated by moral reasons such as to promote character and combat moral and social ills. The issue of prayer in schools is related to civil religion in that it represents the effort to maintain religious rituals which permeate American public life around civic holidays. The prayer-in-schools effort often manifests a nationalist spirit to maintain Christian America. A group which considers itself a moral majority is motivated by the sheer political reality of its loss of power over a paramount American institution. Finally, the movement taps into the issue of local control and states rights in opposition to Federal Court decisions (Kathan, 1989).

The elimination of religious education and religious elements from public schools does not pertain to public colleges and universities. These institutions offer religious studies which students are free to take. The presumption is that students at the college level have the maturity to study religion in a manner that does not threaten their freedom to believe. In many religiously oriented colleges some courses in religious studies are mandatory.

While total secularization of education took place in the United States and elsewhere, in other countries a limited secularization has allowed for some religious instruction and worship. For example, in Britain religious education is still a subject of study in state schools. Since the mandating of religion in 1944 there has been an ongoing debate over the aims, content, and methods of this religious education. In England there has been a shift from a religious education that attempted to nurture the Christian faith to one that attempts to treat religion in an objective or in comparative manner.

While education in the West has been secularized to the extent that religious education is either prohibited or fostered in non-nurturing ways, in many parts of the world, especially in Arab countries there has emerged a powerful movement to center education again around religious beliefs. Also, within Western countries there are still many young people who attend schools where religion is a dominant force. Controversies exist over public support for these schools, acceptable in some countries and prohibited in others. This chapter will now explore the various rationales that are offered by contemporary philosophers for religious education in schools.

PHILOSOPHICAL DISCUSSIONS ON RELIGION AND EDUCATION

Theoretical discussions about education in religion have abounded among philosophers of education. In this chapter the principal theoretical positions in this area will be reviewed and discussed. The issue of education in religion is complicated by the fact that different legal situations in countries are the context for philosophical discussions. Two countries will be treated: the United States where there is complete separation between church and state and England where there only a limited separation.

Teaching about Religion in the United States

The 1962 United States Supreme Court decision *Engel v. Vitale* in which the Court judged a twenty-two word prayer as unconstitutional left the door open for what has been termed the objective teaching of religion. The court stated that

It might well be said that one's education is not complete without a study of comparative religion or the history of religion and its relationship to the advancement of civilization. It certainly may be said that the Bible is worthy of study for its literary and historical qualities. Nothing we have said here indicates that such study of the Bible or religion, when presented objectively as a part of a secular program of education, may not be effected consistent with the first Amendment. (In Engel, 1974, p. 18)

In years immediately after this decision a number of states, including Florida, Pennsylvania, Nebraska, and Wisconsin, developed programs for the teaching of religion in public schools.

The movement for religion in the public schools has made limited progress in the past three decades. Educational systems generally seem to take it for granted that the wall of separation between church and state precludes a serious dealing with the subject of religion. The results of this lack of attention to religion are pointed out by Sizer (1987):

By pretending there is a wall between religious issues and their schools, public school people remove themselves from the argument about the ways that religion must properly exist in their schools, and they leave the field open to unchallenged enthusiasts. (p. 128)

A report issued by the Association for Supervision and Curriculum Development (1987) called for public school educators to accept responsibility for including religion in the public school curriculum. The report made the distinction between the teaching of religion, which can take place in public schools, and religious education, which is the task of families and religious institutions. It stated that it is important for children to learn about the faith of others, something which can happen in schools but does not usually take place in families and religious bodies.

The case for teaching about religion in the public schools of the United States has been made by a number of philosophers. Phenix (1974) argued that religion is too important a dimension of human life for schools to ignore and proposed that it be taught where it is appropriate in the teaching of the secular disciplines. Phenix gave his explanation of what it means to teach religion in an "objective" manner. To teach a subject objectively does not mean to teach in a value free manner but to teach in a disciplined manner. For him it is as possible to teach religion in an objective a manner as it is to teach history or literature where there are also a plethora of interpretations and authorities. He contended that

There is no reason why any person, no matter what his own faith is, may not study theology—Christian, Jewish, or Buddhist—objectively. To do so requires understanding the subjectivities which each particular faith has. (Phenix, 1974, p. 67.)

His proposal is that in the early years of schooling religion would be taught in conjunction with music, dance, art, and architecture. Then religion would be taught in its literature, history, psychology and sociology. In the final stage of education the philosophical and theological issues in religion would be dealt with.

Phenix forthrightly took up the conventional objections offered to the teaching of religion. In his view, rather than creating hostilities and divisions the teaching of religion would foster understanding of religious differences. Although religion cannot do justice to the myriad of religions, it is able to deal sympathetically with the dominant religions in the community and nation. While religion is fundamentally a matter of private belief, it also has public dimensions which are worth exploring. It is possible to teach religion in a non-indoctrinative manner by approaching religion in an open, non-authoritarian and appreciative spirit. Phenix has confidence in the ability of teachers to present faiths other than their own in an objective and impartial manner. Whereas teaching religion may sow doubt in some, this doubt can be constructive if it encourages students to examine religion in a critical manner. Religion treated objectively is not the same thing as religion treated abstractly and impassionately. He also believes that suitable teachers can be found and materials developed to make teaching about religion a valuable experience.

The objective approach to religious education has been subjected to criticism in the United States. The American Jewish theologian Eugene Borowitz (1967) argued that the public school in setting up specific courses of religion may go too far. Borowitz is concerned that the public schools in proposing to teach about religion in separate courses is moving beyond the limited aims which it should have. The teaching of religion in his view is primarily a responsibility for families and religious institutions.

Borowitz also questions the possibility of teachers being objective in the teaching of religion by asserting that religion is not subject to the same sort of public testing that is possible in other academic areas. In his view it is the textbook and the teacher that determine what is objective. His chief objection is to separate courses and not to the treatment of religion in history and literature courses. His suggestion is that public schools should focus on universal human experiences without directly relating these to religion. For him college age is a suitable time for the objective teaching of religion, when students have the intellectual capacity to deal objectively with religious matters.

Borowitz's reservations were echoed by a pamphlet of the American Jewish Committee (1979). The pamphlet contended that the public schools must not be involved in furthering religion. It makes the judgment that the introduction of religion into the schools would inevitably be divisive. It also considers any attempts to treat religions on a comparative basis as undesirable. Although noting that religion should be treated carefully in subjects where it appears naturally, it contends that it is not even possible to teach a common core of religious beliefs. Notwithstanding this, it argues that public schools should continue to stress moral and spiritual values which are found in all religions.

A Roman Catholic statement offered some similar reservations (Pennsylvania Catholic Conference, 1976). The statement contends that the elimination of the teaching of religion in public education resulted in the teaching of secularistic values. The statement does not think it possible to teach a common core of religious values. It proposes that some sort of released time for studying religion off school premises be instituted.

Frederick Olafson (1967), a philosopher at Harvard, argued that there was value to objective teaching about religion, although he too expressed some reservations. He interpreted teaching religion as including imparting information about the world religions or developing in students an understanding of the religious dimension of life. Whereas the first objective is to be achieved through direct teaching, the second objective is best achieved through indirection, that is, through the quality of the teaching and through avoiding approaches which would block the sympathetic power of young people and not allow their care and intelligence to come to the fore. In presenting both objectives for teaching about religion he is confident that such teaching can be justified only if prior conditions are satisfied.

Olafson contends that in order for these courses to be worthwhile and constitutional, they must be taught academically and not in a context of religious affirmation. Such courses must be taught with the same degree of freedom and objectivity that they are taught in colleges. To teach in this manner is to look at religion as "a human and historical reality through secular glasses and without ulterior motives or prettification or edification" (p. 86). Olafson's second condition concerns recruitment and training of competent teachers. Such programs should not interfere with the integrity of the instructional program of the school. His concrete proposal is for a senior elective in religious studies.

Olafston cautions about too high expectations for these programs. While he affirms the intellectual benefits that would accrue from such programs of study, he is doubtful about any beneficial result they might have on the moral character of students. Students may benefit, he grants, from learning about the moral codes proposed by religious institutions but the effect of such learning on moral behavior is unpredictable. Schools can influence moral behavior less by talking about morality and more by providing a moral and caring climate and opportunities for moral experiences.

Finally, Olafson makes the point that although it is possible that teaching religion might favorably dispose students toward it or make them intelligent and critical about it, it could also have the effect of diminishing in them the transcendent dimension of religion as a reality beyond life and culture. He concludes that such programs should not be advocated with expectations of real benefit to the religious life of young people.

Bischoff (1976) has presented a clearly thought out rationale for the teaching of religion in public schools which attempts to deal with some of the limitations suggested by Olafson. He derives his theory from an analysis of the public school and its education. The public school is to serve the needs of the public. In a pluralistic society this demands that the school be ideologically neutral. The educational goals of the school must set its agenda. To deal adequately with the world educationally the school must deal with the order of meaning as well as the order of factual information. To understand others in the pluralistic society students must understand the self-understandings of their follow students.

What belongs in the public school, according to Bischoff, is not theology but religious studies or the science of religion. To study religion in this manner means to bracket the question of the existence of a transcendent being as proposed by many religious faiths. Religion is to be studied rather from the perspective of sociology, psychology, history, philosophy, politics, and economics. Academically speaking, a functionalist approach to religion is preferred over one which focuses on the substance of religion, that is, religion is to be studied more for what it does than for what it is.

Bischoff proposes a historical-hermeneutic approach to the study of religion, one that focuses on self-understanding through engagement with religious texts. Such an approach includes elements of criticism of religious phenomena. Bischoff makes it clear that he does not propose the study of religion through aseptic observation but rather insists on

> Objective confrontation of the student with the authentic claim to ultimate value and meaning in the religious phenomena studied . . . enabling him to come to an informed decision as to their relevance and validity for him. (1976, p. 81)

An examination of language used in discussions about religion in the public schools has been presented by Moran (1989) Moran notes that all parties to the debate avoid the language of "religious education" because this is the language used for education in religious organizations. "Teaching about religion" is the preferred language in the United States since it is the phrase used in a number of Supreme Court decisions. This phrase is used in order to avoid the implication that religion is taught in order to foster religious commitment in students. Moran favors the language "to teach religion" in analogy with such usage as to teach mathematics, science, etc. For him teaching about religion appears to make the teaching of the subject removed and abstract.

Moran compares teaching religion to teaching art, morality, and politics. In these forms of teaching, and also in teaching religion, there are limits to what teaching can do and the actual practice by students of art, morality, politics, and religion. In teaching these subjects the teacher may hope that students transfer what is learned into practice but this cannot be the direct aim of teaching. For Moran religion should also be taught like any other subject—with tests, marks, and credit. He admits that many will not consider this approach religious enough but contends that this is all that should be attempted in the classroom. In brief, for Moran educators in public school settings have the task of teaching students religion rather than of teaching them to be religious. Moreover, Moran seems to imply that this should be the same goal in a religiously affiliated school in asking: "Is there and should there be a difference between the two in the nature of classroom instruction?" (p. 120).

Moran's distinction is an important one but there are other ways to make it that are more appealing to educators. A California handbook uses the terminology "teaching about" and "instructing in."

To teach about religion is not to instruct in religion. Teaching about religion embraces the study of various religions; appreciation of the nature and
variety of religious experience historically and currently; information on
past and present sources, views, and behavior of religious persons or
groups; and the influence of religion on cultures and civilizations. Instruction in religion, by contrast, is to seek acceptance of and commitment to a
particular religion, including a nonreligion like secularism. Freedom to instruct in religion is a treasured part of the American heritage. Instruction
is carried out in the home and in the churches. Although instruction in
religion may help a person achieve a deeply meaningful life, it is prohibited
in public schools. (In Byrnes, 1975, p. 74)

Those dissatisfied with the objective teaching of religion propose
forms of religious education which go beyond the mere imparting of information. In this approach religious education is "the development of a
sensitivity to religious problems, a sensitivity more than the purely intellectual of the philosophical realm." In this approach children are not
only taught beliefs but are "readied, made aware of the religious dimension of life, which . . . is a significant aspect of being human" (Sizer,
1967, p. xvii). This approach to religious education has a psychological
dimension. Religious education fosters an attitude of asking the right
questions about reality and supports children in this quest. Although
Sizer is not sure whether this approach to religious education is constitutional, proponents of religious education in state schools in other countries make similar proposals.

There is no doubt that philosophers of religion and education have
made a strong case for the justification of religion in the public school
curriculum in the United States. The field of religion is vastly important
to people's lives and should not be neglected in education. Yet the movement for religion in public education as yet has not been a successful one.
The teaching of religion as such has a small place in the American public
school curriculum. While there are many advocates for religion in the
schools, there are many who oppose the introduction of religion into curriculum either because of the dangers of indoctrination or the risks of
debasing religion. The legal issues surrounding religion in the schools
have not been adequately clarified, with many seeing little differences between religious practices and the teaching of religion. There is also confusion in many quarters about what the "objective teaching of religion"
actually means. Most school boards and administrators earnestly desire

to avoid the controversies that would ensue were issues of teaching about religion publicly debated.

The reluctance to deal with religious issues carries over into the area of education in values. Any attempt that public schools make to deal with moral values quickly runs into opposition from religious groups. Although a distinction can be made between values and religion, the reality is that most people's values are connected with their religious beliefs. There is no way in which one can carry on a serious discussion of moral values with young people without at the same time discussing the religious sources for their values. Such values as friendship, the sanctity of human and nonhuman forms of life, are rooted for many people in their religious traditions.

Religious Education in Britain

In Britain religious education has been a subject taught in schools since the passage of the Education Act in 1944 which stated that religious education shall be given in accordance with a prescribed syllabus. The act made the teaching of religion compulsory on grounds that religious education could contribute to moral and spiritual growth for both individuals and for society. The act also prescribed an act of collective worship each day in schools. In order to safeguard the rights of children and their parents, the law wisely included a conscience clause whereby parents could withdraw their children both from the act of worship and from religious instruction. Although the act did not explicitly mention the Christian religion as forming the content of religious education, nurture in the Christian faith seemed to have been implied and such nuture is actually what took place in schools through biblically based curricula until at least the 1960s.

In the 1960s with the influx of immigrants of many different religions and with an awareness of the need to respect religious differences, a number of nonbiblical approaches to religious education were introduced. For several years religious education followed the lead of Ronald Goldman (1965) and placed the child's everyday experiences and needs at the center of religious education. Goldman's research had concluded that biblically based religious education was not achieving the desired results. Building on students' needs for love, belonging, trust, acceptance, identity, freedom, self-concept, relations to others, understanding, relationship with the divine, and a sense of stability teachers can lead them to understanding religious teachings which are related to these. This approach still gave a place of prominence to the Christian religion in that the themes for study were related to the content of the Christian religion.

The end of the 1960s witnessed a turn to a more objective and academic approach to religious education. The predominant approach was called objective or phenomenological, so called because it attempted to present religious phenomena without making judgments about the truth or falsity of various religious claims. Ninian Smart's work (1966; 1968) was influential in the development of this widely used approach. He proposed that religion should be taught in an open, descriptive, and even neutral manner. Religions were to be taught not as systems of truths but by discussion, comparison, weighing of arguments, and without prejudice to the outcomes of the teaching. Religious doctrines are to be taught not as if they were true but as existing in continual tension with alternative positions. The phenomenological approach demands that theological assumptions are to be avoided and that the facts about world religions are to be described as much as possible in a value neutral manner. In Smart's view a person need not be a believer to teach a particular religious faith. In fact, he argues that the best teachers of religion may often be outsiders. The teacher must merely be sympathetic towards religion.

What the phenomenological approach to teaching religion amounts to is clarified by a study of the religion curriculum developed for the City of Birmingham, England, in the mid 1970s (Hull, 1984). The aim of religious education is not to foster faith in any particular religion. The purposes of religious education include an awareness of the contributions made by religion to society, the development of a critical understanding of religion, and the formulation of personal philosophies. Religions are to be studied alongside the secular ideologies of communism and humanism. Religions and ideologies are to be presented with fairness, objectivity, impartiality, and balance. The attempt should be made to present religious faiths in a manner with which believers would not disagree. The Birmingham syllabus recognizes that teachers can teach their own religious faiths as well as those of others in a fair and impartial manner. Religion is to be taught not only as a system of beliefs but also in its rituals, customs, and moral codes. The syllabus was adopted after much discussion and debate and after criticism by both religious believers and secular humanists. The syllabus makes it clear that the teaching of religion is a matter of education and instruction and not a matter of nurture and indoctrination.

There still are prominent advocates for the objective approach to the teaching of religion, notably Edwin Cox (1983) who argues that the aim of the objective study of religion is not to nurture or foster religious faith but to promote an understanding of religions. He recognized that in a pluralist society there are limitations to what schools can do in the area of religion. Cox has proposed four main aims for this type of religious education. It will enable students to understand what religions have contributed to culture in influencing the arts. Second, education in religion will aid students to understand what people believe and how their beliefs shape their lives. Third, it will help students to understand that a reasonable approach to life entails making up one's mind on the fundamental issues that religion raises. Fourth, it may help them to make choices about their own attitudes towards religion.

As early as 1967 voices were raised concerning the so called objective or phenomenological teaching of religion. The British philosopher Paul Hirst (1967) argued that the objective teaching of religion does not go goes far enough. He contended that

> It is surely a mistake to think that one can seriously study the history of religion without a clear understanding of religious claims, their implications, and the kind of justification they are thought to have. (p. 337)

The task of religious education for him is to enable students to understand religions from the inside, from the way that adherents to them see the world. Admitting the practical difficulties of finding suitable teachers and materials he argued that religious education is important for promoting religious understanding in a pluralist society.

In the 1970s because of some dissatisfaction with the phenomenological approach's objective and dry style, another perspective called experiential or existential or personal-existential, was proposed by religious educators. The concern of these educators was that religious education be more interesting and especially more relevant to the lives of students. They also believed that religious education could aid students in their search for a faith by which they might live. Their attempt was to develop a form of religious education which could be justified on academic grounds as a personal religious quest just as other academic subjects such as history and literature can be taught in a way to promote personal quests and inquiries. Goldman led the way in starting with student needs and experiences and attempted to probe deeper into what students can learn from religion. Religious education in this mode might be termed education for responsible living.

In this form of education there is a kind of religious nurturing but not a nurturing in any particular religious faith. There is a belief that religion is found in the depths of human experience, manifesting itself in real problems and concerns. This approach underlies the work of the Religious Experience Research Unit at Oxford University which focuses on the religious experiences of children. It contends that room must be made for spiritual experiences within the religious education endeavor. Religious education has as its task enabling children to recognize their spiritual experiences and those of others. Edward Robinson made this case for such experiences in religious education:

> Whatever practical aims any particular programme of religious education put before us, it will achieve little unless we can help young people, through the growth of imagination, the mastery of expression and the breakdown of isolation, to some sense of that form of depth that is the necessary prelude to any awareness of the mystery, horror, and beauty of life. (1982, p. 91)

Grimmitt's (1973; 1987) widely-read works are the most influential of those espousing the personal-existential approach to religious education. Grimmitt contrasted learning *about* religion in which students evaluate the inner logic and meaning of religion from learning *from* religion in which students evaluate personally the role of religion in their own lives. Grimmitt saw religious education as the attempt

> To create in pupils certain capacities to understand and think about religion as a unique mode of thought and awareness; which takes as it starting point the child's own existential experiences and which attempts to help children to build conceptual bridges between these and what they recognize to be the central concepts of religions. (1973, p. 49)

Grimmitt placed great faith in depth experiences of love, hate, and fear to foster a distinctively religious way of knowing. He also made clear that his approach to education is not based on theological principles nor is it concerned with institutional aspects of religion.

Priestly (1985) summarized the major personal-existential propositions, which he termed a spiritual approach. Religious education is to begin and end with the inwardness of students, because the inward and the spiritual are the beginning points for all concrete expressions of religion. This education must be open ended in recognizing that the spiritual cannot be totally contained nor adequately expressed. The teaching style in this form of education is similar to that used in the creative arts where a high degree of self-expression is desired. All dimensions of religion should be drawn on, including the intellectual. Finally, Priestly suggested that

> We who are teachers need to demonstrate that we too are on the endless road of spiritual search. If the purpose of all our teaching is that through all own knowing and our doing we are in the process of becoming fuller persons we must show ourselves still to be traveling. (1985, p. 119)

The continuing debate over religious education in Britain brings out the complexity of issues concerning religion in public education. Religious education is supported by government legislation as recently as 1988 which mandates not only religious education but also school worship. While the seems to promote only the objective study of religion, religious educators contend that such cannot be done unless students are helped to clarify their own beliefs and values. Notwithstanding the many difficulties that surround religious education in Britain, one can only admire a system of government and education that does not shrink from the serious teaching of religion. Communities have learned over the years to come to forms of consensus that safeguard the rights and conscience of religious and nonreligious persons and communities.

Religious Education and Indoctrination

Over the past decades philosophers in Britain and elsewhere have directed attention to the thorny issue of religious education as a form of indoctrination. Anthony Flew (1972) believes that religious education is the paradigm case for indoctrination, viewed as a pejorative practice. Religious education is indoctrinating because religion teachers present as true those doctrines which cannot be known to be true by any ordinary standards with the intention of producing in students unshakeable convictions. Where Flew especially sees indoctrination is in the teaching of religion in denominational schools. In describing indoctrination Flew gives attention not only to methods of presentation but also to the content of what is taught and the aims of the teacher. Flew indicted the widespread indoctrinating efforts of Christian Churches in Britain and the United States. For him indoctrination is not

The teaching of religion in general—any religion, anytime. It is the enormous and generally effective effort made in our own two countries now by a particular highly traditional Christian Church, which seeks to fix in the minds of children an unshakeable conviction of the truth of its specific distinctive doctrines. (p. 114)

White (1972) described two forms of indoctrination which may take place in religious education. The first is the case where the teacher intends to bring about in students certain religious assents and commitments. He saw little chance for teachers to keep their own commitments outside the teaching situation. Indoctrination can also take place in a situation in which a pupil identifies with a teacher who is a believer and comes to believe as the teacher does, without the teacher intending the indoctrination.

John Wilson (1972) admitted that some indoctrination takes place in religious education but argued that this need not be the case. For him it all depends on what the "religious" is. He contended that if religions are viewed as ways of seeing the world, and that if these ways of seeing the world are psychologically desirable for children, they may be justified and not indoctrinatory.

In his philosophical analysis of indoctrination Chazan (1972) concluded that there are three essential elements: the method of teaching, content of instruction, and the intention of the teacher. In his view all three are essential elements of indoctrination. His contention is that though religious education, as moral education or political education, may be carried on in an indoctrinatory manner, such need not be the case. It is at least logically possible to conceive of a

Religious education which does not involve the imposition of beliefs in an arbitrary manner, but . . . which is concerned with the best possible presentation of these contents in order to enable a student to eventually make an intelligible and free decision vis a vis his religious beliefs and commitments. (1972, p. 252)

Chazan is convinced that it is feasible to have a non-indoctrinatory religious education that would deal with ideas, beliefs and behaviors of a specific religion in such a way that these are transmitted and justified and that fosters the free and reasoned decision to accept or reject this inheritance.

While a nonindoctrinatory religious education is logically conceivable, it may be difficult to attain in practice, especially for those who are teaching their own religion. Believers are convinced that what they believes is true, even though there are those who do not share these beliefs. Furthermore, the justification of religious beliefs on a rational basis is a difficult matter about which there is much dispute. In order to avoid the charge of indoctrination religious educators need to be aware of the nature of religious knowledge and the varieties of religious beliefs. They also need to recognize how their own beliefs may influence their teaching. While teachers who attempt to teach religion in such a nonindoctrinatory manner run the risk of teaching without passion and commitment, this is preferable to the risks of indoctrination.

The problem of indoctrination often comes down to the problem of what the teacher is to do with his or her own religious beliefs when teaching religion, in order to avoid both indoctrination and passionless teaching. Hill (1982) has analyzed a number of alternatives for the teacher of religion. Teachers should avoid the stance of "exclusive partiality" in which they teach in such a way that they do not allow a challenge to their views. This approach does not show respect for the views of others in a pluralist society. Teachers should also avoid the stance of "exclusive neutrality" in which they keep controversial issues outside the classroom. Doing this with regard to religion ends up in promoting a form of secular humanism or anti-religion. Hill argues that the position of "neutral impartiality" in which views are presented and the teacher does not present his or her commitments, is scarcely possible and not educationally sound. Such a stance brings an air of unreality into the classroom. What Hill recommends is the stance of "committed impartiality" in which teachers reveal their own religious commitments in the process of teaching. Though all views are presented, the teacher can make known his or her views and the reasons for holding these views.

For John Hull (1984) the issue of indoctrination comes down to the issue of what teachers of religion are to do with their own religious commitments in teaching students of various religious faiths. He believes that it is possible for these teachers to have both open minds and passionate commitment, provided that the type of religious faiths they possess foster the values of learning, autonomy, and inquiry. Hull also makes the case that the Christian religion, properly understood, fosters these values. He concluded his analysis with the following:

> I think religious educators who are Christians should have no fears about the Christian legitimacy of their work promoting an open, secular, critical view of religious education, which will be fully respectable educationally and will contribute to the developing needs of children and young people. . . . We may indeed fully believe that this kind of religious education rather than the evangelistic or the nurturing kind is a responsibility laid upon us by the Gospel and is part of our obedience to that Gospel. (1984, p. 206)

An awareness of the danger of indoctrination in religious education has led some church-oriented religious educators to propose that the teaching of religion in church schools should not have as its purpose nurturing or catechizing young people in the faith but rather the academic study of religion. Rossiter (1982) has made a persuasive case for a creative divorce in church schools between catechesis (education in the faith) and religious education (education in religion). His argument is based on the nature of modern education as open and critical in which students question and challenge teachers and viewpoints. Students also resist attempts to involve them in religious discussions which they view as psychologically invasive. The nature of religious faith as a developing process recommends a less doctrinally and more inviting type of teaching. Rossiter contends that many young people are rightly unwilling "to cooperate with a religious education that seems to be marketing Christian attitudes and values, especially if these are perceived as restrictive" (p. 34). Rossiter allows that other components of religious schools such as retreats and clubs may foster a more nurturing form of religious experience.

While the issue of indoctrination may take place in many school subjects, there is an especial sensitivity to indoctrination in religious and moral education because of differences of opinion among communities about moral and religious matters. Teaching in these areas demands a particular care on the part of teachers to respect the beliefs and opinions of students. The dangers of indoctrination should not deter teachers and schools from dealing with disputed issues.

CHAPTER 6

POLITICAL EDUCATION

Ever since education became a matter for institutions beyond the individual and family there has been a political dimension to it. When the family was solely responsible for the education of the young, the emphasis was placed on the values, knowledge, and skills necessary for life in the family and for work within the family and community structure. When the organization of a social group remained a loose joining of families within a clan, there was only limited need for an education that has a detailed political dimension. Once the social grouping became more complicated and differentiated and something similar to a state or nation developed, there also arose a need for an education that attended to the demands of membership in the broader social unit. Attention also had to be given to an education of leaders for this unit.

Thus more developed social units call for formal modes of education that prepare persons not only for membership or citizenship but also for leadership in the body politic. Every modern system makes provision for this type of political or civic education, with different types of states providing their own forms. While in some nations there is a centralized approach operated through a ministry of education, in others there is much more local control and decision making.

When one, therefore, examines education in modern nations, it is also essential to examine the explicit and implicit political or civic education that is offered. Educational systems, as part of the political structure, not only teach the young basic skills and job skills, they also provide a broad education for citizenship that consists of courses in national history, social studies, as well as organized school activities. Schools also provide for this education through the way in which they are organized, the character of student organizations, and involvement of parents and students in schools.

Philosophers of education have given attention to this dimension of education from the *Republic* of Plato to Dewey's *Democracy and Education*. As in other areas already treated in this book, philosophers have their own approaches to this form of education. Philosophers of education focus on the aims and nature of political education, the possible justifications for political education, the clarification of language used in this area, the criticisms of forms of political education, and such related issues of indoctrination and handling controversial subject matter.

I have chosen to entitle this chapter political education, all the while realizing that other terms such as civic education, civics, education for citizenship are more common in this country. I prefer the term political education over the others because it opens the possibility of including forms of education that take a critical stance towards present societal and political arrangements. The term also connects this education more clearly with such academic disciplines as history and political philosophy. The term political is also valuable because it includes the social and economic sphere.

Political education has been defined as "the cultivation of the virtues, knowledge, and skills necessary for political participation" and as such it "has primacy over other purposes of public education in a democratic society" since it prepares persons "to consciously participate in consciously reproducing their society" (Gutmann, 1987, p. 287). The goals of political education have been outlined by Spring: educating citizens, selecting political leaders, creating a political consensus, maintaining political power, and socializing individuals for political systems (1991, p. 6). These goals can be broadened to include a critique of present political arrangement and education for world citizenship.

In some ways, political education can be viewed as an extension of moral education because many elements of political education also deal with moral knowledge, attitudes, and behaviors. While the political is a realm of moral values and judgments, the moral sphere also includes personal and interpersonal dimensions.

Explicit attention to political education is extremely important at this time in the history of the United States. Social changes within the country and worldwide changes have made education for citizenship a highly controversial matter. The principal questions are how are we to educate in the values of the national consensus while at the same time respecting the diversity of many groups within the nation; and, should we broaden our education for citizenship to include an education for world citizenship.

In this chapter as in others I will first present the perspectives of philosophers and educators from the past. Then I will review the philosophical aspects of the proposals for political education that have been offered in recent years.

HISTORICAL PERSPECTIVES

The Classical Tradition

The origins of political education are found in the writings of the Greeks and Romans. Within these worlds there developed the notion of citizenship that entailed membership in a political community which was regulated by rules, and therefore not based on kinship, religion, ethnicity, or inherited status. In these nations free citizens made laws that recognized the rights and responsibilities of members of the community. In order for such societies to function, members had to be educated for political life while others had to be prepared for leadership in the polis.

Plato wrote the first educational treatise which dealt with the shape that political education should take in a society of laws. He wrote the *Republic* in the context of the failures of Greek democracy and the defeat of Athens by Sparta in the Peloponnesian War. In this work he contended that the defeat of Athens took place because of the tyranny which resulted from an excessive individualism, the rise of traditional beliefs about kinship and religion, a widespread preoccupation with private wealth, and the ignorance of the common people. In order to remedy these failings Plato proposed a state that would be ruled by wise, just, and well-educated guardians who would seek the good of the state and be willing to sacrifice their own pleasures to achieve this good. According to Plato's utopian vision of society all persons in the state were to do the job for which they were best suited: workers were to produce the things needed for life; warriors were to defend the nation from outside aggression; and guardians were to rule the people.

The *Republic* is largely Plato's proposal for an education that would produce the types of persons needed for this state. A rigorous system of state-controlled education was to provide the appropriate education for each group in society. The most thorough education was for the guardians who were to assume the roles of philosopher-kings. The intellectual or liberal arts education which they were to receive was described in chapter one. This education would enable them to contemplate ideal truth, beauty, and goodness through an education in mathematics, metaphysics, and dialectics.

This Platonic vision of the ideal society clearly envisions aristocratic rule. This vision has appealed to many who are concerned with the problems of excessive individualism and freedom in society. Plato has been rightly criticized as the first opponent of a democratic and open society. His views appear to sanction a totalitarian view of the state which controls all aspects of the lives of individuals. One of the enduring values of his theory, however, lies in his insistence that those who are to rule should be prepared for this by a rigorous intellectual training. A contemplation of truths that transcends the ordinary experience of individuals may broaden the vision of leaders to contemplate all political decisions and issues in a wider perspective.

Aristotle's proposals for the political realm and the education suited for it were less monolithic and more pluralistic than those of Plato. He discussed the advantages and disadvantages of the three forms of government: monarchy, aristocracy, and democracy. While he believed that all three political arrangements could promote the common interests, his preference for aristocratic rule was made clear by his eliminating women, children, slaves, mechanics, traders, and farmers from citizenship. He did maintain, however, that citizens, that is, free men were to engage in self-government and share in the ruling of the state.

What Plato and Aristotle agreed on was the necessity of the state for the fullness of human life. They also agreed that education was a public function and not a private matter for families to decide upon. Aristotle made the case for the political education of the young:

No one will doubt that the legislator should direct his attention above all the education of youth; for the neglect of education does harm to the constitution. The citizen should be molded to suit the form of government under which he lives. For each government has a peculiar character which originally formed and which continues to preserve it.

Since the whole city has one end, it is manifest that education should be one and the same for all, and that it should be public, and not private—not as at present, when everyone looks after his own children separately, and gives them separate instruction of the sort which he thinks best; the training in things which are of common interest would be the same for all. Neither must we suppose that any one of the citizens belongs to himself, for they all belong to the state, and are each of them a part of the state, and the care for each part is inseparable from the care of the whole. (Aristotle, 1964, p. 268)

When Aristotle in his *Ethics* described the education that is suited for members of the state, he did not do justice to the demands of a political education. He proposed a liberal education which stressed intellectual and moral virtues and placed less emphasis on the practical reasoning demanded in public and political life. The virtues result from habit formation and are molded in the early years of life in family and school. Higher intellectual virtues result from education in mathematics, logic, natural sciences, and philosophy. The virtues of practical reasoning which have to do with making things or conducting one's life come from a study of politics, ethics, economics, rhetoric, and the arts.

The Greek tradition of education found in Plato and Aristotle, with its emphasis on theoretical learning, formed the Western academic tradition. In this tradition the seeking after truth took preference over seeking after justice and morality. This tradition has tended to devalue practical knowledge and experience. This tradition prevailed until the Enlightenment and the democratic revolutions in the seventeenth and eighteenth centuries.

Yet there were some dissenting voices in the ancient world. It was left to the rhetorician Isocrates to propose a form of education which explicitly prepared citizens for political life. His philosophy assumed that the highest good was the service of the political community and the chief means of accomplishing this was through discourse. In politics he favored a union among the various states of Greece to be achieved through public discussion. His political views did not prevail.

In Isocrates' view, for persons to be citizens and leaders in the public sphere more than philosophy was necessary; what was called for was training in oratory, the art of persuasion. In proposing a new type of statesmen who could deal effectively with practical problems, he argued that leaders were to be educated through a study of logic, literature, history, and ethics. Through this education persons would develop good judgment about the problems of the state and be able to enter into rational discussions about political problems. His belief was that democracy could be promoted through public discussion and discourse.

Isocrates' ideas, like those of other Sophists, were opposed by the philosophers and their followers. Yet, although his ideas were only a minor contribution to political philosophy, Isocrates has actually triumphed in that politics, with few exceptions, has been dominated not by philosopher-kings but by those trained in the art of persuasion, lawyers and barristers.

The concept of citizenship and education for citizenship had a limited existence in the Greek world. The same can be said for the Romans. The early patrifamiliar arrangements gave way to imperial regimes which revived hereditary power. Roman law recognized the absolute power of the sovereign over all groups in society. Through this period and through the Middle Ages the notion of membership in a political community was almost wiped out by the multiple memberships in different groups that characterized this society. A prominent historian writes that

> Kinship had almost as much sway [in medieval society] as it had had in earliest Rome, during the republic, and in earliest Athens, prior to the Cleisthenean reforms. Medieval society was a vast web of groups, communities, and associations, each claiming jurisdiction over the functions and activities of its members. The church was powerful; but so, after the twelfth century, were guild, profession, monastery, and manor. (Nisbet in Butts, 1980, p. 32–33)

Democratic citizenship and education for it consequently had a short-lived existence. The full notion of citizenship education waited until the modern period.

Enlightenment Political Education

The Enlightenment saw the development of a political philosophy which was more clearly democratic in nature. Connected with the revolutions in England, the United States, and France were new ways of viewing the political system and people's participation in it. Many plans were formulated for a new education to suit the new political situation. What began to be stressed in this period were the rights of individuals and of families. These revolutions which attacked the established orders of monarchy, feudalism, aristocracy, and heredity ushered in a new political and educational era that has had repercussions to the present time. The enlarged role of citizens in the countries that underwent democratic revolutions called for an education that would both preserve and foster these new political arrangements.

The political philosophies of Enlightenment figures is a matter of complicated study. Only a few highlights can be given here, with stress on those philosophers who addressed the needs for an education for citizens. Because the main focus in this historical perspective is political education in the United States, those who influenced this enterprise will be given special treatment.

While the classical tradition stressed the authority of the state in providing for the political education of its citizens, John Locke, a British philosopher and classical liberal, challenged this power of the state in asserting the rights of parents to educate their children. The basic unit in society for Locke's classical liberalism is not the family, community, or state but individuals. In Locke's view of the state adult citizens have the right to choose for themselves and for their children what they think is their own good. Locke did not worry that parents might abuse their authority for he believed that

> God hath woven into the Principles of Human Nature such a tenderness for their Off-spring, that there is little fear that Parents should use their power with too much rigour; the excess is seldom on the severe side, the strong bypass of Nature drawing the other way. (Locke, 1960, p. 355)

Locke also felt that if children went to school they might learn bad habits from their classmates.

History has shown that attention has to be given not only to the rights of parents but also to the rights of children and the state. These issues will receive some treatment under the section on contemporary discussions. Locke's views are found in the political philosophy of Robert Nozick (1974) who argued for the greatest possible freedom for individuals.

John Stuart Mill rejected the extreme argument of Locke while still making a defense for individual freedom. While denying that parents have absolute rights over their children, he argued that the state should ensure that parents provide for the education of their children. The state, however, should not direct that education. Mill saw the dangers in state education precisely in the control over the political and religious opinion of members. He considered as evil all attempts of the state to prejudice the opinions of its citizens on disputed subjects. He pointed out that

> A general State education is a mere contrivance for molding people to be exactly like one another; and as the mold in which it casts them is that which pleases the predominant power in the government—whether this be a monarch, a priesthood, an aristocracy, or the majority of the existing generation—in proportion as it is efficient and successful, it establishes a despotism over the mind, leading by natural tendency to one over the body. (Mill, 1966 [1859], p. 129)

Mill equally opposed the despotism of parents and the despotism of the state when it comes to education. If the state conducted education, it had to be only one of the forms offered. While parents had the right to educate children, the state had the right to examine children on what they learned and to impose fines on fathers whose children failed to pass examinations. These examinations, if they treated political issues, merely tested the students' knowledge of political matters and the arguments they gave for them.

By the time that Emmanuel Kant wrote on education it was well established among Enlightenment thinkers that the state had the right to conduct education for children. While he had praise for home education he pointed out that "as a preparation for the duties of a citizen, it must, I am inclined to think, be allowed that, on the whole public education is the best" (Kant, 1960, pp. 26–27). Public education, as opposed to home education, was a better system in which to learn how to measure one's powers with those of others and to know the limits imposed upon us by the rights of others. Kant also urged that children be taught to have an interest in the progress of the world, "although it may not be to their own advantage or to that of their country" (p. 121). (Incidently, Kant gave sound advice to all theorists of education in his remark that "The prospect of a theory of education is a glorious ideal, and it matters little if we are not able to realize it at once.... We must not look upon the ideal as chimerical nor decry it as a beautiful dream, notwithstanding the difficulties that stand in the way of its realization" [p. 8]).

Political Education in the United States

After the Revolution in the United States there were a number of plans for developing a new national educational system, which entailed a new political philosophy. Education was viewed as one of the main forces for establishing a new nation; schooling would lay the foundation for responsible citizenship in a free society. Some of these proposals openly advocated the political and religious indoctrination which Mill and others would eventually condemn. The plan offered to the Pennsylvania Legislature in 1786 by Benjamin Rush called for the indoctrination of the young into the doctrines and discipline of a church since

> Man is naturally an ungovernable animal, and observations on particular societies and countries will teach us that when we add the constraints of ecclesiastical to those of domestic and civil government, we produce in him the highest degrees of virtue and order. (In Spring, 1986, p. 34)

Echoing elements of Plato's political and educational philosophy, Rush ascribed to the view that the child was the property of the state and that the state's rights over children was greater than that of families. For this reason he argued for a rather authoritarian approach to education which included the inculcation of what he called republican virtues. He stated that

> I consider it possible to convert men into republican machines. This must be done if we expect them to perform their parts properly in the great machine of the government of the state. (In Spring, 1986, p. 34)

Children were to be taught that they were public property. Though they were to love their families, they were to forsake them for the good of the country. Students were encouraged to amass wealth but only to increase their power to contribute to the wants and needs of state.

The most philosophical of the approaches to postrevolutionary education is found in the writings and proposals of Thomas Jefferson, a man of classical learning and far-ranging political philosophy. For Jefferson it was impossible for a nation to be both ignorant and free. His political philosophy was based on the assumptions that the purpose of life is individual happiness and that the purpose of government is to advance this happiness. Since he also thought that education is the soundest basis for happiness, he proposed education as a paramount function of government. Jefferson made the case for the importance of a republican form of education for the new nation. In a letter to Washington in 1786 he wrote, "It is an axiom of my mind that our liberty can never be safe but in the hands of the people themselves, and that too of the people with a certain degree of instruction" (In Perkinson, 1977, p. 8). In a plan which he submitted to the Virginia legislature in 1779 he described the new political function which he assigned to education:

> Experience has shown that even under the best forms of government, those entrusted with power have, in time, and by slow operations, perverted it into tyranny and it is believed that the most effective means of preventing this would be to illuminate, as far as practicable, the minds of the people at large. (In Perkinson, 1977, p. 8)

Jefferson saw as the primary political purpose of education the development of an educated citizenry that would prevent the tyranny that had emerged in many countries around the world. He was also interested in the education of new political leaders from all classes in the population (with some limitations, however), leaders who would safeguard the rights and liberties of their fellow citizens. Jefferson's plan clearly entailed a limited vision of democracy, but one considered so radical in his time that most of it was never adopted. In order to establish a national aristocracy of talent he proposed that all free white males in Virginia have the opportunity for early schooling, with the best students going on to grammar schools, and some eventually to the University of Virginia.

When Jefferson spoke of education he meant not only schooling but the other educational instruments of society, especially the press. Nevertheless, when it came to schooling he was very specific about the political purposes of education, for among the aims and purposes of primary education he included: "To understand his duties to his neighbor and country, and to discharge with competence the functions confided to him by either." Among the aims that he ascribed for higher education were these:

> To form the statesmen, legislators, and judges, on whom public prosperity and individual happiness are so much to depend; to expound the principles and structures of government, the laws which regulate the intercourse of nations, those formed municipally for our own government, and a sound spirit of legislation, which, banishing all arbitrary and unnecessary restraint on individual action, shall leave us free to do whatever does not violate the equal rights of others. (In Cremin, 1970, p. 39)

Political or civic education in the early years of the nation took place through the spellers and readers which stressed patriotism, love of country, and love of God. A number of these catechisms indoctrinated into the political opinions of the Federalist Party. Jefferson, who strongly opposed Federalism with his republican views, made a strong case for the study of history as a means of providing civic education. In his view historical knowledge fortified persons with a knowledge of the past that would help them to make future decisions. It enabled persons to judge the past, as well as to recognize corrupt and tyrannical regimes. He recognized that education alone was not adequate to the task of full political education but he thought it so important that he wanted an amendment to the constitution in aid of public education (Butts, 1980, p. 55).

When it came to his beloved University of Virginia, Jefferson became very explicit on the political purposes of education. The university was to include a school of law and a school of government. Jefferson made it clear that the "professor of government should expound Republican doctrines and ideals in order to counteract the Federalist biases of the colleges of the day" (Butts, 1980, p. 56). Jefferson in this proposal raised the critical question of indoctrination into political ideologies, to be discussed later in this chapter.

Although most of Jefferson's proposals were rejected in his lifetime, his political philosophy and philosophy of education have influenced other educators such as Horace Mann and John Dewey. Mann went further in proposing an even more democratic philosophy of education. His main focus was on establishing a public system of schools open to all persons. From his position as superintendent of education in Massachusetts he promoted public education for many reasons, including the advancement of political life. Though a trained lawyer and not a philosopher, his analyses and proposals for education were both profound and influential.

Horace Mann actually used the term "political education" when he expressed his view that citizens of the nation should understand the true nature of their government. He also described the political education which he felt appropriate for the nation's schools. It included a study of the constitution, the threefold powers of government, the mode of electing and selecting officials, and

Especially, the duty of every citizen, in a government of laws, to appeal to the courts for redress, in all cases of alleged wrong, instead of undertaking to vindicate his own rights by his own arm, and, in a government where people are the acknowledged sources of power, the duty of changing laws and rulers by an appeal to the ballot, and not by rebellion, should be taught to all the children until they are fully understood. (In Cremin, 1957, p. 93)

Mann recognized that there were dangers to be faced in political education. Political disputes in society and in schools could lead to violence among social classes and the destruction of national unity. His solution was that schools should teach the common elements of republican faith but skip over controversial matters. No political proselytism was to take place in schools. When teachers came across a controversial text he counseled the same as he did in matters of religious dispute:

> When the teacher, in the course of his lessons on the fundamental law, arrives at a controverted text, he is either to read it without comment or remark; or, at most he is only to say that the passage is the subject of disputation, and that the schoolroom is neither the tribunal to adjudicate, nor the forum to discuss it. (In Cremin, 1957, p. 97)

The handling of controversial political matters in a classroom was one that also beset progressive educators, like John Dewey; it remains a matter of controversy.

John Dewey: Democratic Education

One of the major thrusts of Dewey's philosophy of education was the development of a character in children which was needed by a democratic society. This character, which was marked by a social spirit, would be developed only if schools were organized as cooperative communities in which children participate and to which they contribute. Teachers were also to participate in the cooperative inquiry which characterized the school community. The goal of Dewey's democratic education was to turn out for society exemplary young adults.

While previous educational systems were designed to pass on the values of society, Dewey assigned to the schools another social and political task: to be instruments for the fuller democratization of American society. Schools were not merely to adjust individuals to social institutions but were "to deepen and broaden the range of social contact and intercourse, of cooperative living, so that the members of the school would be prepared to make their future social relations worthy and fruitful"

(Dewey, 1896, p. 361). For Dewey the schools were institutions for facilitating the growth of cultural, technological, and scientific forces that were necessary for a truly democratic society.

In *Democracy and Education* (1916) Dewey made the case for an education which he thought appropriate for a democratic society. The goal of the democratic school was to initiate children into democratic communities of inquiry. Some, however, have charged Dewey with promoting democratic ends through undemocratic means of social control. Except in one case involving the education of Polish-Americans Dewey appears to have remained committed to democratic methods. Furthermore, he strongly opposed George Counts' proposals for indoctrination into a socialist vision of society.

Dewey viewed as one of the major obstacles to democratic education class privilege, a system which found it philosophic basis in Plato's distinction between working with one's hands and working with one's mind. He argued against the philosophy and the practice of distinguishing between two forms of education, industrial and intellectual, theoretical and practical. For him a democratic society had to be committed to combatting this philosophical and social dualism.

Dewey's maturest ideas on political education appear not in *Democracy and Education*, written in 1916, but in a number of articles written in the 1930s when the specter of fascism and Naziism cast its shadow over the world and the democratic philosophy of life was challenged. In his view the maintenance and flourishing of democracy demanded an increase in social knowledge and forms of social engineering. Even at this time, however, he remained convinced that education was the primary means for ensuring the survival of democracy. Education, Dewey said

> Is not the only means, but it is the first means, the primary means and the most deliberate means by which the values that any social group cherishes, the purposes that it wishes to realize, are distributed and brought home to the thought, the observation, judgment and choice of the individual. (Dewey 1966 [1938], p. 37)

Dewey was not hesitant to point out some of the failures in the political education conducted in the schools. The schools, he contended, were not doing enough to combat prejudice against Negroes and Jews. He asked "what are our schools doing positively and aggressively and constructively to cultivate understanding and goodwill which are essential to democratic society" (1966 [1938], p. 42). He questioned whether the schools had done an adequate job teaching about allegiance, loyalty, liberty, justice, public spirit, and citizenship.

In another article Dewey argued for forging a closer connection between social studies and social action. He was critical of the way in which the school still attempted to educate persons for political citizenship, merely by giving a great deal of information about the government. In order that people might not be manipulated he called for more teaching about precisely how decisions are made in democratic societies through power machines and party bosses. In this article Dewey attempted to find a middle way between aimless education and reprehensible indoctrination by proposing the alternative of an

Education that connects the materials and methods by which knowledge is acquired with a sense of how things are done and of how they might be done; not by impregnating the individual with some final philosophy, whether it comes from Karl Marx or from Mussolini or Hitler or anybody else, but by enabling him to so understand existing conditions that an attitude of intelligent action will follow from social understanding. (1966, p. 56)

During his entire life Dewey argued for the political rights of teachers as well as for their duty to be informed about public issues. He was a strong proponent of academic freedom on the part of both teachers and students, for he saw this right as needed for them to explore the forces at work in society. He realistically recognized that in troubled times such as the 1930s training for good citizenship was not simple. Yet he argued that

Every force that operates to limit the freedom of education is a premium put upon ultimate recourse to violence to effect needed change. Every force that tends to liberate educational processes is a premium placed upon intelligent and orderly methods of directing to a more just, equitable, and humane end the social changes that are going on anyway. (1966, pp. 79–80)

As did many other educators at this time Dewey grappled with the issue of political indoctrination. While he shared the view of George Counts that teachers and schools should take on a more socialist orientation, he raised serious questions about the methods by which this orientation was to be presented in schools. His commitment to the values of intelligence made him sensitive to any method which offended free and open inquiry. He also advocated that teachers adopt an aggressive stance against what he thought was propaganda in the press. The school's task in such a situation was, in his view, to foster a critical understanding of both propaganda and social forces.

Radical Political Education: George Counts

While Plato and Rush present a conservative view of political education and Dewey and Mann, a liberal or reformist view, George Counts may be considered both a political and educational radical in that he called for revolutionary change in the United States. In the midst of the depression in 1932 Counts addressed the convention of the Progressive Education Association and accused the movement of having failed to confront the deep problems of industrial democracy. Counts also challenged teachers to reach for political power themselves and to become the revolutionary group that was needed to lead the country to socialism.

The most controversial part of the Counts' plan was clearly what he urged teachers to do in their classrooms. What he proposed was that they should indoctrinate children into a radical socialist vision of society. Teachers should also indoctrinate children about the evils of capitalism and the values upon which it depended. Counts dramatically proposed his thesis in these words:

> I am prepared to defend the thesis that all education contains a large element of imposition, that in the very nature of the case this is inevitable, that the existence and evolution of society depend upon it, that it is consequently eminently desirable, and that the frank acceptance of this fact by the educator is a major professional obligation. (In Gross, 1963, p. 180)

Many who shared Counts's call for radical change doubted that teachers could be the revolutionary force or that teachers should directly use classrooms to promote such a vision. They also questioned the morality of the means that he urged teachers to use in the classrooms.

In later writings Counts presented a Marxist analysis of the causes of the Depression, laying the blame for it on the values of capitalist businessmen and socially conservative groups. Those who followed Counts's lead came to call themselves social reconstructionists. For a number of

years a heated debate took place among educators on the merits of
Counts's Marxist analysis and his proposals. While Dewey and other
progressives sympathized with many of the aims of the social reconstructionists, they remained unconvinced that direct indoctrination was compatible with the principles of democratic education.

The social reconstructionists have left us a legacy of a radical form of
political education. They challenged what many viewed as the value-free
vision of the school by implicating it in the larger social, economic, and
political problems of society. They also introduced into political education curricula which were critical of injustices in American society. John
Childs, a forceful social reconstructionist, explained that

> Many teachers believe that in a democratic society they should seek to ac-
> tively nurture in the young the emotional and intellectual dispositions
> which will prompt them to put the welfare of the many above the privi-
> leges of the few. In doing this they recognize that they are using the school
> as a positive agency to bias the young in favor of the values of social de-
> mocracy. (Childs, 1935, pp. 8–9)

The social reconstructionists did not limit their efforts to public schools
but also put their ideas at the disposal of labor unions, churches, neigh-
borhood organizations, and the press.

The theories of the social reconstructionists caused a great stir in the
1930s. But as the nation returned to normalcy with the advent of the
New Deal, radical educational thought had few followers. The situation
changed somewhat in the 1960s with a number of radical theories on
political education being advanced. Radical political education did not
come strongly to the fore until a new voice was heard from Latin America.

Revolutionary Political Education: Paulo Freire

In 1970 the educational world was suddenly greeted by a powerful
philosophical voice from the Third World. Paulo Freire, a Brazilian philosopher of education, presented in his *Pedagogy of the Oppressed*
(1970), a truly radical theory and practice of political education, based
on a number of philosophical traditions including phenomenology and
Marxism. Freire developed this approach while he led a campaign to
eliminate adult illiteracy in the early 1960s in his native Brazil. Because

of his involvement in this program he was forced to go into exile, along with other radicals. In the past twenty years through books, lectures, and interviews he has described his theory and practice in many countries of the world. He was asked by various government in developing countries to assist them in literacy and political education (Elias, 1994).

The purpose of the Freirean approach is to bring about in oppressed people, conscientization, that is, a keen awareness of the causes of their oppression and a firm commitment to struggle against the forces of oppression. In order to accomplish this Freire joined education in political literacy to basic adult literacy education. Consequently, in the process of teaching illiterates to read and write he also raised their consciousness about oppressive social and political realities in which they lived. He did this by using politically charged words and pictures in the literacy education. These words were chosen after a period of time spent living with the people who were to attend the literacy courses.

It is Freire's view that there is no neutral education. Education is either for domestication or for liberation. He contends that the traditional education through didactic methods merely reinforces the structures and values of the dominant classes in society. The books which are used and the "banking" method of education treat students as things into which the ideas and ideologies of the dominant classes are deposited. To counteract this form of education Freire proposes a problem-centered approach which used dialogical methods, stressing the relationship of equality between teachers and learners and challenging people to study, reflect, communicate, and act.

Freire describes the role of the teacher as the coordinator of the educational processes. Coordinators arrange for the learning by leading the group through dialogic processes. They are not to impose their ideas on the students but to draw out the ideas or perceptions of students. Freire has manifested great faith in the ability of oppressed people to correctly analyze and discuss the social and political situation in which they lived.

Freire's theory of political education focuses on the education of adults in oppressed situations. Transferred to school situations the theory runs some of the same risks of ideological indoctrination that beset the social reconstructionists. Some radical educators have attempted to apply his ideas, together with the critical social theory of the Frankfurt school, to school situations. Their proposals for a radical theory of citizenship education will be presented later in this chapter.

In conclusion, political or civic education in the United States can be seen in terms of educators' response to the social situations and problems. While at certain times there has been great attention to political education, at other times, it has received little notice. The high points in thought and ideas on political education were immediately after the Revolution with the proposals of Thomas Jefferson and Benjamin Rush. During the pre-Civil War reform movement Horace Mann proposed a political education that stressed political consensus as one of the justifications for the common school. The political reforms during the Progressive period produced the democratic education of John Dewey. Social reconstructionists such as George Counts proposed a radical form of political education to respond to social and economic upheaval. In more recent times the Cold War produced an education that stressed the values of democracy over communism and socialism. During the turmoil of the sixties various proposals—conservative, liberal, and radical were presented.

CONTEMPORARY APPROACHES

The present moment in American history affords a new challenge to political education. As American society becomes more of a multicultural society, there is great debate over the meaning of citizenship. As the world has increasingly become a global society, many are proposing a new form of citizenship, world citizenship. In this section I will explore contemporary issues with regard to political education. There are a number of scholars who argue against political education in the schools. Other scholars point out the elements of political education which form the basis of a hidden curriculum for the schools. There has been a revival of civic learning associated with the bicentennial of the birth of the nation. Other scholars propose a radical and emancipatory form of citizenship education. Finally, the beginnings of a new paradigm are found in the efforts of some to propose a political education for life in a multicultural and global society.

Arguments against Political Education

In the midst of contemporary discussions about political or civic education a number of voices are heard that are strongly opposed to political education in the schools, in the tradition of John Locke and John Stuart Mill. These voices include radical historians, socialists, anarchists, and even political conservatives. Offering various arguments both philosophical and empirical these scholars urge schools to desist from both moral and political education, maintaining that the family and public discussion are adequate to the task of political education.

From the perspective of Michael Katz, a radical historian, the schools should be value neutral and merely teach basic academic subjects because only these are free from the danger of imposition and indoctrination. In his view of American history, schools have always imposed upper class values on lower classes by reinforcing political, social, and moral structures. He favors no program of civic or moral education because these would only serve to maintain a system which is exploitative and class based. In his view the right of the state to impose its political and moral values on students is questioned. This rather pessimistic perspective on education would leave political education to forces outside the schools (Katz, 1971). The arguments of these scholars is similar to arguments presented by those socialists who oppose political education in capitalist countries.

Some neoconservative critics of American society arrive at a similar conclusion on other grounds. They contend that schools do not have the right to engage in political education, something that should be left to the family and voluntary associations of society. Wanting to avoid state intrusion into education, they prefer the schools to rely on informal customs and spontaneous tradition. Neoconservatives are critical of government interference in schools, believing as they do in a free market system. One can question this absolute right that these philosophers give to parents, given cases of neglect and abuse of children. On the other hand the state's rights in education are also limited. Children are neither the exclusive property of the state nor of the family.

This position comes almost down to an anarchist position which finds little support at present but which has been a force at times in United States history. What individualists want to preserve is the freedom of individuals and the ownership of self. Included among this group are Leo Tolstoi and Ivan Illich. Many opponents of national systems of schools have seen schools as state sponsored means of controlling people's minds.

Another variation of this approach is found in the writings of British and American analytic philosophers of education. They believe education should serve the goals of understanding and not serve any other purpose outside of this. The educational needs of individuals are paramount, to be met by a study of publicly acknowledged forms of knowledge. There appears in this view to be a latent commitment to conservative or liberal values because of the stress on knowledge of how the system works and on understanding how the citizen can act within a system. No attention, however, is given to developing skills beyond the analytic skills needed for understanding.

The beliefs of those who oppose civic and political education caution us to the difficulties involved in any education where there are serious controversies or differences of opinion. By asserting the rights of the individual in education they force us to think about the limits that should be placed on the state's right to both compel the young to attend school and to determine what the young shall study. The rights of individuals, however, have to be balanced with the needs of a society to maintain its basic values, which protect the freedom of members. If one over-stresses the freedom of individuals, then it becomes difficult to justify even compulsory school, let alone political or civic education.

One can seriously question whether the schools can give an adequate education if little or no attention is given to the political dimensions of life. How can even history and literature be taught unless one explains differing political ideas? Is it really advisable, or even possible, for teachers to exclude the political from the classroom? Given that those who have examined the hidden curriculum of the schools have demonstrated the political messages that schools send out, a strong case can be made for explicit political education.

Hidden Political Education

In recent years a great deal of attention has been given to the hidden curriculum of the schools, including the inculcation of political and social values. The hidden curriculum is viewed as the "tacit teaching to students of norms, values, dispositions that goes on simply by their living in and coping with institutions and routines of schools day in and day out for a number of years" (Apple, 1979, p. 14). Through a process of political socialization, political views and character of students are formed by the very constitution and conduct of schools. The behavior of teachers—how they speak about students, school, the political realm— provide a political education. These scholars have shown that teachers possess a political philosophy and that this political philosophy guides teachers' practice (Bricker, 1989).

Of the two competing philosophies of liberalism and communitarianism, the practices of the school are clearly in the liberal tradition which emphasizes the values of freedom and justice at the expense of the values of friendship and generosity. Bricker argues that schools should also stress the good of the community as well as the good of the individual. The liberal political philosophy is rooted in the philosophy of Kant and the theory of justice proposed by John Rawls (1971). The communitarian position has been defended primarily by Sandel (1982).

Through his extensive interviews with five teachers Bricker was able to glean some elements of civic education which these teachers offered to their students through the hidden curriculum. From the fact that teachers do not encourage students to work together, Bricker makes certain conclusions about their political and educational philosophy. Teachers espouse the theory of individual freedom and justice at the expense of communitarian viewpoints. They stress the value of individual possessions that exaggerates the distances among people. They prefer that students do their work alone rather than cooperatively in groups. Teachers often engage in comparing students with one another through many means of assessment. They accept without question the current system by which students compete with each other and are deeply concerned with rankings. What students learn from schools is the excessive individualism and overriding concern with individual freedom that characterize American society. The virtues of community life are, in Bricker's view, not sufficiently manifested in the organization and management of education. Bricker's conclusions are reinforced by the analyses of Bellah (1985; 1991) on the political character of the United States as well as the individualist values and aims of education in the United States.

There are many other practices in schools that in a hidden way foster a political education. Are the virtues of democratic citizenship fostered by tracking arrangements? What political and social effects result from the low esteem in which vocational education is held? What message is there in the continued existence of racially segregated schools and classrooms? What lessons are there in breaches of the rights of academic freedom? What political messages are there in the gender makeup of schools with predominantly male principals and female teachers?

Only limited conclusions can be drawn from a study such as Bricker's, based as it is on interviews with five teachers. Other empirical studies on political socialization have tended to stress the role of families and media. The research, however, by a philosopher of education, does have relevance at a theoretical level in illustrating the types of values which are found in schools. Bricker attempts to do justice at a theoretical level to the values of personal freedom and community responsibility. In this way his ideas are similar to feminist scholars such as Carol Gilligan and Nel Noddings, whose work was treated in the chapter on moral education.

Revival of Civic Learning

Around the time of the bicentennial a revival in civic education occurred in United States education. Professional organizations, foundations, and government agencies were part of forces for this revival. Such a revival was also necessary no doubt because of the drop in patriotic feeling and the increase in public criticism connected with the civil rights movement, the unpopular war in Vietnam, and the Watergate scandals. Educators joined with politicians as well as scholars of history and political science to take another look at citizenship education as the United States moved into the third century of its existence.

In the revival of civic learning the school, as was to be expected, was assigned a distinctive role in education for citizenship. This role comprises three tasks: "1) providing a study of and commitment to the value of political democracy; 2) imparting realistic and scholarly political knowledge; 3) teaching the participation skills required for the maintenance and improvement of the democratic political system" (Butts, 1980, p. 126). It is noteworthy that neither criticism nor a rethinking of citizenship in multicultural or global terms was a stated goal in this revival.

Advocates of civic learning described ten value concepts or claims that should form the basis for a cohesive civic education. The five values of justice, equality, authority, participation, and personal obligation for the common good are directed at providing for a cohesive and unifying dimension in public life, while the values of freedom, diversity, privacy, due process, and international human rights stress desirable pluralistic or individualist elements in a democratic political community. For an explanation of these values Butts draws on the political philosophy of John Rawls, Alexander Meiklejohn, James Madison, Robert McIver, Lawrence Kohlberg, and John Dewey (Butts, 1980, 132-155). Though these are sound values, what is lacking in Butts's treatment is a discussion of the many possible conflicts that exist among these values both in the practical and theoretical spheres, for example, between freedom and equality or authority and privacy.

The new civic education attempts to make use of the scholarship that is available in the many disciplines that contribute relevant knowledge about the political life of the nation. Fortunately, in many of these disciplines there has been a turn to dealing with the political relevance of the scholarship. The social sciences have added to the behaviorist and positivist tradition of scholarship a respect for participation and judgment, recognizing that they have a role to play in dealing with the problems that face the nation. Civic educators tend to make use of the humanistic scholarship in sociology, political science, history, and other disciplines, a scholarship which sees individuals and groups playing a greater role in political events than rigid laws and material forces.

Civic education also covers the skills of political participation, to be learned through realistic involvement in school and community affairs. Such skills include speaking effectively, running a meeting, the arts of negotiation, compromise, the use of power, and decision making. While some educators stress political action that uses the indirect route of influencing representatives and public officials, others favor direct participation with like-minded persons through the mediating institutions of families, neighborhoods, churches, and voluntary organizations. Those who favor indirect participation point out that since there are many interest groups in society and many values to consider, the persons elected to represent all the people are in the best position to make decisions. Those who favor methods of direct participation contend that such action is a check against situations where representatives are influenced only by special interest groups and party politics.

A Communitarian Civic Education

In recent years scholars have attempted to develop an ethic of civic life that places more emphasis on the values of group decision making, community participation, and social justice in order to balance the values of freedom and autonomy of individuals (Sandel, 1982; MacIntyre, 1984). Richard Pratte (1988) has used this new ethical and political orientation in developing a civic education with an emphasis on community. This approach, which also draws on the ideas of John Dewey, places as much emphasis on developing the good person as it does on developing the good citizen. Pratte sets as the goal of civic education "developing virtuous citizens who view their good as individuals as being one with the good of the human community" (p. 9). This education stresses the values of civic compassion and decency, caring for others, service to others, as well as tolerance and respect.

Communitarian civic education entails three broad goals. First, it attempts to develop historical perspective by helping students to gain a knowledge of their own cultural traditions in order that they might appreciate democratic citizenship as well as be critical of present political arrangements. Second, it entails the development of social-action skills such as the ability to confer, discuss, debate, argue, negotiate, and compromise. Students can be aided in this by being given opportunities to role play situations. Third, it attempts to reduce ethnocentrism by making students aware of cultural prejudices.

One of the characteristics of this communitarian approach in education is the stress placed on community service, which is viewed as "the driving force, the unifying base for a moral civic education" (Pratte, 1988, p. 107). Community service is a way to bridge the separation between public and private life. It is in community service that students have the opportunity to exhibit the virtues of trust, kindness, concern, caring, tolerance, and respect. Such service enables students to move beyond themselves and to feel responsibility for community development. The community service envisaged by communitarian proponents is not make work but

Life in earnest, engaging students in the formation of social habits of willing action beneficial to others. To be a good citizen is to pursue self-interest in ways compatible with enriching and edifying community life. Personal self-interest is adapted to, and not pursued at the expense of, the community purpose. (Pratte, 1988, p. 183)

This form of civic education has received support from many educators who have proposed service programs to help students meet social and civic obligations. Some political leaders have also endorsed such programs. This approach brings into the school neglected elements of moral and religious traditions.

Education for Radical Emancipatory
Citizenship Education

The radical tradition in political education, originated by George Counts has recently been utilized, as well as other sources, by Henri Giroux and others in developing an approach to political education which can be called radical, critical, and emancipatory.

These critics fault conservatives with proposing a citizenship education directed at inculcating an uncritical patriotism which ignores the pervasive problems in the United States: racism, sexism, manipulation, classism, elitism, and chauvinism. In Giroux's view what citizenship education has failed to develop is

> The imperative of educating students to affirm moral principles that renounce social injustice and encourage students to become involved in the world in order to change it. What is missing from these approaches is any notion of a public philosophy that gives credence to an emancipatory form of citizenship that puts equality and human life at its center and equates democracy not with privileges but with democratic rights that ensure meaningful participation in the political, economic, and social spheres of society. At the same time, meaningful democracy and its attendant notion of emancipatory citizenship points to the construction of new sensibilities and social relations that would not allow for political interests to emerge in everyday life which support relations of oppression and domination. (1988, p. 15)

These critics also point out that their fellow radicals have engaged only in destructive criticism and have not offered viable alternatives.

Giroux faults traditional teaching of history for failing to make enough use of the element of struggle in United States history, found in trade union struggles, civil rights struggles, and feminist struggles. Social studies fail to analyze the false ideologies that operate in United States political life. The social studies curriculum, does not, in his view, do justice to the diversity and difference that exists in the United States. Indeed, the term patriotism is used as a code word for explicitly excluding the diverse and the different. Not only the schools but also the mass media, especially Hollywood films like *Rambo*, are indicted for contributing to the lessening of United States democracy.

These critics are especially critical of the recent school reform movement which they see as rooted in the effort to make citizenship education serve the narrow economic interests of the nation. They decry the lack of political vision in such documents as *A Nation at Risk*. Barbara Finkelstein has uttered this stinging attack on school reformers:

> Contemporary reformers seem to be recalling public education from its traditional utopian mission to nurture a critical and committed citizenry that would stimulate the process of political and cultural transformation and refine and extend the workings of political democracy. . . . Reformers seem to imagine public schools as economic rather than political instrumentalities. Instead, they call public schools to industrial and cultural service exclusively. . . . Americans . . . seem ready to do ideological surgery on their public schools—cutting them away from the fate of social justice and political democracy completely and grafting them instead onto elite corporate, industrial, military, and cultural interests. (Finkelstein, 1984, pp. 280–281)

A number of principles are proposed for developing a critical theory of citizenship education. First, since the achieving of democracy is a constant struggle among competing ideas of power, politics, and community, students must be educated to be *active agents* in defining, questioning, and shaping relationships in the political sphere. Students must learn to face up to the fundamental antagonisms that exist in United States society. They should be encouraged to participate in all political spheres. A second principle entails the recognition of a need for a *radical pluralism* that will result from strengthening the bonds among citizens in such a way that the demands, cultures, and social relations of diverse groups can be involved in public discourse. This education should attempt to create a politics of trust and solidarity that will support a common life based on democratic principles.

Third, educational efforts should not only engage in criticizing social, political, economic, and cultural structures but must also develop "a *language of possibility*, one that combines a strategy of opposition with a strategy for a new social order" (Giroux, 1988, p. 31). The vision that Giroux holds out for schools is that they can be "democratic public spheres committed to forms of cultural politics aimed at empowering students and enhancing human possibilities" (p. 32). Fourth, educators must strive to make schools places of popular engagement and democratic politics. They should strive to make them places that foster civic literacy, citizenship participation, and moral courage.

The role of teachers in this education for emancipatory citizenship is to be radical intellectuals who link political struggles with broader social issues, and forge political relationships with others to deal with social issues. In this role they should attempt to combine the pedagogical with the political. Teachers in colleges and schools should see themselves as involved in developing a public philosophy that defines the meaning of citizenship in a democratic society, which is in a special way dedicated "to uncovering sources of suffering and oppression, while legitimating social practices that uphold principles of sociality and community that are dedicated to improving the quality of human life" (Giroux, 1988, p. 36).

Giroux has valiantly attempted in his writings and talks to keep the radical critique alive in educational debates. He has applied his particular mode of criticism, first critical social theory and now postmodernist critique and radical feminism, to educational issues. In his criticism of citizenship education, though he makes some valid points, he sets up persons of straw on both the Right and the Left. He does not give ordinary teachers credit enough for avoiding extremist positions on either side, in their attempts to deal both with their own political stances and those of the community in which they work. Unfortunately, Giroux never gets close enough to dealing with the realm of practice to offer any really helpful proposals to improve political education. He does not deal sufficiently with problems of indoctrination and manipulation that might plague the strong ideological positions which he takes. Finally, he does not attend sufficiently to the unitive elements in a public philosophy, as seen in the advocates of civic learning. Notwithstanding his efforts to develop a language of possibility, he is much clearer on what he is against—things which educators on the entire political spectrum would most likely condemn, than he is on concrete proposals to fulfill these aims.

Education for Citizenship in a Multicultural and Global Society

In recent years some scholars have rethought political education in light of changes in the United States and the world. Until recently citizenship education focused on producing citizens who are committed to the common values of the nation. Since it is now more clearly recognized that the United States has become a multicultural society with large number of immigrants from foreign countries, scholars debate how this factor should influence the type of political education that takes place, especially in the schools. The chapter on intellectual education treated this matter as part of the debate over the canon.

Furthermore, with the heightening awareness that the world has become a global society, the issue of education for world citizenship alongside national citizenship has been raised. Many other subjects of study in schools are considered under the umbrella of political education: environmental studies, peace studies, global studies, women's studies, and black studies. This new situation in the minds of many calls for an expanded or reconstructed political education, an education for global democracy.

The education for citizenship recognizes that individuals must now operate, at least in their thinking, at local, national, and international levels. Political education should also include attention to social, cultural, environmental and economic domains. This education attempts to address issues of human rights, social responsibility, and power. It is not enough to think merely in terms of a just society; attention must also be directed to the needs of a just global society. An eloquent spokesperson for this education for world citizenship presents these overriding goals:

> I propose a concept of education for democratic citizenship for local, national, and global responsibility which is embedded in human rights and a commitment to social responsibilities. . . . [I propose] to release the concept of citizenship education from the intellectual and political bondage that has passed historically for citizenship education and to liberate it from the exclusive economic and political interests of nationally and internationally dominant groups. (Lynch, 1992, p. 6)

In this view of citizenship education, nationality plays only a partial role. This rethinking of citizenship education is taking place in many parts of the world.

Those who call for this new form of citizenship education are aware of the arguments against it. How does this education fit in with the rise of an aggressive nationalism in many parts of the world? Will not such an education fail to develop a healthy spirit of national pride and patriotism in students? Will not an emphasis upon diversity weaken the bonds of unity which are necessary for civic peace and public order? Is there really any meaning to the concept of global citizenship? Are not these proposals rather idealistic when one considers that citizens expect national leaders to seek the national welfare? Is not an education based on such a vision an abstraction at best and a distraction at worst?

Those who advocate education for world citizenship respond to these questions by pointing to changed realities in the world. Education for a narrowly conceived national citizenship runs the danger of being perverted in times of national and world crisis by preventing legitimate criticism and fostering selfish nationalistic aims. World citizenship recognizes that individuals have rights and responsibilities beyond the territory of nations, rights which have been recognized by the International Declaration of Human Rights and international law. Because of increased international communication and education, violations of human rights are now known throughout the world. Increased international transportation, the internationalization of business and industry have brought about a great interdependence among nations. Some major problems that are connected with the environment cannot be dealt with except through cooperation among nations. Finally, the cessation of open hostilities between East and West has resulted in calls for a new world order to replace the order dominated by the United States and the Soviet Union.

In this new situation it is not enough to teach young people about United States history, government, and domestic problems. A knowledge of the Declaration of Independence and the Constitution must be supplemented by a knowledge of the Declaration on Human Rights and a study of international law. Education in the core values of national consensus will take students far in understanding world problems but these must be examined in the light of other traditions and value consensuses. A knowledge of skills for political life and involvement must also include attention in dealing with problems beyond national borders.

Concluding Observations: Indoctrination

The issue that plagues all forms of political education, as well as moral and religious education, is the danger of indoctrination. What does the teacher do in the classroom or lecture hall with his or her own particular political views. Although this is a problem at all levels of education, it is particularly sensitive in teaching the young. Interestingly, this issue is not usually discussed in terms of parent-child relationships for it seems to be assumed that parents have some right to pass on their own views on controverted issues.

The literature on indoctrination from a philosophical perspective is an extensive one. Indoctrination is distinguished from education in a number of ways: content, intention, and methods. Indoctrination involves handing on *beliefs* as true or uncontroversial, when the teacher knows them not to be such, while education presents all sides of an issue. The intention of the person indoctrinating is that persons will hold the beliefs that have been presented, while the intention in education is that persons will weigh all views and make up their own minds. Indoctrination utilizes methods which inhibit freedom of inquiry and judgment in students, while education makes every effort to use methods that respect the dignity and rationality of persons.

With regard to the stance that teachers should take in a classroom about their own particular views, there are a number of possibilities. Teachers can make every effort to remain neutral, not offering their own opinions on matters on which there is a political difference. It may or may not be possible to do this. Usually students will probe the opinions of teachers, at least out of curiosity. Attempting to do this as a matter of policy may make an unreal situation out of the classroom. Although I have occasionally attempted this stance, at times I have been forced to abandon it.

Teachers may also make very clear what their political positions are on all topics. I think that this should be done judiciously and as late as possible in the teaching process. My method, especially when I taught in high schools, was to allow students to present their own ideas, gathered through study and interviews on an issue, debate them among themselves, and then enter the debate or forum as late as possible, never in such a way that my views were the correct views. On most issues there were some who arrived at what I thought.

The teaching of history presents particular problems because it is regarded by many students as purely objective knowledge. Students should be made aware of the position of the textbook they are using by bringing in alternative interpretations of events. I have found that students can be brought to realize how events receive different interpretations by having them interpret an event which they have all experienced.

The ideal of the political educator is to take the stance of one who is both committed to causes and interpretations while at the same time fair to all decisions and interpretations that others make. There is some slight danger in this. I once had a teacher who presented the views of those he opposed with greater persuasion than he did his own interpretations. This seems to go against the well known axiom that people are more to be believed for what they affirm than for what they deny. In this matter, as in others, the main line of defense is constant vigilance and the willingness to submit to self-criticism and criticism from others, especially one's students.

CHAPTER 7

VOCATIONAL EDUCATION

Philosophers have not given as much attention to vocational education as they have to the other dimensions of education that have already been treated. Perhaps the bias against this form of education enunciated in the classical tradition has been responsible for this. Nevertheless, there is a tradition of philosophical thought on aspects of vocational education that can be examined. There are also aspects of vocational education that both need and receive some treatment from philosophers.

In this chapter a number of issues relating to vocational education will be treated. A historical review of philosophical positions will indicate some of the areas of dispute. Among the arguments for having vocational education in the curriculum have been philosophical ones, even though most justifications are economic. The aims of vocational education certainly fall within the purview of philosophy of education.

There has been a variety of language used to describe the education which is related to preparation for entry into employment, as well as for retraining for employment. "Manual training" was used in the early days of the movement in this country. "Vocational education," the preferred term for Dewey and the progressives, has the advantage of being used by the federal government in its funding acts. In the 1970s "career education" was widely used. Some have used the language of "technical education" to indicate that the education is directed toward skills. It should also be noted that some prefer not to use the word education but the word training to indicate the narrower focus of such education.

While most of the debates surrounding vocational education concern secondary education, there have also been debates about vocational education in colleges and universities. Although the treatment here is mainly concerned with pre-college years, one might extend some aspects of the discussion to education for the various professions in society.

The questions that concern us with vocational education are whether or not it should be part of general or liberal education. In many countries these subjects are not taught in schools, or at least in regular schools. The American tradition has been to include them. What is the justification for this? Is it an example of American pragmatism or egalitarianism? Can philosophic justification be offered.

One of the fundamental issues in debates over vocational education is the meaning that is ascribed to work. Forms of work are valued differently in different cultures. Views on particular forms of work also change over time. It is clear that philosophies of work and education for work are influenced by social and cultural understandings.

HISTORICAL PERSPECTIVES

The Classic Position

For Plato education is a major concern of the state. People are to be educated in accordance with the needs of the state and according to their natural endowments. Three forms of education are proposed for the three classes that make up the state: artisans, military, and rulers. Persons should be educated and trained in accordance with what they were good for, a practice that would also secure the good of society. A physical, military, and moral education is suited for the warriors or guardians. A full intellectual education should be given to the rulers of the state. In Plato's opinion people should stay for their entire lifetime at the position for which they are suited. A vocational training is appropriate for the working class, in the form of apprenticeships.

Since Plato believed that the mind was superior to the body, he considered the lowest form of education to be for those who worked with their hands and not with their minds. This form of education was called "technical" (from the Greek *techne*—to make) education. Plato thus made a considerable distinction between intellectual and practical or industrial activities. As seen in the chapter on aesthetic education, this viewpoint extended even to those who performed with musical instruments. In point of fact Plato would not have used the word education for this form of activity.

Aristotle enunciated basically the same viewpoint as Plato. He accepted the situation that some people were marked out to be slaves from the hour of their birth. While the highest form of activity is contemplation by the mind, the lowest form of activity is working with one's hands. This no doubt reflects the social arrangement in ancient Greece according to which slaves worked with their hands and free men with their minds. Thus, although farmers and artisans are necessary for the life of the state, they should not enjoy the rights of citizens.

Aristotle's preference was clearly for the life of leisure over the life of work for gain since he considered the latter an unfortunate absorption and impoverishment of the mind. He made this contrast in speaking of who shall be citizens and who shall rule:

> . . . in a state which has an ideal constitution . . . the citizens must not lead the life of mechanics or tradesmen, which is ignoble and far from conducive to virtue. Nor . . . must they be drawn from among the farming class, because leisure is necessary for the growth of virtue and for the fulfillment of political duties. . . . No one can rule satisfactorily without the leisure derived from easy circumstances. (Aristotle, 1964, p. 60)

In the Greek literature where there is little praise for work, the word for work is *askolia*, the lack of leisure. It was only in Roman times, when slavery declined, that work was taken more seriously (Watts, 1983, p. 123).

This classical position of viewing activities of the hand as inferior to activities of the mind has had a long history in Western education. The Greek concept was reflected in Christianity within the monastic traditions where the lay brothers and sisters did the menial work while the monks and nuns could devote themselves to the higher concerns of contemplation and study.

The classic tradition contained another relevant idea for understanding vocational education. Education for particular professions, vocations or jobs, even including physician, lawyer, and rhetorician was considered technical and thus a lower form of education. The classical tradition made a sharp distinction between education of the mind and education for work. This intellectual education as enunciated by classical authors had little use for technique; it attempted to educate the whole person, meaning the mind of the person. Only medicine managed to separate itself as a special kind of learning, but the ancient physician

> was dogged by an inferiority complex. From Hippocrates to Galen they go on saying: "The physician is a philosopher as well." They had no desire to remain walled in within their own particular culture. . . . They tried to be educated men like all the others, men who know their classics, men who could speak like the rhetors and argue like philosophers. (Marrou, 1956, p. 303)

Thus the classical tradition offers us a distinction between education for leisure and education for work, liberal and illiberal occupations, technical and humanistic education, general and professional education. These contrasts and dualisms have plagued Western education to our day.

Vocational Education in the Western Tradition

While succeeding educators and educational practices have extolled the classical preference for education of the mind, it should be noted that education as developed in the West has always had an element of education for work. The first schools in the early Middle Ages had the vocational goal of training priests and monks to perform the services of the church and to read the Bible and Christian writers. Education in the Middle Ages was designed not only for church men and women but also for future knights. Although it is true that this education was designed for specific classes, its vocational dimensions should also be noted.

While the medieval universities were places where the classical education for leisure was dominant, these universities were actually organized for the practical purposes of preparing clergy, teachers, lawyers, and physicians for society. Though this education had few practical components, its purpose was certainly vocational and the materials used bore on the practice of medicine and law. Thus the medieval universities departed from the institutions of higher learning in the ancient world which did not educate for work. Accordingly, the ancestors of our present day colleges and universities were the practically oriented medieval universities of Paris, Bologna, and Salerno (Haskins, 1957).

Whereas the medieval universities clearly had vocational objectives, this cannot be said of the lower schools of the time. These were designed to teach a basic literacy, form moral character, and nourish spiritual life. The practical skills needed for earning a livelihood in society were learned through various types of apprenticeship arrangements.

With the beginning of the industrial age education for vocations became an even more prominent part of education. New vocational academies were established in England and the United States to prepare the rising merchants of the middle class for their professions. While those who were to enter the older professions of clergy, law, and medicine still received elements of a classical education, a more practical and vocational education began to take root in these academies.

It was Enlightenment educators that first drew attention to the importance of manual or vocational education and it was to these educators that John Dewey and other progressives looked for support for their ideas. The English philosopher, John Locke, proposed a vocational education with a pragmatic outlook because all learning for him was to have some practical worth. Education must concentrate on what is most useful to the person.

Rousseau in the educational classic, *Emile*, advanced the importance of "the pursuit of the industrial arts" arguing that "man in society is bound to work, rich or poor, weak or strong, every idler is a thief." This education is to take place through an apprenticeship, preferably in farming, forging, or carpentry. Rousseau praised manual work as the occupation which comes the closest to the state of nature. This education consists not merely in knowing what to do, for Emile must also know "the mechanical principles underlying the crafts" (Rousseau, 1956, pp. 85–90). Rousseau was insistent that education consisted more in practice than in precepts. He also saw a connection between education of the hand and education of the mind, pointing out that employment in a workshop aided the development of the mind. While Rousseau preached the values of manual education, the Swiss educator, Johann Pestalozzi, put this form of education at the service of his education through love when he showed how the loving heart was made effective by developing the powers of the hand and the head. The powers of the hand were to be developed through training in manual skills and the tasks of home industry. The German educator, Friedrich Froebel, advocated manual arts education for children in kindergartens.

Developments in the United States

It was in the United States, however, that the strongest case was made for vocational education within the structure of the school. It was here that the apprentice system failed to produce all the workers needed for the fast growing society. From the earliest days there were calls for vocational and professional education in the schools. It was also in the United States that the strongest philosophical argument was offered for the inclusion of this form of education, an argument associated with philosophical pragmatism and experimentalism.

Though many voices were raised in defense of the vocational education movement in the early years of the republic, the philosophic justification for this movement awaited the philosophy of John Dewey. In the following sections I will focus more on the history of this development, putting off to my treatment of Dewey the philosophic arguments for the inclusion of vocational education in the curriculum of schools and colleges.

There was an element of practicality in Benjamin Franklin's Academy. His goal was that youth should come out of the academy fitted for learning any business, calling, or profession. In the plan for his academy he gave his reasons for preferring a practical curriculum. He noted that it would be well if students were taught

> Everything that is useful and everything that is ornamental: but art is long, and their time is short. It is therefore proposed that they learn those things that are likely to be most useful and most ornamental, regard being had to the several professions for which they are intended. (In Cremin, 1970, p. 376)

The curriculum for Franklin's academy was to include, besides the traditional three R's, drawing, writing, gardening, field trips to farms, scientific experiments, and physical exercise. Franklin's goal was to produce men of affairs and not poets, scholars and scientists. Showing his lack of interest in an education in the classics, he concluded

> Thus instructed, youth will come out of this school fitted for learning any business, calling or profession, except such wherein languages are required and qualified to pass though and execute the several offices of civil life, with advantage and reputation to themselves and country. (In Cremin, 1970, p. 376)

Other "adventure schools" existed in the colonies where modern subjects were taught: commercial subjects (arithmetic, accounting, bookkeeping, penmanship, letter writing, pure and applied mathematics, including engineering, surveying, navigation; modern foreign languages, as well as geography and history). Although Franklin wanted his academy to be a permanent school, in a few years it became a Latin School causing Franklin to sever his connection with it and to lament that the academy he founded was no longer concerned with education for such a country as ours (Perkinson, 1977, p. 7). However, Franklin was somewhat vindicated because in the the nineteenth century many of the academies had a practical orientation (Sizer, 1964).

At the level of college education concerns of practicality were raised in the famous Yale Report of 1828. Accompanying the establishment of many colleges in the early part of the nineteenth century was a concerted attempt to include in the curriculum practical subjects along with the classical curriculum to which colleges had long been committed. The Yale Report, however, rejected many of the proposals for a more practical curriculum. It also rejected the proposal that a single college provide both practical and professional studies. The report asserted that

> The great object of a collegiate education, preparatory to the study of a profession, is to give that expansion and balance of the mental powers, those liberal comprehensive views, on every topic of interest, and those fine proportions of character, which are to be found in him whose ideas are always confined to one particular channel. (In Spring, 1985, p. 64)

The Yale Report had such weight in United States colleges that it was not until the time of the Civil War that a large infusion of practical concerns entered into them. Vocational concerns motivated the Land Grant College (Morrill) Act of 1862 which led to the founding of a number of colleges for practical arts, such as mechanics and agriculture. For several years previously, some reformers had called upon colleges to become of greater service to the needs of the nation. What the reformers actually desired was a large infusion of science into the college curriculum because of science's role in agricultural and industrial development. The Morrill Act by giving public land to states provided federal money for the industrial classes to pursue education in agriculture and mechanical arts. The act definitively introduced the practical into the college curriculum, not withstanding vocal defenders of the traditional classical curriculum.

Manual Training Movement

The successful efforts of the Land Grant colleges encouraged all educators to look for other ways to bring the practical into the curriculum. It also made educators press for the extension of vocational education to the schools. The needs of industrial United States together with increased immigration into urban areas made the calls for practical education even more urgent. The first effort in this regard was an attempt to justify manual training as just another aspect of general education.

The manual training movement and the later vocational education movement were part of the progressive reforms in urban areas in the latter part of the nineteenth century and early part of the twentieth. The motivation with which refomers promoted vocational education as a solution to problems of urbanization and immigration are a matter of dispute. Although many interpret their motivation as essentially humanitarian in attempting to help immigrants enter into the mainstream of society, others regard their efforts as attempts to maintain the basic class and power structure in society by channeling immigrants into working class jobs. As will be seen, radical critics of vocational education have taken the second interpretation as the more valid one.

The manual education movement, like other movements in educational reform, received part of its impetus from abroad. Victor Della Vos, a Russian engineer and educator, exhibited the work of Russian students at the Centennial in Philadelphia in 1876 where he organized a construction shop for each art or trade, for example, blacksmithing, carpentry, etc. Attempting to abstract, systematize, and teach mechanical processes, Della Vos developed a series of graded exercises designed to teach the skills necessary for engineering. Practical skills were arranged in an order sequence and thus could form the basis of a school curriculum.

John Runkle witnessed this demonstration and introduced its concepts into a newly founded School of Mechanic Arts at Massachusetts Institute of Technology. Becoming an enthusiastic proponent of manual training, he argued that education in this form would take the place of the time consuming apprenticeship of earlier years. His view of manual training was that it combined education of the hand with education of the mind.

Runkle attempted to justify manual education in the public schools according to the reigning philosophies of education:

> There is a growing feeling that our public education should touch practical life in a larger number of points. . . . It is not meant that. . . . our education should be lowered mentally, but that it should be based, if possible, upon those elements which may serve the double purpose of a mental culture and discipline—a development of the capacity of the individual with and through the acquisition of artistic and manual skill in the graphic and mechanic arts which most largely apply in our industries. (Runkle in Lazerson and Grubb, 1974, p. 59–60)

Around the same time Calvin Woodward of Washington University introduced the teaching of tool work without any immediate vocational goal. He criticized the public schools for adhering to the outmoded ideals of gentlemanliness and culture which fostered teaching students to think without teaching them to work. In his view the old education was useless not only because it did not fit persons for the world but it actually unfit them. He started a Manual Training Institute at the University in 1879 which combined manual training as part of liberal education. Its goal was education and not production, principles rather than narrow skills, art rather than the tradesman's competence. For Woodward, manual training would redress the imbalance between the literary humanist curriculum and the need for handiwork in society. Seeing such training as part of a wholesome intellectual culture, he argued that it would also bring dignity and comfort to the work of clerks, bookkeepers, salesman, poor lawyers, etc. When he presented this training as a means for increasing mental discipline, he may have exaggerated its benefits in order to make it appealing to various reform groups. The arguments of these reformers did have some effect, seen in the fact that Nicholas Murray Butler, President of Teachers College, accepted the concept that "manual training is mental training through the hand and eye just as the study of history is mental training through the memory and other powers" (In Kliebard, 1987, p. 132).

Woodward in an address before the National Teachers Association in 1883 presented a comprehensive review of the arguments for manual training. Many of the same arguments have also been used for vocational education.

1. Larger classes of boys in the grammar and high schools; 2. Better intellectual development; 3. A more wholesome moral education; 4. Sounder judgments of men and things, and of living things; 5. Better choice of occupations; 6. A higher degree of material success, individual and social; 7. The elevation of many of the occupations from the realm of brute, intelligent labor, to positions requiring and rewarding cultivation and skill; 8. The solution of labor problems. (Woodward in Lazerson and Grubb, 1974. p. 61)

Although leaders of the National Education Association at the time accepted that manual education belonged in the universities, they at first rejected it for the public school. William Harris, the idealist philosopher and educator, was the main spokesman against the introduction of this education into the schools. For him, since the distinctiveness of the human person lay in rational powers, it was the responsibility of schools to foster these. In his view, to teach a person carpentry in schools is to give a limited knowledge of self and nature. He contended that the early imposition of manual training on children could not be accomplished "without dwarfing their human nature, physically, intellectually, and morally, and producing arrested development" (Harris in Kliebard, 1987, p. 132). Harris also denied the intellectual value of manual training, contending that manual processes soon become habit and do not continue to exercise the mind.

The value of manual training in education became a debated issue in the argument over what type of education the freed black slaves and their children should receive in the schools. The values of manual training were espoused by Colonel Armstrong at Hampton Institute founded in 1867 and at Tuskagee founded by Booker T. Washington in 1881. While Armstrong claimed that the training of the hand was the same as the discipline of the mind and will, Washington contended that through manual training "the downtrodden child of ignorance, shiftlessness, and moral weakness would be converted into a thoroughly rounded man of prudence, foresight, responsibility, and financial independence" (Armstrong in Kliebard, 1987, p. 133).

On the other hand, William Dubois, a Northern black educator and activist, considered the education provided at these institutes anachronisms in an industrial society and argued that this form of education actually hurt the intellectual and professional chances of blacks. He also raised broad philosophical questions about manual training:

Industrial schools must beware of placing undue emphasis on the "practical" character of their work. All true learning of the head or hand is practical in the sense of being applicable to life. But the best learning is more than merely practical since it seeks to apply itself, not simply to present modes of living, but to a larger, broader life which lives today, perhaps, in theory only, but may come to realization tomorrow by the help of educated and good men.... The ideals of education, whether men are taught to teach or to plow, to weave or to write must not be allowed to sink to sordid utilitarianism. Education must keep broad ideals before it, and never forget that it is dealing with Souls and not Dollars. (Dubois, 1902, p. 81)

Echoes of this debate are still heard in present day arguments over vocational education.

Vocational Education

Although the manual training movement spread in the schools, men of business began to call for an education that would train students for particular jobs in the economy. This demand for a highly practical instruction led some educators to propose a form of vocational training that was not part of general or liberal education. Arguments concerning economics and industrial needs convinced school boards of the need for a more specific vocational education. The movement for this kind of vocational education prevailed with the federal legislation of the Smith-Hughes Act of 1917. By this time the movement for general vocational education had given way to specific vocational education.

The struggle to introduce widespread vocational education into the schools is a complicated one, with the key players being educators, politicians, the business community and labor unions. In the analysis of Katznelson and Weir (1985) professional educators prevailed over the interests of other parties at this time. Whereas business wanted separate trade schools which labor opposed, labor unions were willing to settle for vocational education within public schools, advancing both educational and economic arguments. As will be detailed later in this chapter, vocational education became a site of a class base battle over whether the ideal of the common school would give way to a highly differentiated form of public education.

Vocationalism triumphed in American education for many reasons.

Because this form of education was first introduced to provide training for immigrants in large cities, its proponents connected it to the notion of democratic equality of educational opportunity. Many advocates argued that it would foster economic efficiency and growth, expand the possibilities of upward social mobility, assure the retention of pupils in school, and teach more efficiently the moral values previously attributable to manual education.

Despite its triumph, the origins of vocational education have left a lasting legacy. Many progressive reformers advocated the scientific testing of students and the placement of students in tracks according to their achievements on these tests. While vocational education and training in skills were added to the curriculum of less able students to "fit the level of capacity of students to their future requirements in adult society," the curriculum of the "able" students was also enriched (Chapman, 1988, p. 121).

John Dewey and Vocationalism

John Dewey was at the center of the debates over what kind of vocational education should be introduced into the schools. Although a proponent of vocational education, Dewey criticized the effort of many boards to turn schools at public expense into preliminary factories. He was especially critical of the effort to set up separate vocational schools, arguing that this arrangement would foster separation of classes and foster business interests at the expense of educational values. For many years Dewey argued for a broader view of vocational education, opposing narrow forms of skill training. In his opinion industrial education should emphasize "acquisition of specialized skill based on science and a knowledge of social problems and conditions and not the acquisition of specialized skill in the management of machines" (Dewey, 1915, p. 42). In this vein, Dewey was critical of the Smith-Hughes Act for subordinating educational interests to industrial interests. He contended that the bill did little to increase the industrial intelligence and power of the worker but rather was designed to add to the profits of employers by promoting the avoidance of waste and greater efficiency in the use of machines and materials.

Dewey objected to what he perceived as a narrow vocationalism for social, political, and educational reasons. He remarked

The kind of vocational education in which I am interested is not one which will adapt workers to the existing industrial regime; I am not sufficiently in love with the regime for that. It seems to me that the business of all who would not be educational timeservers is to resist every move in this direction, and to strive for a kind of vocational education which will first alter the existing industrial society, and ultimately transform it. (Dewey, 1915. p. 42)

Dewey in *Democracy and Education* (1916) attempted to clarify his stand on vocationalism by separating himself from social efficiency educators such as David Snedden and Charles Prosser. His basic philosophy enunciated that

Both practically and philosophically the key to the present educational situation lies in a gradual reconstruction of school materials and methods so as to utilize various forms of occupations typifying social callings, and to bring out their intellectual and moral content. (p. 369)

Dewey proposed using "the factors of industry to make school life more active, more full of immediate meaning, more connected with out of school experience" (p. 370).

In his attempt to distance himself from social efficiency educators, Dewey came rather close to the older view of manual training as part of liberal education. While opposing separate schools for liberal and vocational studies, he wanted schools so reorganized that students would have respect for useful work and would develop an ability to render meaningful service in society. He advocated that motor and manual skills be developed in an active, constructive, inventive, and creative manner. The goal of such education, for Dewey, was not so much skilled workers but persons with industrial intelligence, a knowledge of the conditions and processes of manufacturing, transportation, and commerce. A knowledge of science, especially laboratory science, was necessary. He contended that his view of industrial intelligence "will prize freedom more than docility; initiative more than automatic skill; insight and understanding more than capacity to recite lessons or to execute tasks under the direction of others (Dewey, 1917, p. 335).

A major debate among progressives over the philosophical aspects of education engaged Dewey with David Snedden and Charles Prosser, proponents of social efficiency education. Snedden and Prosser supported a technocratic training model marked by a conservative social philosophy, a methodology of specific training based on principles of stimulus-response psychology, and a curriculum designed according to the job needs of industry. Their doctrine of social efficiency contained an image of persons, a vision of the good society, and recommendations for school practice which affected not only vocational education but all of education. Education was to select and prepare people for specific roles in society. The philosophy amounted to a job efficiency approach (Kliebard, 1987, ch. 4). These educators even wanted vocational schools to avoid the discussion of controversial social economic questions, including that of collective bargaining. Dewey of course saw vocational education imparting not only practical skills but also the sociological and cultural background of vocations (Curti, 1966, pp. 558–558).

Dewey's defense of a certain kind of vocational education for the schools represents the strongest philosophical case that has been made for this education. As in many other areas of thought and practice, Dewey searched for the unifying ideas. Although he recognized the potential for vocational education in an industrial society, he also realistically faced the dangers of introducing industrial education into the schools. He remained the champion of educational values over industrial values. True to his democratic vision he wanted all children to be exposed to all forms of education. He wanted industry's influence in the schools not in order to make the schools the tools of industry but for industry to aid in the reorganization of schools around occupations and practical activity.

Recent Developments

There have been many criticisms of vocational education over the years. It has been criticized for its narrowness and inability to keep up with the demands of industry. It has in fact created a dual educational system in many parts of the country. It may have led to the stifling of equality of educational opportunity for working class and poor. Studies in the 1960s showed that vocational education has little long-term economic benefit as measured by income, job stability, and employment rates. The economic justification is no longer strong (Lazerson and Grubb, 1974, p. 48).

Philosophical criticisms of vocational education have come from a number of quarters. Those committed to the ideals of a general or vocational education have never accepted vocationalism in schools or colleges. Robert Hutchins (1968), president of the University of Chicago, is typical of classical humanists who argue that vocational education has no place in schools and colleges. Such an education in his view treats people as instruments of production and not as valuable in themselves. For him the same education—an intellectual and moral one is to be given to every person. He also argued that vocational education did not lead to economic development in countries which introduced it.

Interest in vocational education increased in the 1960s when it was proposed as a way to deal with increased unemployment and with the problems of the economically disadvantaged. In federal legislation vocational education took on a broader meaning to include technical education and basic literacy skills. This broader view of vocational education continued into the 1970s with the broader vision of career education proposed by many educators, a concept which bears some resemblance to Dewey's view of vocational education.

In the early 1970s a novel approach to vocational education was proposed by the federal government under the name of career education. Sidney Marland, United States Commissioner of Education, proposed this form of education as a response to student rebellion, delinquency, and unemployment. Arguing against general education programs in schools which prepared students for neither college nor the job market, he proposed a form of education that would be related to career objectives. According to this approach to education for work "all educational experiences, curriculum, instruction, and counseling should be geared to preparing each individual for a life of economic independence, personal fulfillment, and an appreciation for the dignity of work" (Marland in Spring, 1989, p. 154). Marland was especially insistent that the community college philosophy be centered on career education. Career education was also proposed for the educationally disadvantaged and as a way to solve some of the manpower problems in the economy (Spring, 1989, pp. 153–155).

In the educational reform movement marked by the 1983 manifesto *A Nation at Risk* vocational education has received little attention, since the call has been to strengthen teaching and learning in the academic disciplines. Also, studies have shown how vocational education has failed many students by preparing them for outdated jobs. At the same time there is evidence of increased interest in vocational education as one way to address the need for a more trained workforce, and a way to combat high unemployment, especially among minority youth. Even with 25 percent of high school youngsters in vocational classes a philosophic debate still goes on between academic and vocational educators over the continued emphasis on preparing high school students for college. Vocational education still struggles with its image of a second-class education (*The New York Times*, July 15, 1992, B 7).

In recent years the ideal of the common school at the secondary level has also been considerably weakened with the introduction of magnet schools, many of which have specific vocational goals. Whereas the ideal of the common school remains strong at the elementary and junior high school level in all areas, the existence of magnet schools, especially in large cities, signals the need that young people have for a more career-oriented education. Since vocational education in these schools remains within the structure of general education, these schools are not comparable to the trade schools for secondary students which are found in other countries. Although these schools have had the effect of maintaining a larger number of students in school, more study is needed to assess their value in preparing students for work.

CONTEMPORARY DISCUSSIONS

Although the great debate over vocational education in the United States took place in the years preceding the First World War, periodically the issue is joined anew. In times of high unemployment vocational education is criticized for not providing the trained persons needed for the workforce. In times of high employment it is criticized for educating people for the wrong kinds of jobs. Thus although vocational education has achieved a permanent status in education, primarily because of the infusion of federal monies, this very fact makes this form of education vulnerable to criticisms at all times from many quarters, namely, from economists, politicians, and educators.

Because a discussion of vocational education necessarily hinges largely on economic facts, it appears that philosophical or theoretical arguments have less place in contemporary debates. Also, the arguments of philosophers often appear to be the justification for some economic proposal or reality. Although this is no doubt true in other areas of philosophy, it is understandable that philosophical rationalization would be prevalent in an area of great practical interest since all ideas have their origin in social constructions. Acknowledging this fact makes us more aware of the limitations that philosophy of education has by its very nature. While decisions in the practical realm need the clarity and the argumentation that philosophers bring, there are many other often more relevant factors to be considered.

Given these limitations, I will still make an effort to tease out some of the current theoretical issues that surround the whole area of vocational education. I will begin with a discussion of the philosophy of work, the continuance of the classical position, and other issues.

Philosophy of Work and Leisure

Any concept of vocational education must deal with broader philosophical issues about the meaning of the language of work and leisure and philosophical traditions which attempt to explain work.

Philosophers are concerned with distinguishing between various words such as job and work. Job implies simply earning a living; it is labor; work is characterized by the involvement of the worker's purpose in life, the exercise of style and craft. This distinction was at the basis of two approaches to vocational education. The social efficiency movement wanted to prepare people for jobs. This perspective of work accepted the need for a differentiation of labor based on a natural inequality. The task of education in this viewpoint is to prepare people to be functioning units in society. Schools will also serve to sort out people according to their various capacities.

It is important to recognize that there are many forms of work in society which are not paying jobs. Work is essential for persons throughout their entire lives, including the years of retirement. Through work the young achieve some sort of independence, gain a greater self-image, learn to work collectively with others, and attain a sense of responsibility. There are many forms of community work that people involve themselves in specifically for the good of others. Also, we have all heard the retired speak of their continued involvement in work after they have left their jobs.

The concept of work is a broader concept which is connected to the notion of a personal career or vocation. Career focuses on the individual's life and deals with advancement, promotion, and satisfaction. Vocation brings in a greater social dimension with the sense of a calling to do something for the common good of society. The concept of vocation implies some greater moral purpose in the human activity. The use of the term vocational education over job training is an attempt to deal with this distinction.

This continuing debate within vocational education must not be seen as a choice between job training and vocational education. Obviously the schools can do something in both of these areas. Many who leave the schools and colleges need some specific skills which can be provided through job specific education such as trade education and computer programming. But schools as institutions of broader learning must also attempt to provide a comprehensive vision of life within which to see one's work. Because today many opportunities exist for persons to be reeducated or retrained, persons who receive job training along with general education, are not as greatly disadvantaged as past generations.

Philosophical issues relating to education for work are connected with issues relating to the very nature of work. Religious philosophies have differed from the classical tradition by ascribing a high value to work. Work is viewed by theologians as an opportunity to share in the divine activity of work. Through work one learns to discover and understand not only oneself but also the divine. Even those forms of work which are drudgery and pain are interpreted in religious and philosophic traditions as redemptive of the human spirit and instrumental for the betterment of the world. Many religious philosophies look upon humans as endowed with mind and hands, both of which can be employed for useful purposes. Through work persons can fulfill their obligations not only to God but also to the human community. Another religious viewpoint sees work as contributing to religious obedience and resignation (Anthony in Watts, 1983, p. 131ss).

A particular approach to work has been developed within Protestant-ism, an approach which sees work as part of one's religious vocation or calling. Each person is believed to have a calling to a specific work assigned by God to the individual so that in performing this work one does one's duty both to God and to the community. This viewpoint has encouraged people to apply their talents to the particular work to which they were called. These ideas are considered by some scholars as essential to the development of capitalism. This Protestant work ethic also exists in a secular form according to which individuals see their own self-work and their contribution to the community in terms of the qualities and achievements of their work.

Not all philosophies, however, are positive in their analysis of work. The existentialist and the Marxist traditions have pointed out that much of modern work has become an alienation and a drudgery for many people, especially those involved in work that entails routine. Although such work is deemed dehumanizing, Marx, as will be developed later in this chapter, held to a rather idealistic understanding of the possibilities of work. The interpretations of these scholars appear to reinforce a notion within the Jewish Scriptures that looks upon work as a curse for sin.

Any examination of a philosophy of work must consider the relationship between work and leisure. One of the legacies of the classical theory of education in the West is that education is for leisure and not work; it is for living and not for earning a living. Persons, in this view, are truly human when they are engaged not in instrumental activities such as work but in activities that have no goals outside themselves. In this view education must be primarily concerned with leisure. Such a viewpoint fails to understand the intrinsic value of work and its relationship to leisure.

Although work and leisure are often contrasted, there are important connections between them. Persons fulfill themselves through activities both in work and in leisure. When working one looks forward to leisure; while at leisure one anticipates a return to work.

Some present the relationship between leisure and work as a matter of leisure redeeming workers from the ill effects of work which is boring, monotonous, and draining. Although there are situations in which leisure is the salvation of persons, generally leisure activities will not compensate for unsatisfying and unfulfilling work. It is more the case that there is some correlation between the quality of one's work activities and one's leisure activities. The French sociologist Emile Durkheim noted that people can handle the combination of interest and dullness only if it is found within work rather than between work and leisure. He raised this question:

> Who cannot see, moreover, that two such exigencies are too opposed to be reconciled, and cannot be held by the same man? If a person has become accustomed to vast horizons, total views, broad generalizations, he cannot be confined, without impatience, within the strict limits of a special task. (Durkheim, 1964, p. 10)

No matter what philosophers, religious or non-religious, might think of the philosophy of work and its relationship to leisure, the question remains how should one be prepared for work. If it is contended that people should be educated for work in institutions of learning rather than on the job or in technical institutes, what sort of philosophical justification can be given for this? This justification can be given in the context of examining the major philosophic opposition to vocational education.

Critiques of Vocational Education

A philosophy of work and leisure is at the foundation of any effort to justify vocational education in the schools. Everyone recognizes that people need training for particular jobs; they question whether doing this constitutes education and whether or not this preparation for work belongs in schools. One gets at the heart of the debate over justification by first looking at a contemporary version of the classical position and by examining radical Marxist discussions about vocational education.

As long as Mortimer Adler continues to direct his philosophical attention to education, the classical position on education for work will endure. In his most recent writing, a collection of essays written over a long life, Adler makes the case against vocational education. Calling vocational training education for the sake of earning and not learning, he contends that "school is a place for learning and not for the sake of earning" (1988, p. 105). The training for earning a living should be received on the job. In even stronger language, which appears to come directly from Aristotle, he asserts

> Vocational training is training for work or for the life of a slave. It is not the education of the future citizen, of the free man who has leisure to use. Liberal education, as distinguished from vocational training, is education for freedom, and this means that it is education for the responsibilities of citizenship and for the good use of leisure. (p. 216)

Let me note that in the *Paideia Proposal* (Adler, 1982), of which he was only one of the authors, Adler softened his standpoint to include manual training in cooking, sewing, typing, machine repair, not, however, for any vocational purpose but because "learning to do things with one's hands is just as much a matter of mental agility as learning to do things with words." It is interesting that the proposal justifies manual training by appealing for justification to the older arguments of the manual training movement.

This latest position of Adler's is echoed by John Goodlad (1984) who, in his examination of schools in the United States, found that at least a quarter of teachers in public schools were employed in what he considers vocational education. He argues that 15 percent of the curriculum should be dedicated to vocational education of all students, but as a component of general education conducted in the same way that other subjects are perceived and conducted.

Though Adler's voice is an important one in stressing the values of a liberal education that all should to some degree receive, he fails to recognize the serious limitations of his philosophical position in addressing both the needs of individuals and the needs of society. Far from being exploitative, vocational education can meet the needs of individuals to earn a living in society with the talents and capabilities they possess. Making vocational education solely the function of corporations, businesses, and factories runs the danger of depriving workers of the broader perspectives on work which schools are in the best position to offer.

The contrast that many opponents of vocational education in the schools make between vocational education and liberal education also needs examination. Many forms of liberal education have utilitarian and vocational goals. In fact institutions of higher education have added internships and practicums to their liberal arts studies in order to enhance the vocational values of these studies. Perhaps what is needed is a concept of liberal education that focuses not on particular studies such as the humanities but a concept of liberal education in which studies are seen to be liberal and liberating if they aid persons to become free, intelligent, sensitive, and skillful people.

In this age old debate over liberal and vocational education we must not contrast a liberal education which presents a wide view of human culture with a narrow technical education which teaches only the particular activities of a job. We must recognize that humanities can be taught illiberally, focusing on minute points of grammar, history, and literature and vocational subjects can be taught liberally in such a way that one learns general principles and the broad cultural context in which one's work is situated. Entwistle (1970) makes this point persuasively:

> Vocational education, as well as the learning of techniques, requires an
> awareness of the wider cultural dimensions of work in general and one's

own job in particular. When approached in this way vocational education
constitutes a liberal experience. (p. 67)

Vocational education in schools is better prepared than other training
arrangements to place job training in a context where it can truly be a
liberal experience.

The justification of vocational education must be made not only in the
face of the continuing influence of classical education but it must also
deal with criticisms that come from radical philosophers, chiefly Marx-
ists, who see vocational education as the repressive action of a capitalist
system. This viewpoint can be understood only by an examination of the
Marxist reading of the history of the vocational education movement as
a class struggle in which upper classes used schools to maintain their position. The needs of industrial United States, together with increased immigration into urban areas, made the calls for practical education even
more urgent. The first effort in this regard was an attempt to justify manual training as just another aspect of general education.

The manual training movement and the later vocational education
movement were part of the progressive reforms in urban areas in the latter part of the nineteenth century and early part of the twentieth. The
motivation with which refomers promoted vocational education as a solution to problems of urbanization and immigration are a matter of dispute. Although many interpret their motivation as essentially humanistic, the movement from the beginning had the strong support of the
National Association of Manufacturers which advocated vocational education as a way to weaken the power of labor unions over skill training.
Recognizing this, labor unions opposed vocational education in the early
years and attempted to influence the shape of federal legislation once the
passage of legislation was insured. According to these historians, labor
unions prevented the more harmful solution of separate trade schools being established in favor of vocationally oriented tracking within the comprehensive high school (Lazerson and Grubb, 1974, pp. 17–25).

The radicals' opposition to vocational education is thus based on their
view that such education results in the sorting and training of certain
classes of students for labor. This is accomplished through the vocational
guidance that occurs in the schools. Vocational guidance and career education as advocated by many is seen by radicals as manpower training of
individuals for certain roles in society.

It must be noted that the Marxist criticism of vocational education is not a criticism of vocational education as such but of how it has come to be used in capitalist societies. Marx saw an important place for vocational education in a future socialist society, asserting that

> There can be no doubt that when the working class comes into power, as inevitably it must, technical education, both theoretical and practical, will take its proper place in the working class schools. (Marx, 1967, p. 258)

Marx was insistent on the value of work in society as an activity that made persons truly human. Through work people fashion a civilization. Marx's objection was to the nature of work in a capitalist society, as forced and imposed. The solution to these problems for Marx was not in escape from work to leisure but in a choice among creative forms of work.

Radical critics of education have also expressed misgivings over the involvement of the business community with the schools, particularly the involvement with vocational education. Business involvement in educational endeavors runs the risk of serving the interests of business at the expense of the interests of students and broader societal needs. Radicals are critical of those educators and political leaders who

> argue that the traditional arm's length relationship between schools and business be dismantled for the purpose of overhauling schools in order to align them more closely with short and long term business and corporate interests. (Aronowitz and Giroux, 1985, p. 209)

Radicals have been especially critical of the increasing influence of corporations in education, citing the promotion of texts and school supplies by corporations, the takeover of textbook publishing houses by corporations, and the growing number of business-school partnerships that have emerged in the past decade. The danger in such arrangements is that the school curriculum, not only vocational education, will be shaped totally by what employers want. Corporations that make gifts to schools may attempt to exercise inordinate control over them.

According to radical educational critics, the driving business interest in vocational education in the past decade has been to increase the number of qualified employees for entry-level jobs in order to keep down wages of such workers. Radicals also charge that business attempts to influence the schools in producing workers who are compliant and loyal to the company (Spring, 1991, p. 27).

The radical critique of the involvement of business and education is a useful one in pointing out some of the dangers in the relationship between business and education. It is also true that present economic problems have produced increased involvement of business in schools. What is missing from the radical analysis, however, is a realistic approach to the needs of students. The reality is that since one of the goals of education remains the preparation of young people for work, educators must be sensitive to the needs and demands of business. Radical critics, however, serve to remind educators that business is not the only client of the schools.

Opposition to vocational education has also come from another quarter, from economists who have argued that there is little economic benefit from vocational education. The connection between education and work has become a matter of great debate at the present time. The manifesto A Nation at Risk in 1983 tied the United States economic failures to a lagging educational system. Since that time many studies have reported the relative inferiority of graduates of schools in this country. A reform movement, mainly at the state level, has attempted in the past ten years to bring about changes in the educational systems. One notable reform has been the development of partnerships between businesses and education where business skills and methods are brought to the service of the schools.

Reforms in vocational education have not figured largely in any of the reform proposals of this period. Attention has been given more to education in basic skills, mathematics, and the sciences. What this seems to indicate is that the outcomes of vocational education may be more at the personal and community level than at levels relevant to national economic development. It has become increasingly difficult to make the case that the vocational education in secondary schools contributes greatly to economic development.

Economists have long recognized the difficulty of making the connection between vocational education and work. Lester Thurow, an economist at MIT, concluded a number of years ago that vocational education was not a useful tool in addressing the problems of unemployment because there is a surplus of skilled labor in this country. He also contends that most skills are learned on the job. Thurow also concluded that vocational education is equally unlikely to increase economic growth. It is

Thurow's point that what employers want is not trained workers but trainable employees at the entry level. Thurow's argument supports those who have argued against specific job training or occupational education (Thurow, 1977).

Not everyone has the same faith that Thurow has in the ability of on-the-job-training without adequate vocational education to provide the skilled workers needed. Education can provide a variety of information, concepts, and skills for individuals at entry level positions. Secondary education, community colleges, and even colleges engage in this type of training. What vocational education can provide future workers with is an adequate and flexible knowledge base that can give students entry level jobs while preparing them for future development both on the job and through additional schooling.

The Case For Vocational Education

Notwithstanding these criticisms of vocational education, it is safe to predict not only that vocational education is here to stay but also that it will continue to know the ebbs and flows that it has known in the past. What kinds of arguments can be given in favor of continuance of vocational education in the curriculum? A number of valid arguments justify vocational education in the schools, some of which have already been addressed. There is some advantage in grouping these together in one section to assess the full weight of the philosophic justification for vocational education.

Before making the case for vocational education in the schools there should be some clarity about what constitutes a proper vocational education. It should be viewed as part of the general education of all students in society. In other words, it is truly educational, and no one's education is complete without it. Vocational education must include an exposure to the broader cultural meaning of work in one's own job and in other jobs and professions. Vocational education should also include a technical education which entails a knowledge of the theoretical principles that enable persons to apply their knowledge to new and changing situations. Finally, vocational education may also include technical training in a particular occupational skill or technique.

Thus the justification of vocational education lies in the kind of education given, the way in which it is given, and the context in which it is placed. It is not enough to supply merely technical training in some skill such as carpentry, brickmaking, or computer programming. Students must also be taught the principles that underlie the procedures that they utilize. It is the theoretical explanations that separate education from training. What vocational education adds to technical education is a sense that through work one is involved in more than earning a living or producing goods and services for others. The vocational aspect of vocational education attempts to help students to see "their job through words like commitment, concern, service, or having a social as well as a purely personal significance" (Entwistle, 1970, p. 55).

Vocational education brings into the schools an essential dimension of human life that schools omit only at great risk to their students and to society. If schools are to prepare students for all of life, they must prepare them for the world of work. The presence of vocational education in schools brings students into contact with the world of work and professions which open to them future possibilities. Vocational education serves to close the distance between school and work which many in society have seriously criticized. Many sociologists and psychologists have contended that the segregation of young people in schools, with total separation from the world of work, increases psychological problems and fails to prepare youth for the realities of the world of work.

Vocational education, as it focuses on the moral and cultural purposes of human work, can be a force for education in morality and values. The school has the opportunity to present students with the dignity of work for human development and for social betterment. The context of work is a valuable one for probing important moral values such as diligence, perseverance, self pride, and self worth. The context of work is a suitable place to discuss the common values of society and the need for all to labor for social justice. School is in a position to provide students with a place to discuss the deeper meaning of work and to probe the moral issues which are connected with work.

The presence of vocational subjects in the school curriculum brings a concreteness that should aid teachers and students in other school subjects. Connections can more realistically be made between abstract principles in mathematics and sciences and their applications in practical and technical areas. The study of the humanities, especially those themes which bear on work, can be enhanced if attention is drawn to concrete aspects of the world of work. The study of foreign languages can benefit from an understanding of the language of work and how it is applicable in different cultural situations.

Vocational education is a way in which schools can address the various forms of intelligence that students possess. Cognitive psychologists have now broadened our view of human intelligence beyond the ability to manipulate numbers and language, as important as these are in a person's education. The practical intelligence of being able to do and to make things gets more attention if vocational education is included in the curriculum. If schools begin to recognize practical intelligence as another form of intelligence and not a lower form of intelligence, perhaps the class stigma that has been attached to vocational education from its introduction into the curriculum will be erased.

Vocational education has the social advantage of encouraging more students to remain in school, especially those students who at this time in their life lack interest in the purely academic subjects of the curriculum. All forms of human intelligence do not emerge at the same time. Many have had the experience of overcoming earlier distaste for school subjects at a later time of life. Remaining in school through interest in vocational education may have the added benefit of keeping students open to other forms of education. For other students extracurricular activities such as sports and the arts can serve the same purpose.

The presence of an explicit vocational education in schools may encourage teachers and students to examine the vocational possibilities of all subjects. Every school subject has career potential about which teachers may inform their students. This does not mean that one should always seek to connect school subject with practical endeavors. Other justifications can be given for the various subjects in the school curricula. But anyone who has taught high school youth knows that for a large number of students utilitarian concerns are often important.

Education in and through Work

A final issue to be discussed is the potential of work itself as an educational experience. There has always been a tradition in education that emphasizes that one learns by doing, one learns in and through one's work. As a teacher I often learn what I truly think about an idea or a book by using it with students in my workplace. The interaction with students and colleagues brings out concepts and relationships about which I was either unaware or only vaguely aware. This is true for people in all forms of work. It is for this reason that one can applaud, with some caution, the present emphasis of involvement of business and industry in the schools. In this last section I wish to explore ways in which persons learn in the workplace.

One of the major changes that has taken place in the past thirty years is the involvement of corporations in the education of workers. There are three ways in which every education is involved in the workplace. The experience of working is a learning experience in itself. This is the reason why many jobs require experience, for presumably persons who have worked at some position have acquired necessary knowledge, attitudes, and skills. Because this type of experience cannot be gained in schools, we have seen the expansion of cooperative education, work internship programs, and work-study programs. In this first type of workplace learning there is a clear difference between school learning and work-place learning.

A second type of learning that occurs in the workplace is job-specific training, which takes various forms. In many workplaces there are formal programs while in others there is a dependence on informal learning. Some educational activities are conducted in-house while others are under contract. Some corporations have even developed residential corporate education centers where courses are offered for all types of employees. Since this type of program can only be offered within corporations, there is little conflict between this form of training and that offered in schools and colleges.

The newest development in corporations is forms of education that are almost the same as those in schools. Many corporations offer courses that are usually taught in schools. The extent of this educational effort is enormous. Large corporations have huge educational budgets, employing many trainers and educators. Everything can be part of the curriculum from basic literacy and remedial education to a college education. Furthermore, a number of corporations have schools which confer bachelor's degrees, and even master's degrees. Many corporation courses are accredited through colleges and state agencies.

These developments and collaborations raise issues about the relative value of the school and the workplace in education. They bring up questions about the special competencies of each and the best types of collaboration that should exist. Ethical issues also come to mind with these new developments. For some these developments indicate that the schools should abandon vocational education altogether, while for others they are incentives to make greater efforts.

These developments have taken place for several reasons. Corporations see the advantages of group instruction in specific areas. Financial reasons induce other corporations. Still others feel that the schools do not produce the educated employees that are needed.

This new development suggests questions of a philosophic, ethical, and political nature. The first question concerns the role of the schools and colleges with regard to this development. How close a relationship should schools forge with corporations in educational endeavors? Should schools shape their knowledge base, attitude formation, and skills training to the needs of industry? Should the schools ignore the needs of the workplace, as the classical position maintains, and continue to educate persons liberally and not vocationally?

The schools are in a difficult situation with regard to these developments. If they collaborate extensively with corporations or attempt to educate students to meet the demands of industry, they run the risk of losing their identity as institutions that provide a broad-based education. By forging close relationships they also run the risk of failing to produce students who are critical of what is in the best interests of industry. Dewey's statement that the schools should not prepare students just to fit in but to attempt to bring about change is as valid today as when he first uttered it. The schools have larger educational responsibility to educate students in values that are not particularly industrial values. They also have the responsibility to encourage critical thinking and a healthy skepticism about what takes place in a culture. In doing this the schools assert that the primary responsibility of educators is to students and to society and to a lesser degree to specific institutions of society.

It is not only educators that need to be concerned about these developments. Although one might applaud the efforts of industry to do more in the field of education, one can question with Lewis Branscomb and Paul Gilmore some side effects of this development. What these developments make more difficult than ever, they assert is for "the committed, disciplined, and managed environment of highly structured [corporate] training to be affected by the skeptical attitude of the scholar and the innovative imagination of the researcher" (Branscomb and Gilmore, 1975, p. 232).

There is no doubt that developments in the world of work, described

either as the coming of the information age or the advent of a postindus-
trial society entail that there must be a rethinking of what institutions
such as schools need to become and what might be the future relationships between school and work. In the midst of these developments
schools must think through their task in a more profound manner. There
is much that schools can learn from corporate education, especially in the
area of self-instruction, participation, and teamwork. Yet the schools
must remain true to their primary tasks of preparing people for all of life,
which includes work in a broader understanding. Schools cannot be in-
sensitive to the realities of the job world and continually attempt to educate students for this world. The task is not an easy one but one that
demands constant vigilance. Vocational education should continue but
always within the context of an entire educational endeavor.

CHAPTER 8

PHYSICAL EDUCATION

General works in philosophy of education in recent years have not treated in an extensive manner physical education and sports. Yet in many school systems throughout the world physical education and sports play a major role in the curriculum. In the state of New Jersey, as in many other states, all students in elementary and secondary schools are required to take physical education for five periods a week. When a number of years ago a popular governor attempted to cut the number of periods from five to three, the public clamor from parents and teachers prevented this action. In fact, in New Jersey students must spend more time on physical education than on mathematics for their graduation requirements.

Physical education has always played some role in the education of the young and various justifications have been given over the years for its inclusion in the school curriculum. Also, while sports have always been a part of education, it is only in recent years that a philosophy of sport has been enunciated. The novelist John Updike described in *Rabbit Run* how high school sports might provide a moral justification for the young. Some scholars see in sports a high form of personal enlightenment as well a high form of civilization.

While it is certainly difficult to focus on the lofty aims of physical education and sports in a culture in which physical fitness has become an idol for many and sports have been excessively commercialized, those involved in the physical education of the young have always had some appreciation of the intrinsic value of such activities. Most educators and citizens recognize that a complete education in our times entails attention to physical fitness and the values of games and sports.

Although there is some ambiguity about what is included under the rubric of physical education, there is general agreement that it includes health, physical education, recreation, and athletics. Others include under physical education safety education, driver education, dance, physical fitness, movement education, and park administration (Ziegler, 1977, p. 54). There are difficulties defining physical education precisely because of the diverse activities which are now included in the school curriculum.

In this chapter, as in the previous chapters, my purpose is to trace the main philosophical ideas about the values of physical education and sports. The second part of the chapter will discuss contemporary philosophical justifications for the inclusion of physical education in the curriculum. As in other chapters, the discussion will be primarily about physical education in the school curriculum. This is especially important to do because physical fitness and sport have become vast enterprises in many societies and cultures.

HISTORICAL PERSPECTIVES

Like other forms of education, physical education has its own particular history and philosophy. It has had both its defenders and its detractors. In this brief historical perspective my purpose is to focus on the questions of philosophical justification and educational aims. To be sure, the various ways in which physical education has been justified are closely connected with the needs and values of particular cultures and societies. A review of the historical justifications of these activities will offer the context for a contemporary discussion of physical education and sports in our culture.

The Classical Justifications

While there is evidence of sports in the ancient civilizations of Egypt and China, it is in ancient Greece that one finds the first philosophical justifications for physical education. In Homeric Greece sports were part of the education of the aristocratic knights and served to introduce these future warriors and leaders into a particular way of life. Sports were instrumental in forming an ethical ideal by which great men and women were to live. Through sports the young were prepared for life as a great competitive event in which the goal was to achieve success by vanquishing others. The heroes of the Homeric epics are depicted as achieving the virtues which made them suitable to serve as an inspiration for others to rival and imitate.

In the city-state of Sparta, which won many medals in Olympic games, both boys and girls were early introduced into riding, athletics, gymnastics, and sports. These activities were, of course, to promote physical strength for future warriors. The goal of Spartan education was to produce not individual heroes but an entire city of heroes. In Sparta there is evidence of the first close connection between physical education and the art of warfare; even gymnastics were joined with military training. Physical education included an austere and ascetic atmosphere, an instruction to children to endure pain, and a minimum amount of food. However, as Sparta became excessively militaristic and totalitarian, both the arts and athletics were denounced as detracting from purely militaristic goals, demonstrating that there is something in sport that resists a totally militaristic culture. Sparta is remembered today as an example of a distorted approach to physical education and sport, one that fails to recognize the intrinsic values of activities that cannot be totally subordinated to such extrinsic goals as national reputation, national defense, and military prowess.

Physical education and sports were also important in early Athenian society, though they were not so closely connected with military life as in Sparta. In Athens physical education became more popular and democratic because sports there were considered as a form of competition (Marrou, 1956, p. 65). The young were trained by coaches in sports grounds or palestras for athletic contests such as racing, discus and javelin throwing, long jumping, wrestling, and boxing. The guiding ideal of this education was ethical, to produce the beautiful and good man—the superb mind in the beautiful body. The moral ideal was to be achieved in and through sport because in this education a primary aim was to develop the mind and character as well as the body. The moral or character justification for sports is one that often appears in the history of education; it was a dominant theme among progressive educators in early twentieth-century United States.

With the rise of the purely intellectual education offered by the Sophists, the importance of physical training and sports declined in Athens.

Sports then became an enterprise only for specialized experts who underwent long and arduous training. In fact sports even became a commercial racket and athletes were nearly professional. Many of the youth began to show less interest in sport and physical education. (Marrou, 1956, p. 93)

In contrast to the views of the Sophists, voices in Athens stressed the obligation of citizens to become and remain healthy for their own well-being as well as for the good of the state. Xenophon, a disciple of Socrates, placed these words in the mouth of his master:

> No citizen has a right to be an amateur in the matter of physical training; it is a part of his profession as a citizen to keep himself in good condition, ready to serve his state at a moment's notice. Finally what a disgrace it is for a man to grow old without ever seeing the beauty and strength of which his body is capable. . . . And in all the uses of the body it is of great importance to be in as high a state of physical efficiency as possible. Why even in the process of thinking, in which the use of the body seems to be reduced to a minimum, it is a matter of common knowledge that grave mistakes may often be traced to bad health. (In Rice et al., 1969, p. 26)

These words connect good health with good citizenship, healthy physical functioning, and even intellectual well-being. Each of these themes is expressed in the history of physical education and sport. What is new in the view of Socrates is the connection of physical fitness with the ability to think.

In addressing physical education and sports in his dialogues, Plato made use of various justifications, especially the ideal of education for moral character. Of the education of children he wrote

> Then they send them to the master of Gymnastic, in order that the bodies may better minister to the virtuous mind, and that they may not be compelled through bodily weakness to play the coward in war or on any other occasion. (In Rice et al., 1969, p. 27)

Although Plato attributed the greatest importance to intellectual education, he also assigned an important task to physical education. For the early years of education Plato advised gymnastics (which included hygiene and nutrition) for the body and music for the soul. However, he argued strongly against the competitive spirit in gymnastics. Because he also wanted athletics to be restored to their original purpose of preparing the young for life, he favored wrestling as the best preparation for combat. Furthermore, Plato advocated dancing as a means of producing moral discipline, since he believed that it would bring a harmony into natural movements. This sport, in addition to running and field events, was to be engaged in by men and women. All of these forms of physical education were to be given in facilities under the control of professional instructors paid by the state.

In the Hellenistic culture physical education and sport were important activities. They were not only forms of relaxation but complex activities which involved hygiene, medicine, aesthetics, and ethics (Marrou, 1956, p. 165). These activities had a prominent place in the ephebia, the Hellenistic school in which physical education accompanied literary education, from the earliest years for both girls and boys. Hellenistic physical education was characterized by a sporting spirit of emulation and competition as children were trained for the many competitions in the Hellenic world. Besides gymnastics children engaged in swimming, boat races, running, field events, wrestling, and boxing. Children even engaged in loosening up exercises, performed to the sound of an oboe. Special teachers, pedotribes, supervised the instruction in special buildings dedicated to this instruction.

The stress on physical education declined with the rising importance of literary subjects in schools and with the increasing prevalence of professional athletes in society. When Christian culture became a major force in the Greco-Roman world, physical education seems to have disappeared from the educational scene in the Hellenic world, as sports became merely a pastime (Marrou, 1956, pp. 184–185). Christian writers attacked not sport itself but the frivolity of spectators spending long hours watching sports. In the authentic Christian tradition, however, there is no opposition as such to sports, but there are many comments on the potential abuse of sports, especially when connected with professionalism and religious rites (Freyne, 1989). A less positive assessment of Christian influence contends that "the Christian ideal left but little room for the organized practice of sport and the cultivation of bodily exercise, except insofar as the latter contributed to general education" (Huizinga, 1950, p. 19).

The educational ideal of classical humanism of the Greeks was to educate the whole person, body and soul, sense and reason, character and mind, in a harmonious balance. The ideal was a person who could go in many directions during his or her life. The Latin poet Juvenal expressed this ideal: *Orandum est ut sit mens sana in corpore sano* (One should seek a sound mind in a sound body). The ideal was honored even if it was not always possible for individuals to achieve. This ideal was not observed when the mind was left uncultivated while persons were trained to become merely sports champions. The ideal was also not observed when a purely literary education was offered to the young. Physical education in the classical ideal is seen as an accompaniment and an aid to intellectual, moral, and aesthetic education. Yet Greek culture was aware of the ambiguity of sports because of the excesses to which it might lead.

Renaissance Humanism

The next period of history which saw significant attention to physical education and sports was the Renaissance when the ideals of classical humanism were again extolled. Sports had not received great attention from educators with the fall of the ancient Hellenistic and Roman cultures. Christianity, which had become the dominant cultural and educational force in the western world, preached the salvation of souls and the need for an asceticism of the body in order that it might not lead the soul astray. In monastic education and in the medieval university little attention was given to athletic sports or physical education. Physical education did, however, have a role in the education of the medieval knight, who received little intellectual education. Thus the classical ideal of the harmony of body and mind was not operative in medieval Christian education and the education of medieval knights (Rice et al., 1969, chs. 4 and 5).

During the Renaissance, however, the reborn interest in classical ideals brought a renewed attention to the education of the body. Physical exercise, hygiene, and sports all were included in the revival of classical ideals. In the Renaissance humanism of many writers physical education was promoted as a preparation for warfare. Sports were also advocated as a way to develop the competitive spirit of young boys. Renaissance educators stressed disciplining the body as a means of improving health and preparing for the rigors of war. Since these educators also recognized that the general ability to learn depended on one's physical condition, they considered hours spent in rest and recreation as valuable means for promoting the learning of other lessons. This harmony in education was expressed by Pietro Vergerio, a humanist from Padua and Florence:

But where an active frame is conjoined to a vigorous intellect a true education will aim at the efficient training of both—the Reason that it may wisely control, the Body that it may properly obey. So that if we be involved in arms we may be found ready to defend our right or to strike a blow for honor or power. . . . Now war involves physical endurance as well as military strength. (In Rice et al., 1969, p. 49)

By this time even religiously oriented educators had begun to recognize the value of physical education. Pope Pius II, a Christian humanist, in a letter to a young prince extolled the values of physical training as a means of cultivating grace of attitude, sound health, relaxation, and renewed strength for learning. The great English humanist, Roger Ascham, in his influential book, *The Schoolmaster*, stressed the importance of physical education. The education of the courtly gentleman was to include physical training as a training exercise for war or a healthful pastime for peace. Ascham also made the connection between recreation and learning: "The best wits to learning must need have much recreation and ceasing from their books, or else they mar themselves, when base and dumpish wits can never be hurt by continual study" (In Rice et al., 1969, p. 51).

Religiously oriented educators tended to stress the moral value of both sports and the arts. Martin Luther in advocating schools for every church in Germany, expressed his preference for music and gymnastics as moral forces in stating that

the Great reason for these pastimes is that the people may not fall into gluttony, licentiousness, and gambling as is the case, alas! in courts and in cities. Thus it goes when such honorable and manly exercises are neglected. (In Rice et al., p. 52)

He also recognized the value of these activities for driving away care and melancholy and preserving an elastic and healthy body.

The value of physical training is expressed also in the writings of such humanists as the Frenchmen Francois Rabelais and Michel de Montaigne, the Bohemian John Comenius, and the Englishmen John Milton and John Locke. Locke repeated the classical humanist formula: "A sound mind in a sound body, is a short but full description of a happy state in this world; he that has these two has little more to wish for" (In Rice et al., 1969, p. 56). One-third of his treatise on education was taken up with physical education, including exercises, hygiene, and eating habits.

While the writers of the Renaissance and religious reformers extolled the values of body training, their emphasis was on individual perfection and not on groups or classes. Bodily training in the view of religious reformers was in the service of moral and intellectual development. The recognition that bodily exercises and games were in themselves important cultural values came only at the end of the eighteenth century (Huizinga, 1950, p. 19).

Enlightenment and Physical Education

As has been shown in other chapters, the Enlightenment thinkers made significant contributions to the advancement of educational theory in many aspects. Their contributions to physical education are equally significant, emphasizing as they did the goodness of natural development. Rousseau in his *Emile* proposed an education based on natural development. Emile's early education was directed at growth and physical welfare. According to Rousseau, Emile should be free to learn from nature as well as free to exercise his limbs, senses, and organs, which are the tools of intelligence. In extolling the importance of free play and movement Rousseau laid the foundation for a view of physical education as having a value in itself. Only at the age of twelve, when Emile's natural desire for physical activity abates, is he ready to learn moral rules and technical skills. Recognizing a close connection between physical education and intellectual education, Rousseau gave this advice: "If you would cultivate the intelligence of your pupil, cultivate the power which it is to govern. Give his body continual exercise; make him sound and robust in order to make him wise and reasonable" (Rousseau, 1956, 62).

The naturalistic philosophy of physical education espoused by Rousseau was also enunciated by Johann Basedow, a teacher in Denmark, and Johann Simon, a German teacher of physical education, who both contended that nature and natural growth demanded that the child be given time for play and bodily exercise. In their view normal physical growth is more important in early years than mental training. They also contended that there are intellectual and moral values to be derived from playing games (Rice et al., 1969, p. 63). These ideas influenced the practice of many schools in Europe.

The most significant Enlightenment theorist and practitioner of physical education was Johann Friedrich Gutsmuths, who in *Gymnastics for the Young and Games*, produced a high quality manual which was also influential in the United States, when it was published here in 1802. This educator recognized that proper physical education demanded a knowledge of physiology and medicine, that swimming should be included in this education, that there was much to learn from classical humanism, and that nations should promote physical well-being. Gutsmuths also spoke of other benefits of physical education such as self-reliance and courage. His program included the education of young women.

Although Enlightenment scholars such as Emmanuel Kant and Friedrich Froebel also wrote on the benefits of physical education, this section concludes with the influential ideas of Johann Heinrich Pestalozzi who gave an important role to physical education. In his experimental school this Swiss educator gave attention to the recreative and competitive value of sports and games. Physical education was recommended for the strength, skill, endurance, hardihood, and command that it produced in the body. Pestalozzi saw physical education in unity with other forms of education in aims and methods. In his school one hour a day was given to games and sports. He developed a scheme of bodily movements and exercises with increasing difficulty.

The Enlightenment educators, especially their emphasis on natural development, were all influential in shaping educational theory in the United States because nineteenth-century educators looked to Europe for ideas, as did scholars in other fields. German, British, Swiss, and Swedish approaches to physical education all found support in this country. In time, as with other subjects, distinctive approaches to physical education emerged in the United States.

Physical Education in the United States

Because education in colonial America was under the auspices of churches and was established primarily for moral and religious purposes, one finds little consideration of the values of physical training and sports in early schools. In fact, the Puritan culture of New England was hostile to play, sports, and physical exercises. In the middle of the seventeenth-century laws were passed against shuffle board and lawn bowling. Such activities were regarded as inappropriate in a colony in which people were to work hard and avoid the waste of time involved in popular festivals (Coleman, 1989, p. 24).

The first notable exception to this negative view came from the secular and practically oriented Benjamin Franklin who in his proposals for academies in Pennsylvania called for schools which included fields on which students could engage in games, running, leaping, wrestling, and swimming. There is also ample evidence of the involvement of children and adults in games and sports outside of school settings, most of which came from the English world of sports. Soon afterwards both Noah Webster and Thomas Jefferson recommended athletic exercises as a part of a person's education.

With the growth of the common school movement in the United States in the first part of the nineteenth century, increased attention was given to physical education. Immigrant groups brought their own traditions to this country. The German and Swedish traditions in gymnastics were particularly influential in many schools. Gymnastics was added to the tradition of sports which had been brought from Britain. At this time physical education or gymnastics was considered separate from sports among educators.

An example of a particular United States contribution from this period is found in the innovations of Catherine Beecher, a leader in the education of girls. Beecher introduced a form of calisthenics for girls at the Mt. Holyoke Female Seminary, a system of physical education based on twenty-six lessons in physiology and two courses in calisthenics. The aims of these exercises were to produce grace of motion, good carriage, and sound health. Because of her books on physical education Beecher has been acclaimed the first American to originate a system of gymnastics and the first woman's physical education leader in America (Rice et al., 1969, p. 149).

The most widespread effort in physical education at this time was led by Dr. Dio Lewis, a temperance and health lecturer. Arguing that free play was not adequate for the physical development of children, he contended that the gymnastic teacher was as important as the subjects teacher in the education of the young. He preferred gymnastics to the military training and the athletic sports that were proposed by others. Lewis developed an extensive system of exercises to be used in place of military drill, riding, and dancing. Lewis was influential in popularizing physical education throughout the country, especially through a training school which he established. Dr. Lewis is only one the many medical men who proclaimed the importance of physical training and fitness.

As might be expected, with the growth of cities after the Civil War and with increased immigration by the end of the nineteenth century, greater attention was given to education, including physical education, in all sectors of society. Physical education, including health education and exercise, was an important part of the reform program of progressive educators in their effort to meet the needs of individuals and society. While the earlier advocates of physical training tended to come from the medical profession, in the progressive movement educators began to dominate as advocates of this form of education.

Progressive educators introduced new terminology to describe the widespread efforts to produce healthy individuals. Some colleges of a strong classical tradition like the University of Chicago, began to refer to physical *culture*. Other departments refered to military and physical *training*; but the term that eventually prevailed was *physical education*, because an identifiable group of educators began to propose physical education in the schools. Since the time of the progressives the term physical education has been in vogue. Previous to this what is included under this term was found in

> physical activity, physical training, military training, gymnastics, calisthenics, hygiene, physical culture, physical fitness, sports and games, recreation, health education, athletics, sports education, movement education, and physical education. (Siedentop, 1980, p. 30)

Early in the progressive period a historic conference was held in Boston to determine the status of physical education in the schools. Various systems of gymnastics were debated. The conference arrived at the conclusion that physical education should be introduced into the schools provided it took little time, was conducted within the classroom, and required no equipment. Sports and games were not discussed at the conference, even though sports had by then made their way into schools as extracurricular activities. (Williams, 1964) Once physical education was included in the schools there was an advancement in emphasis, facilities, and activities.

Progressive educators made a significant contribution to the development of educational theory when they introduced the concepts of work and play as educational activities. The new physical education which they proposed gave a prominent place to play in the schools. Play and work were not introduced as ends in themselves, however, but as means of achieving other educational aims. Clark Hetherington, the father of modern physical education, expressed this new approach to physical education as follows:

> This paper aims to describe the function and place of general neuromuscular activities, primarily general play activities, in the educational process. . . . To present the thesis four phases of the education process will be considered: organic education, psychomotor education, character education, and intellectual education. (Hetherington, 1962, p. 160)

These four phases became the four objectives of the new physical education also called education-through-the-physical, to contrast it with the older education-of-the-physical of the gymnastic period. In a contemporary theory of physical education play as an activity in its own right is used as a theoretical basis.

The pragmatic goals of the progressives, including education for physical fitness, were given great prominence in 1919 when the National Education Association published its seven cardinal principles of education: health, command of fundamental processes, worthy home membership, vocational competence, effective citizenship, worthy use of leisure time, and ethical character. The three objectives of health, worthy use of leisure time, and ethical character were interpreted by physical educators as especially relevant to their discipline. This statement of objectives went against the traditional justification of education according to academic disciplines.

Athletics and physical education received another justification from the progressives who connected these activities with the needs of industrial society. Charles Eliot, the president of Harvard University, gave this as a reason for including physical education in the schools:

> . . . it would give the boy the best preparation he could receive at that time of his life for a soldier's future, and it would also give the boy the best preparation the schools can give in the industrial army. . . . What we want in the form of discipline in the army is just what we want in the industries; it is the cooperative work, it is the sense of comradeship, fellowship, which in sports we call "team play." (Eliot in O'Hanlon, 1980, p. 97)

Those progressives who emphasized the importance of practical studies focused on physical education as "one of the most social of all pedagogical enterprises . . . bound to thrive in an age of social reform" (Krug, 1964, p. 277).

John Dewey, who made a strong case for the value of work in education, also made the case for play activities as educationally valuable. According to Dewey, the play activities of children were important starting points for educators. For him play was not merely to relieve the tedium of regular school work, but a way to engage the whole child. Play had a place in the curriculum for intellectual and social reasons. Although Dewey also recognized that play activities engaged children outside school life, he insisted that it was the special task of the school to present play activities in such a way as to separate them from the crudities of adult play activities. In his view

> It is the business of the school to set up an environment in which play and work shall be conducted with reference to facilitating desirable mental and moral growth. It is not enough to just introduce plays and games, hand work and manual exercises. Everything depends upon the way in which they are employed. (1916, p. 196)

While Dewey saw a value in play for mental growth through providing experiences, it is clear that he valued it equally for its moral capacity for recreating individuals and keeping them from idle and dangerous amusements. Dewey believed that

> If education does not afford opportunity for wholesome recreation and train capacity for seeking and finding it, the suppressed instincts find all sorts of illicit outlets, sometimes overt, sometimes confined to indulgence of the imagination. Education has no more serious responsibility than making provision for the enjoyment of creative leisure; not only for the sake of immediate health, but still more if possible for the sake of its lasting effect upon habits of mind. (1916, p. 205)

While Dewey made it clear that he considered the natural development of the child one of the aims of education, he did not agree with Rousseau that good natural development will take place in a spontaneous and automatic manner. In accepting natural development as an aim of education he states that parents and teachers should "make health an aim; normal development cannot be had without regard to the vigor of the body—an obvious enough fact but one whose due recognition in practice would almost automatically revolutionize many of our educational practices" (1916, p. 115). In his view the mind is developed by exercise of the muscles of the body. The aim of the natural physical education he proposed "means in the concrete, regard for the actual part played by use of the bodily organs in explorations, in handling of materials, in plays and games" (1916, p. 115).

It is clear that the field of physical education greatly benefited from the reforms introduced by progressive educators. These reformers proclaimed that character training as well as ethical and moral development were fostered by participation in sports and games. This same belief was responsible for the development of sports in nonschool situations such as public playgrounds and church sponsored programs. Sports were also thought to provide the same recreative and moral values for adults, especially for those who worked in industrial areas. For some historians, physical education and sports acted at this time to maintain existing economic and social conditions which needed to be directly confronted. Sports, they believed, became a compensation for much of the meaningless work in the urban industrial areas. In this interpretation sports, recreation, and physical education became a conservative force in society (Spring, 1974, p. 484).

Because there is still considerable dispute about the motivations and achievements of progressive educators, it is difficult to come to a final judgment about the social and cultural role that physical education has played since the progressive era. Sports is a complex cultural phenomenon, playing different roles in different societies. While some can point to places where sports and physical activities have hampered societal growth, one can also point to examples where sports have become a mechanism for social growth. Sports are deeply involved in the ambiguities and contradictions of every society and culture. A whole academic field, the sociology of sports, has developed to examine such questions.

Physical education received a boost during the First World War when it gained support both for its own merits and as a substitute for military training. When President Wilson spoke favorably of the importance of physical training, many educators lobbied politicians to enact new regulations requiring more physical education in schools. The result was that a number of states enacted such legislation. Physical education was even promoted at this time as an antidote for the spread of un-American political propaganda. One of its advocates asked "Did you ever hear an unhealthy, un-American doctrine proceed from a normal healthy body" (In Krug, 1964, p. 413).

Physical education and sports also played a part in the life adjustment educational movement which was dominant in the years before the Second World War. Adjustment to life included meeting certain health and physical needs. The broader educational aspect of this education was subordinated to technical competence and skills. What developed in this movement was a reliance on technique without a full consideration of the goals and consequences of an education which placed paramount emphasis on technique. It was only with the Second World War that physical education again received the justification of education for physical fitness that it has usually embraced in times of military struggle (Lawson, 1977, p. 81). This emphasis on techniques and technologies has continued to dominate in certain forms of physical education.

The progressive view that people are to be educated through the physical for extrinsic purposes was espoused by many prominent professors of physical education in the twentieth century. Charles Bucher described as the objectives of physical education: physical development through activities that build physical power in an individual by the development of various organic systems of the body; motor development by making physical movement useful and with as little expenditure of energy as possible and being proficient, graceful, and aesthetic in this movement; mental development through an accumulation of a body of knowledge and the ability to think and to interpret this knowledge; social development by helping individuals to achieve personal adjustment, group adjustment, and adjustment as a member of society. This theory is still well accepted today even though it has been criticized for failing to produce the adequate empirical demonstration of its validity (Siedentop, 1980, ch. 4).

This historical treatment has uncovered three main heritages for contemporary physical education. One aspect of the *fitness heritage* focuses on bodily development and health as ends in themselves. Another aspect sees bodily fitness as a means of promoting intellectual and moral goals. Various kinds of physical fitness have been promoted: motor fitness and cardiovascular fitness. While physical education can be justified as advancing physical fitness, educators warn against making claims for it that cannot be scientifically proved. Although periodically physical educators turn to fitness as a justification, most now believe that there is much more to physical education than fitness. President Kennedy initiated the most recent call to fitness in the 1960s.

The progressive heritage of *education through the physical* is still a force in the justification of physical education. In this theory physical education serves intellectual and moral aims. Some educators, however, question whether or not there is adequate proof that physical education has actually advanced physical, motor, mental and social development.

From the 1940s on, the moral justification for physical education prevailed among educators. Siedentop (1980) is particularly skeptical about claims that physical education promotes development of character. He thought that

> It sounds good in an after-dinner speech at athletic banquets. We would be better off if we defined clearly and unequivocally what we consider to be good sportsmanship in specific sport situations and then taught these specific behaviors. (p. 80)

Notwithstanding these criticisms, claims are still made that physical education promotes various forms of development.

Contemporary physical education must also deal with the *sports heritage* in education. Physical education in the twentieth century has been greatly influenced by sport and athletic programs. Sports have become so dominant, especially in secondary schools, that fitness and health have become subordinated to them. It may be that competitive athletics firmly established physical education in the curriculum of schools and colleges and led to the growth of the field and discipline of physical education (Lewis, 1969). In the view of others, however, an imbalance is in place since interscholastic sports programs have become more important than physical education (Spring, 1974).

CONTEMPORARY DISCUSSIONS

Among contemporary physical educators are found a number of philosophical justifications for physical education and sports in schools. Whereas many of these justifications have their origins in past theories, others are found in twentieth century philosophies of existentialism, phenomenology, and Zen.

Before analyzing these philosophies it may be helpful to look briefly at the debate among physical educators about whether physical education should be viewed as a discipline or as a profession. The effort to establish physical education as a discipline began with educators entering the field once dominated by medical persons. When academic degrees were offered in physical education, it was necessary to point to a basis in academic disciplines. To establish physical education as a discipline it was necessary to point to a body of knowledge which is not the concern of any other academic discipline. The content of the discipline is revealed in the academic subfields of physical education: exercise physiology, kinesiology, motor learning, sport psychology, sport sociology, history of sport, and philosophy (Siedentop, 1980, p. 110). Those who teach and do research in physical education at the college and university level are especially concerned with establishing a discipline of physical education.

Those who view physical education as a profession stress the activities of the physical educator, because a profession is characterized by the use of knowledge in the performance of specific tasks. A profession is prescriptive of actions while a discipline merely describes phenomena. The academic discipline provides the knowledge base for the profession. The task of the professional physical educator is to teach the primary subject matter of physical education, that is, sport, games, dance, and exercise to students in the context of a school or other educational institution.

No matter where the emphasis is placed—on the discipline or on the profession—physical education is presently in the midst of debates about the best way to ground its theory and practice. This is a particularly important task because physical educators suffer from a stigma that is not found in other areas of education. The root cause of this may be ambiguity towards all things relating to the physical or to the body. The body and the physical have been presented in some religious traditions as sources of sin; play and leisure have even been called sinful activities. The physical is regarded as the lower part of human nature and as an aspect of persons that interferes with higher intellectual, artistic, and spiritual activities. Furthermore, physical movement is viewed purely as a subjective or individualistic experience and not as important as the objective experience of reason. This stigma attaching to the body and the physical carries over to physical educators who suffer from uncomplimentary stereotypes (Oglesby, 1977, pp. 112–113).

The attempts to deal with these stigmas and stereotypes are found in contemporary efforts to establish a rational or philosophic justification for the inclusion of physical education in the school curriculum. To accomplish this physical educators draw on those Western and Eastern sources that take a more positive approach to the body and the physical.

Physical Education as Human Movement

Physical education as human movement traces its origins to Rudolph Laban, the German educator, who came to England during Hitler's rise to power in Germany. Laban contended that human movement in physical education, taught through the discovery method, could have a strong effect on emotional quality, inner resources, and personality awareness (Siedentop, 1980, p. 137). These ideas were especially appealing to women physical educators and primary school educators. Diana Jordan, an English physical educator and dance instructor, described how "women teachers began to understand the fundamental aspects of movement—how physical skill and agility as well as dance and drama could grow from a common root in all human movement" (Jordan, 1966, p. 137). Advocates of human movement contended that skill in basic movement was all that was needed to learn any specific sport skill (Siedentop, 1980, p. 139).

This particular rationale has given rise to various terminologies for physical education: educational dance, educational gymnastics, discovery teaching, creative movement, and developmental movement. Those committed to the human movement approach to physical education have also used such terms as kinesiology and homokinetics in an effort to distance physical education from the alliance with health and recreation and from techniques used in various sports.

Although this approach to physical education has found favor among physical educators in the United States, there are differences both in terminology and description of movement. Eleanor Metheny, an influential leader, described the physically educated person

> As one who has fully developed the ability to utilize constructively all of his potential capacities for movement as a way of expressing, exploring, developing, and interpreting himself and his relationship to the world he lives in. (Metheny, 1954, p. 27)

Another attempt to define movement education is presented in Brown and Cassidy's (1964) definition:

> By definition, therefore, human movement is the change in position of man in time-space as a result of his own energy system interacting within an environment. Human movement is expressive and communicative, and in the interactive process changes both the individual and the environment. (p. 24)

Physical education as human movement has become a way of expressing what is done in all forms of physical education. In primary schools movement exploration takes place in dances, gymnastics, and games.

Sports and games are seen as manifestations of human movement. At the college level educators speak of movement arts. Educators have also begun to speak of movement therapy for emotionally and mentally disturbed people.

Physical education as human movement studies has been favored by those who want to establish a theoretical and disciplinary basis for scientific research in physical education. Proponents of this approach contend that

> Human movement studies will provide a theoretical base for practice in many health-related areas, in special education, education, physical education, sports, industry, . . . recreation and leisure. (Higgins and Arend, 1977, p. 194)

The relationship between human movement studies and physical education is that between a science that discovers ideas and a technology that puts ideas into practice.

While many look to theories and research in human movement to provide the theoretical basis of physical education, others committed to physical education for fitness or for sports tend to resist these efforts. These differences led at one time to the creation of separate departments of human movement and departments of sport. Carole Oglesby (1977) notes that

> Often these departments had gender identifications, with women suggesting that human movement was central to physical education concerns and men countering with the argument that sport was the core of the body of knowledge identified as physical education. (p. 132)

Although human movement would appear to be a necessary basis on which to view the task of physical education, it can be questioned whether it provides a sufficient philosophical basis for all the activities presently included within the field of physical education. Advocates of human movement studies seem to assume that there is some transfer of learning from general movement skills to the more advanced skills needed in particular games and sports. A more specific type of human activity, or a broader vision of the human, may be necessary for establishing a firm theoretical framework for physical education.

Humanistic Physical Education

A dominant force in education in recent years has been forms of humanistic education that have their origins in humanistic or Third Force Psychology and more remotely in existentialism and phenomenology. Psychologists such as Carl Rogers and Abraham Maslow have applied their psychological theories to the theory and practice of education. The goal of humanistic education is to actualize the full potential of individuals. The values stressed in this education are openness to experience, risk taking, creativity, spontaneity, acceptance of self, compassion, and autonomy.

Some physical educators have attempted to describe their work in terms consonant with the theory and practice of humanistic education, contending that this theoretical approach moves beyond physical movement to embrace many aspects of human life. The goals of humanistic physical education have been described in this manner:

1. To help students improve their self-perceptions of their physical abilities to the point that self-esteem is improved, at least in relationship to their physical abilities.

2. To contribute to self-actualization through physical development, creative self-expression, and total involvement in activities.

3. To contribute to self-understanding by helping students to analyze their needs and abilities in physical education.

4. To help students improve interpersonal relations with specific emphasis on cooperation and sensitivity. (Hellison 1973, p. 68)

Humanistic educators set high standards for teachers of physical education. The teacher is a facilitator who cares deeply for all students and is keenly interested in their growth. This teacher strives to be open and honest with students in all situations. This image of the teacher is contrasted with the view of the traditional physical education teacher as the authoritarian and competitive taskmaster.

One of the characteristics of the humanistic approach is its negative attitude toward competition in sports and games. Some humanistic educators have attempted to introduce the notion of cooperative games. These educators propose an ethic countercultural to what is called the

"Lombardian" ethic which teaches that winning is everything. Jack Scott, a vocal advocate of humanistic sport contended that

> In fact, the counterculture ethic reverses every value of the Lombardian ethic. Cooperation replaces competition, an emphasis on the process replaces an emphasis on the product, sport as a coeducational activity replaces sport as a stag party, a concern for enjoyment replaces a concern for excellence, and an opportunity for spontaneity and self expression replaces authoritarianism. (Scot, 1974, p. 159)

While some humanistic educators have stressed the well known abuses of competitive sports, others point out that the competitive struggle is an integral part of sports.

A powerful humanistic statement on the educational value of physical education has been offered by George Leonard (1975), who proposed that "the physical education department stands at the center of the campus, the foundation stone of the educational enterprise" (p. 19). For him sports and physical education are powerful forces for transforming some of the myths of United States culture and for leading to personal and social transformation because they emphasize cooperation, process, enjoyment, and spontaneity (pp. 19–20).

Leonard ascribes an almost religious quality to athletic and physical experiences. He defines the Ultimate Athlete as

> one who joins body, mind and spirit in the dance of existence;
> one who explores both inner and outer being;
> one who surpasses limitations and crosses boundaries in the process of personal and social transformation;
> one who plays the larger game, the Game of Games, with full awareness of life and death and willing to accept the pain and joy that awareness brings;
> one who, finally, best serves as a model and guide on our evolutionary journey. (1975, p. 287)

Leonard presents this ideal of the Ultimate Athlete as a possible goal for all, even the overweight, sedentary, and middle-aged person who is willing to make some initial attempts to begin physical activity. He goes so far as to state that

> if that person, recognizably transformed in body, mind and spirit takes this experience as the impetus for further explorations and boundary crossings

and the heightening of awareness, then he or she must be said to have embodied the ultimate athletic ideal. (1975, p. 288)

A humanistic approach to sport and physical activity is also found among some religiously oriented philosophers and theologians who forge a connection between physical or athletic activities and spiritual activities. The qualities of discipline, dedication, enthusiasm, and perseverance are considered valuable both in athletics and in one's spiritual life. According to this viewpoint the traditional religious and ascetical practices of fasting and doing penance become the artful shaping of one's body.

> The spiritual person is the one who is interested in and dedicated to the artful handling of the world, the artful shaping of one's self, and the artful handling of one's life into something beautiful for God. (Ryan, 1989, p. 111)

In this perspective activities such as running become spiritual disciplines since they bring about a deep self-awareness and a valuable self control.

Many athletes have made the connection between athletic activities and spiritual experiences. Both are described as experiences in which persons transcend their ordinary selves. Some have described athletic activities in terms of deep prayerful and meditative experiences. Others speak of the experiences as bordering on the mystical or paranormal. While cynics rightfully see some elements of superstition in religious practices of athletes, there is no denying the testimony of many who are genuinely both religious and athletic.

Another variant of the humanistic approach to physical education is found in existentialist analyses of sport, offered by such a scholar as Howard Slusher (1967). For existentialists, sports are not merely an extension of life but essential manifestations of human existence. Human beings become whole when they take part in sport. Through sport people establish and reveal their personal existence, as well as manifest their individuality and personality. Inner authenticity can be achieved only through the decision making in which individuals are challenged to bring out or even transcend themselves.

For existentialists, athletes have the potential of realizing through almost religious experiences that there is something that is not mortal. Athletes experience more than they can express. The transcendence possible in athletic experience is expressed by the philosopher Karl Jaspers

(1957) who explained that "through bodily activities subjected to the control of the will, energy and courage are sustained, and the individual seeking contact with nature draws nearer to the elemental forces of the universe" (p. 58).

Other existentialist themes found in sport include the necessity for total commitment to discover one's authentic self, the requirement to find oneself through risk, and even the willingness to deal with the possibility of death. As in other existential analyses, sport is interpreted in a highly individualistic manner and in a way that ignores the relevance of sports to society.

Criticisms leveled against humanistic education and existentialism in education have also been directed against humanistic physical education and sport. This approach to education runs the risk of focusing too exclusively on individual development, ignoring the social aspects of the person. The language in which educational ideals are expressed, for example, self-actualization, fully functioning and total commitment, sound vague, general, and lofty. Furthermore, it is difficult to determine how such aims are realizable and through what means. One can also point out the risk entailed in asking educators to deal with the emotional and affective dimensions of persons if they have not been adequately educated for this. Finally, this form of education may at times blur the distinction between the educational and the therapeutic.

Holistic Physical Education

Some physical educators have in recent years looked to Eastern thought systems as a way of explaining the goals and objectives of physical education. In this approach the Western model of the person as made up of a separate body and soul is rejected in favor of the concept of the fundamental unity of the person. In this view the body and the person are one and there are no clear divisions among body, spirit, mind, and emotion. The goal in such an educational approach is to focus on the entire experience of persons and to master oneself.

Proponents of this theoretical viewpoint recognize that Western existential and phenomenological philosophy offer similar perspectives to Eastern thought. Kleinman (1972) expressed the objectives of physical education in this theory as follows:

1. To develop an awareness of bodily being in the world;
2. To gain understanding of self and consciousness;
3. To grasp the significance of movements;
4. To become sensitive of one's encounters and acts;
5. To discover the hitherto hidden perspectives of acts and uncover the deeper meaning of one's being as it explores movement exercises;
6. To enable one, ultimately, to create his/her own experience through movement which culminates in meaningful, purposeful realization of the self. (p. 72)

Although the ideas of Eastern philosophy have been applied to a number of sports in the West, it is in the martial arts that one gathers a sense of the philosophical framework of Eastern thought. Eastern thought, in both Indian Buddhism and Chinese Taoism, stresses the union of the self with all of nature. Persons attempt to transcend self to achieve the basic union with nature that makes a person free from anxiety, suffering, and fear. Oneness with nature entails a sensitivity to the ebb and flow of life. This union also leads persons to allow things to happen as they will and not to hinder them from occurring.

Zen Buddhism, a combination of Taoism with Buddhism, contains the injunction that individuals must learn to give up self in order to experience wholeness. Zen advises that persons leave such desires as fame and ambition behind in order to achieve inner freedom, simplicity, and harmony with nature. A goal of Zen is to be totally absorbed in present experience. This practice is found in Eastern movement forms such as aikido, kendo, and tai-chi and has also been advocated for sports such as tennis and golf.

The Eastern contribution to physical education and sports has included a number of activities. Persons are advised to practice *centering*, "both the ability to maintain dynamic balance and also a mental state where the mind is cleared in order to be fully alert and responsive to the immediate action." Connected to this is *blending*, "a fluid quality of motion that utilizes the action generated by an opponent in order to change the course of an attack" (Siedentop, 1980, p. 206).

Other activities advocated by Eastern practitioners of physical education include meditation and yoga. These activities which feature concentration, total absorption within an activity, and a sense of oneness with one's opponents have similarities to such Western practices as biofeedback training and relaxation therapy.

With the worldwide interest in running showing little signs of abating, Zen ideas of meditative running have become widespread. Fred Zohe, a Zen guru of running described his meditative philosophy of life in this way:

> The experience of meditative running has shown me that it is possible to live my whole life meditatively. . . . Thus a viewpoint of meditative running is the joy of the moment, another viewpoint is the learning process, in which running serves only as an allegory for everything that life means. . . . There is no standard to attain, no victory, only the joy of life in the dance of your run. There is joy in every life; only in the moment—now. So you too will know in the flow of your dance. You cannot run for a future reward; everything that is yours you receive *now*. (Zohe in Lenk, 1989, p. 119)

Similar ideas are expressed by individuals involved in other Zen inspired activities. Zen ideas have been used by athletes in tennis, cross-country skiing, and golf.

The Eastern influence on sports and physical education has been subjected to the same kinds of criticism that besets humanistic physical education, to which it is closely related. It tends to emphasize the personal self at the expense of the social self. It is overly present-experience oriented. There is also an apparent contradiction between the philosophy of spontaneity which is proposed and the rigidity of many of its practices. Finally, the use of such procedures in training for competitive sports makes such goals as inner wholeness and peace subordinate to winning in competitive events.

A holistic approach to sports and physical activity is also promoted in other intellectual traditions. The behavioral scientist Csiksxentmihalyi characterizes the holistic experience felt by people when acting with complete abandon as flowing. From his study of people who have engaged in strenuous activity such as mountain climbing, he concludes that people experience a total integration. He reported the experience of one mountain climber:

> One must give oneself over to climbing, fusing one's thinking with the rock. It is the ultimate in commitment in sport, in endeavors to participate. It is the Zen feeling, like meditation and concentration. One strives to direct the intellect to a single point. . . . But when things become automatic, it is to some extent like a thing without an ego. Somehow the thing gets done, without one's thinking about it or even doing anything. . . . It just happens. And yet one is more concentrated. (In Lenk 1989, pp. 124–124)

Physical Education as Play

A number of theorists in physical education have attempted to establish play as the fundamental meaning and basis for physical education. They contend that when play is viewed in this way one can see both what physical education is and what its possibilities are (Siedentop, 1980, ch. 14).

In this theory leisure is a central concern for human life. Leisure is seen as a value in itself according to the definition of the philosopher Paul Weiss (1974):

> Leisure, then, is the time when men can be at their best, making it possible for them to make the rest of their day as excellent as possible—not by enabling them to work with more zest or more efficiency but by enabling them to give a new value and perhaps a new objective to whatever is done. The good life is a life in which a rich leisure gives direction and meaning to all else we do. (p. 86)

Physical education which has as its goal to promote the intelligent use of leisure time thus adds an important element to human life. It is often in leisure activities and play life that persons express their individuality in a meaningful way.

While philosophers of all schools have written of the role of play and leisure activities for the full human life, the existentialist philosopher Karl Jaspers has strikingly connected sport to the quest for personal freedom in the face of what is often an alienating technocracy.

> Contemporary man, when engaged in sport, does not indeed become a Hellene, but at the same time he is not a mere fanatic of sport. We see him when he is engaged in sport as a man who, strapped in the strait-waistcoat of life, in continuous peril as if engaged in active warfare, is nevertheless not crushed by his almost intolerable lot, but strikes a blow in his own behalf, stands erect to cast his spear. (Jaspers 1957, p. 79)

The philosophical examination of play received its classic treatment in Johan Huizinga's work *Homo Ludens* (1950). Huizinga gave a succinct definition of play:

> Play is a voluntary activity or definition executed within fixed limits of time and place according to rules freely accepted but absolutely binding,

having its aim in itself and accompanied by a feeling of tension, joy and the consciousness that it is "different" from "ordinary life." (Huizinga, 1950, p. 6)

This concept of play included the play of animals, children and adults, games of strength, skill, guessing, games of chance, dance and sports. Thus play included sport but also many other types of activities.

Play for Huizinga included three conditions, as contained in the definition. Play must be entered into freely, for being forced into an activity changes its very nature. Second, play must take place within its own boundaries of time and space. Play time is separate from work time. Play spaces such as tracks, fields, boards, and casinos are separate from other places. Third, play must be regulated by rules and conventions that suspend the ordinary rules of life.

The meaning of play and sports has been further analyzed in the work of Roger Callois who added conditions to Huizinga's definition and also provides a classification of sports. Callois accepts the three conditions of freedom to participate, fixed times and places, and rules of play. To these he adds that the outcome and course of action of play are not predetermined. Also, play does not aim to produce goods or wealth. It has an element of make believe or fantasy. The absence of one element does not necessarily mean that there is no play (Callois, 1961, pp. 9–10).

Before classifying the types of play, Callois placed play, on a continuum based on the degree of spontaneity, orderliness, and regulation in the play form. At one end of the continuum (*paidia*) are children's activities of noise, laughter, and agitation; on the other are more skilled games of sport, puzzles, etc. (*ludus*). Play thus includes both instinctive and spontaneous activities as well as sophisticated and skillful human interactions.

An examination of classification of types of play activities sheds light on the nature of physical education as education for play. Callois described four forms of play. *Agon*, competition, is a rivalry in which a person or a group of persons seek to win over another in speed, endurance, strength, skill, and ingenuity. Such an activity includes races and athletics as well as games like checkers and chess. It should be noted that while physical education focuses on competitive activities, there are also expressive activities within physical education. *Alea*, a game of chance such as heads and tails, betting, and lotteries, is a form a play in which the outcome is determined by chance and not by any skill. These games do not come under the rubric of physical education. *Mimicry* or make-believe is a imitation of others, seen in children's games and in forms of dance and mime and in theater productions. *Ilinx* or dizziness is the experience of pleasure, shock, or seizure that comes from tumbling down a hill, mountain climbing, and skiing.

If play is seen as the essential element in physical education, then the definition offered by Siedentop (1980) best describes the discipline: "Physical education means any process that increases a person's tendencies and abilities to play competitive and expressive motor activities" (p. 253). This definition specifies the goals of physical education as increasing playful motor abilities of a competitive and expressive nature. The advantage of this definition is that it connects physical education with the arts, places a value on human play, deals with different motivations, includes activities outside a school setting, and focuses on the irreducible concept of play (Siedentop, 1980, pp. 253–254).

For the concept of play to provide the theoretical basis of physical education it must be expanded beyond the idea of child's play or frivolous activity. Play is an activity that people engage in throughout life. Whereas some play is spontaneous, other forms of play demand a sophisticated education and training that entails skill, effort, patience and ingenuity. There is a great difference between swinging an imaginary sword and skilled fencing.

Those who advocate play as the theoretical basis for physical education are insistent that play justifies itself and needs no goals extrinsic to itself, such as fitness, building character, and learning teamwork, even though these might result from some forms of play. The existentialist philosopher, George Kneller expressed this concept when he explained

> The function of play is one of personal liberation—personal release; in sport man abandons himself to his own freedom, personally choosing the values and rules of his own physical activity, and the desire to play corresponds with the desire to be a certain type of person. (1958, p. 138)

Any consideration of sport as play must face the reality that there are a number of abuses that might destroy the spirit of play within sport. First, there is a danger of exaggerating the importance of victory over another. Though there is a place for the competitive spirit in sport, winning at all costs may eliminate the element of play from sport, lead to a lack of appreciation for good performances, and brutalize both players and spectators. Second, there is a danger that athletes and their coaches may make excessive demands on athletes to achieve victory. This may lead to both physical and psychological harm. The third danger comes from the desire to satisfy spectators and commercial interests. The existence of contracts, strikes, and holdouts all tend to lessen the play value of sports. These dangers exist not only in professional sports but also in interscholastic sports.

It is clear that the advocates of physical education as education for play have made a strong case for their philosophical viewpoint. However, a number of criticisms can made of the play theory of physical education. The concept of play is so closely connected with children's activity that it is difficult for it to form the basis of a theory that embraces activities during one's entire life. Also, play does not readily appear to be a sufficiently serious activity upon which to base all the activities included in physical education. Furthermore, the close connection of play with sport narrows the concept of physical education to sports and ignores other aspects of physical education such as safety and health education.

Notwithstanding arguments that can be offered against play education, this approach does appear to offer the best theoretical basis for physical education. Physical education thus becomes related to an essential dimension of human life, which has relevance during individuals' entire life. It focuses on an area of human endeavor that it shares only with the arts in the curriculum. The curriculum of physical education can grow in sophistication as children develop physically and intellectually.

Conclusion: The Ambiguity of Sport and Physical Education

For years those involved in physical education and sports could point to the idealism of an internationally accepted philosophy of the Olympic movement to encourage both themselves and their students to greater physical and athletic achievement. When the modern Olympic Games were reconstituted in 1896 the ideal was thus expressed:

The aims of the Olympic Movement are to promote the development of those fine physical and moral qualities which are the basis of amateur sport and to bring together the athletes of the world in a great quadrennial festival of sport thereby creating international respect and goodwill and thus helping to construct a better and more peaceful world. (Clark, 1974, p. 364)

The goals of the movement are expressed in physical, moral, spiritual and even political terms.

It is also clear that the movement had a pedagogical goal. The Olympic ideal includes the goal of holding up the achievement of some in order to encourage governments, educators, and the general public to demand the establishment of physical education and amateur competition sport (Clark, 1974, p. 365). The reason for the insistence on only amateurs competing was to reinforce the goal that achievement was possible for all persons, not just for those whose profession was sports.

The professionalism and commercialism of recent Olympics, together with the introduction of political ideology, no matter how understandable or justified or not, sends another message to teachers and students in physical education. The same message is sent by the overemphasis on intercollegiate and interscholastic sports. Physical athletic achievement are only for the highly skilled and trained. The more compelling moral message about physical education and sport may have to come from another Olympics, the Special Olympics, where the ability of every man and every women is celebrated.

CHAPTER 9

SPECIAL EDUCATION

The previous chapters in this book have focused on the various forms of education which take place both in schools and to a lesser degree in other institutions of society. These chapters have treated the history of philosophical ideas and current discussion in curricular areas. This chapter, on the other hand, examines the education of a particular group within society, special children.

This institutional form of education has had many names, with the most accepted name now being special education. Special children can be described as those who because of physical, psychological, cognitive, or social factors, need particular attention for meeting their needs and for realizing their full potential. Special children include the deaf, the blind, the speech disabled, the crippled, the mentally retarded, and the emotionally disturbed. In recent years children with high IQs or gifted children have also been included within the category of special children.

In this chapter it is my intention to bring some historical perspectives to special education, focusing both on the development of the practice of special education as well as on the ideas which have undergirded this form of education. As in other chapters, I will also present a discussion of contemporary issues of a philosophic nature which bear on this subject. This field has not received the same degree of attention from philosophers or theoreticians as other areas. Theoretical consideration has been given to the fundamental bases for special education as well as to the social, political, and legal issues that abound in this field. It is only proper that issues of social philosophy predominate, for if it is true that a society is to be judged by how it treats its least advantaged members, then an educational system and philosophy should stand under this same judgment.

HISTORICAL PERSPECTIVES ON SPECIAL EDUCATION

The development of special education as a particular concern awaited the emergence in society of a social philosophy that recognized the dignity of each child in his or her own right and called for their humane treatment and protection. This philosophy did not arise in any clear form until the seventeenth century with the emergence of an attitude of positive appreciation for children.

A certain progression of thought in the development of this social philosophy can be traced. First, some members of society, notably medical practioners, were motivated by humanitarian values and concerns for those considered less fortunate because of handicaps. This was followed by the espousal of humanistic values which recognized the dignity of human persons and their need for a certain degree of independence and development. More recent efforts in special education have been grounded in the awareness and assertion of individuals' moral and legal rights to dignity, courtesy, and respect, as well as the right of persons to equal opportunity for developing themselves as productive and socially acceptable human beings.

Emerging Concept of Childhood

In earlier times of human history children were not recognized in their own right. They were considered either as the bearers of intellectual and religious traditions or as servants of the state who were destined to meet its needs. Thus in ancient Rome children were clearly under the absolute responsibility of the family according to which the father actually had the right to reject the child at birth. In Roman society, as well as in other societies, children had no rights of their own but were passive recipients of adult values and knowledge. In Spartan society the child was reared by parents till the age of seven and then handed over to become the property of the state (Suran and Rizzo, 1979, pp. 9–10).

Within Christianity during the Middle Ages the viewpoint prevailed that children should be highly valued for their potential service to God and the Church. The treatment of children at this time was mixed. While some children were rejected, exploited, and sold into slavery, others were encouraged to join in the religious fervor of the times, such as in the Children's Crusades.

With the emergence of the commercial and industrial revolutions in the sixteenth and seventeenth centuries, children were increasingly considered an economic advantage for their work potential and consequently were frequently purchased and sold as apprentices, slaves, and servants. While some individuals protested these customs, especially in the name of religion, economic interests prevailed to support these practices.

It was during the Renaissance that the very idea of childhood was invented (Aries, 1962). Childhood was presented as a clearly delineated stage. Children appeared on their own as subjects in art; a literature arose that addressed their needs. The role of the family as the rearer and protector of children received greater attention from writers at this time.

In the seventeenth century with the spread of the ideals of equality, natural goodness, human perfectibility, and the rights of individuals, as found in the philosophy of John Locke and others, writers began to advocate even better protection, treatment, and education for children. Included within this range of thought was the recognition that human deficiencies were attributable to bad environments, incorrect rearing, and corrupt social and political institutions. It was one of Locke's concerns that children be raised with thoughtfulness and empathic understanding. He advised parents to reason with their children (Locke, 1956, p. 181).

In the eighteenth century, an Enlightenment thinker, the French philosopher, Jean Jacques Rousseau, pressed for a recognition of the rights of children to learn freely in environments that were not overly controlled by adults. Rousseau placed the child at the center of education as had no educator before him. Rousseau called for an explicit study of childhood:

Nothing is known about childhood. With our false ideas of it the more we do, the more we blunder. The wisest people are so much concerned with

what grownups should know that they do not consider what children are
capable of learning. They keep looking for the man in the child, not thinking of what he is before he becomes a man. (Rousseau, 1956, pp. 5–6)

Rousseau's stress on the innocence and spontaneity of childhood in his
classic *Emile* led to more humane methods of child rearing, especially
when the Swiss educator Johann Pestalozzi put his ideas into practice in
his experimental school.

Humane attitudes towards children emerged in the New England
colonies where parents were by law charged with responsibility to care
for their children. The office of tithingman was established to oversee
family government and the behavior of parents and children towards
each other. Though the motivation for these laws was no doubt religious,
by the beginning of the nineteenth century, Enlightenment ideas also had
their influence.

It is in the context of this Enlightenment-inspired social philosophy's
recognition of the human rights of children and responsibilities of parents that there emerged the first efforts to deal with special children.
More humane attitudes towards these children replaced former explanations of deviance in terms of

Demoniacal possession, retribution for parental sins, inborn perversity,
punishment for individual delinquencies, inherent moral weaknesses, defective genes, or the inevitable accidents of normal life. (Telford and Sawrey, 1977, p. 26)

Beginnings of Special Education

The treatment of persons with physical and mental deficiencies in the
ancient world was characterized by a great deal of cruelty and mockery.
In ancient Greece and Rome, as well as in the medieval world, such persons were often kept as fools for entertainment. When deformed persons
appeared in the literature of these times, they were most often connected
with murder and mayhem. In the view of many the handicapped were
cursed. The Bible, the Koran, and the Talmud urged a care for the handicapped.

During the Renaissance the prevalence of Christian charity, benevolence, and concern for fellow humans led to the establishment of some
asylums near convents and monasteries for the protection of persons with

physical or mental deficiencies. Such persons were also present in society as beggars who roamed the country side. During this time, however, the mentally retarded were often the object of exorcisms and were at times treated cruelly.

The treatment of handicapped persons improved somewhat in the early 1600s with the emergence of a more positive concept of the human person. A hospital for emotionally disturbed persons was established in Paris. A manual for the deaf was developed. A differentiation was made between those who were emotionally disturbed and those who were mentally retarded (Berdine and Blackhurst, 1985. p. 14).

The first documented account of an attempt to educate a special child was Jean-Marc Itard's effort, starting in 1799, to educate Victor, a boy discovered living in the forests near Aveyron (Itard, 1932). Itard, a French physician, described his efforts to establish the right environmental conditions that would humanize Victor. Believing that learning begins in the senses, he educated Victor to recognize sounds, to feel heat, and to respond to tickling and electric shock. Itard also instructed the boy to make signs and gestures for communicating his wants, to solve simple problems, to recognize a few simple words, and to relate in a highly limited manner to other human beings. What is remarkable about his account is the caring relationship that developed between teacher and pupil. Itard is noted for beginning the movement to train the mentally retarded.

Edouard Seguin, a physician and also a disciple of Itard, continued this work and became a teacher and leader in the field of mental retardation. In his published work, *Idiocy and Its Treatment by the Physiological Method* written in 1846, he documented that retarded children could benefit from medical, physical, and educational treatment. Seguin came to the United States and founded in Syracuse, New York, the first residential state institution with an educational program for mentally retarded persons. Seguin was also involved in the establishment of a number of other schools in the United States. His approach emphasized training of the whole child and used physiological stimulation in addition to training of specific senses. Though Seguin did not achieve his goal of curing mental retardation, he did advance educational efforts in behalf of special children.

An early approach to special education was the placement of special children in residential schools where they were separated from their families and communities. Such schools were established on a small scale

230 PHILOSOPHY OF EDUCATION

in Europe from the middle of the eighteenth century. A residential school for the deaf was established in 1817 in Connecticut by Rev. Thomas Gallaudet with an appropriation from the state legislature. In 1829 a school for the blind was established by Dr. John Fisher. Special schools were established for children with other disabilities.

In the United States an early effort at special education was Samuel Gridley Howe's work with the blind in 1831. In the school which this Boston physician established he showed a unique ability to penetrate the inner world of blind children. His documented efforts with the blind and deaf Laura Bridgman were a milestone in special education. Howe offered a number of suggestions on the education of the blind: the blind should be educated in schools with their seeing peers; blind children are individuals who should be educated to the limit of their abilities; the blind and the sighted should as much as possible have the same curriculum; the main purpose of education for the blind should be to train them to be socially and economically self-sustaining (Farrell, 1956). The development of a special method to teach reading and writing to blind persons awaited the efforts of the Frenchman, Louis Braille.

Special Education in Public Schools

The institutionalization stage of special education gave way to the formation of day schools, special classes, and public school involvements. Most of these developments took place in cities where there were more special children. For the most part special children remained in regular classes and consequently received little attention.

The day school, an alternative to the residential school, was introduced as early as 1871 in Boston with the establishment of a school for the deaf. This type of school had the advantage of keeping children within familial and community settings while also providing special education.

Provision for special education was advanced through developments in the testing movement. In 1905 Binet and Simon devised an intelligence test (IQ) to measure mental age. Because of their work it became recognized that mental retardation, while representing less than normal intelligence, does not prevent all learning. Many felt that this learning should best take place in institutional settings, under the control of a medical staff.

The problem of what to do with special children became more acute with the passage of compulsory education laws from 1852–1918. Pragmatic considerations demanded that provisions be made for such children.

> Educators in the public schools, unable to handle the exceptional children arriving in record numbers and realizing that no special provisions were available for these youngsters, began a movement for the establishment of special classes. Special classes came about, then, not for humanitarian reasons but because exceptional children were unwanted in the regular public school classroom. Feelings against mainstreaming, that is, placing exceptional children in regular classes, were strong. (Chavis, 1977, p. 30)

An important event in the history of special education took place in 1898 when Alexander Graham Bell suggested in an address before the National Educational Association (NEA) that special children should

> Form an annex next to the public school system, receiving special instruction from special teachers, who shall be able to give instruction to little children who are either deaf, blind, or mentally deficient, without sending them away from their homes or from the ordinary companions with whom they associate. (In Gearheart, 1972, p. 1)

Being deaf himself, Bell was determined that every effort be made for the education of these children in as normal situations as possible. Partly as a result of his efforts the Department of Special Education of the NEA was born.

In the early years of the twentieth century the major theoretical and practical concerns of special educators focused around

> Utilizing the "natural" activity of the child, the use of social activities to improve and enrich language ability, an attempt to correlate different kinds of learning activities as a means of reinforcing learning, individualizing instruction by adapting it to individual needs and capabilities, attempting to make learning lead to utilization so that it affects real life, trying to relate experiences preceding instruction to formal learning, and training the attention span and thinking capacity of the special learner. (Baker and Bender, 1981, p. 39)

Many of these formative ideas in special education were derived from the theories of progressive educators. The Progressive Era provided an impetus to the advancement of special education because of its stress on social responsibility and its trust in the power of scientific treatment and control to remediate individual problems. Progressive reformers saw in education a powerful tool to deal with individual and social needs. They saw in science and in the newly developing psychology a means for dealing with problems of special children (Rothman, 1980).

The Progressive period also brought into focus the use of tests for determining which children should be placed in special classes in the public school. Lewis Terman, a psychologist at Stanford, was concerned with the large number of children who were left back or retarded in their schooling progress. He proposed his newly developed IQ test as a way of determining who among the students were likely to be retarded and who had unusual ability. In 1911 he did a survey of "mentally defective children" in a California town. Terman declared that the students who fell below the norm were mentally deficient and should be placed in a special class where they would be given manual training and education in domestic science. This influential psychologist advised schools to identify the feebleminded and choose the most efficient methods for their education. In his view, their separation from normal classes would remove a demoralizing effect on normal children (Chapman, 1988, p. 26–27). Policies such as these have been the cause of many disputes. It has been determined that

> From 1915 to 1930, the number of special classes in public day schools increased greatly, but from 1930 to 1940 there was a halt and even a decline in this trend. The financial burdens of the Depression, dissatisfaction with the premature establishment of inadequately planned special classes with untrained teachers, and misinterpretation of the assumptions of progressive education (typified by the notion that any basically good teacher could teach any group of children) combined to dampen public enthusiasm for special education. (Robinson and Robinson, 1965, p. 460)

With the end of World War II special classes were again promoted, especially by parent groups. While these events were taking place in the United States, a distinctive method of dealing with special children was being developed in Europe.

Maria Montessori and Special Education

Maria Montessori, the Italian physician and educator, began her professional life with a concern for the welfare of children in insane asylums in Italy. Having studied the pedagogical treatment of these children begun by Jean Itard and Edouard Seguin, she came to the conclusion that their deficiency was chiefly a pedagogical and not a medical problem. Through experiments she devised methods of teaching reading and writing to special children. Montessori devised a course for training teachers of Rome to be special educators. Gradually she came to the conclusion, borne out through her work with both retarded and normal children, that the same methods that she devised for the education of retarded children could be applied to normal children.

The Montessori Method is based on a number of principles which she enunciated in her writings. Teachers must teach the whole child, with special attention to diet, exercise, mental health, as well as to intellectual and social environment. Teachers are to be patient observers of children and their activities in environments. The learning environment should be prepared to provide security and promote interest in learning. Children need the freedom to move about in the environment. Interest will be sparked through the use of concrete and manipulatable materials. Education of the multiple senses should be provided. Learning is promoted by self-help, independence, and cooperation. Teachers should give careful attention to language development. Children should be allowed to learn at their own pace, with teachers remaining flexible. Children need to be provided with opportunities for success. Repetition and practice are essential to achieving this success (Orem, 1969, pp. 22–26).

Montessori, like her predecessors Itard and Seguin, stressed that the work with special children was essentially a spiritual task. She thought that the spirit of the child could be awakened only through love, respect, understanding, and patience. In keeping with this view she gave paramount importance to the moral preparation of teachers. Montessori's work has been influential in many countries, in both special and ordinary education.

Special Education Comes of Age: The Legal Battle

In the United States the realization that a large number of retarded persons were present in the population became apparent during the two world wars. Massive testing and screening of young men for military service revealed not only a large number of illiterates in the country but also the extent of the population of physically, mentally, and behaviorally handicapped or disabled persons. The return of many disabled veterans from the wars made the population more sensitive to persons with such disabilities.

In the second half of the twentieth century a movement began to ensure the rights of special children in public school classrooms. This movement attracted a number of advocacy groups: parents, educators, and political leaders. Many arguments were advanced for promoting these rights, some philosophical, others legal, and still others pedagogical. Philosophically, the movement was based on respect and equality for all persons. Legally, the movement took impetus from the 1954 Supreme Court decision of *Brown v. Board of Education of Topeka Kansas*, which declared separate but unequal arrangements in schooling unconstitutional, thus asserting the right of all children to equal educational opportunities. For many educators the argument was clearly pedagogical: special children would benefit from being in classes with normal children.

The effort to mainstream children in regular classrooms included the effort to eliminate all handicapping categories or labels. It also attempted to bring into the normal classroom persons who had mild educational handicaps. An effort has been made to place such children within the least restrictive environment and to utilize many educational programs, including academic remediation, social skills training, auditory training, speech correction, physical therapy, occupational therapy, small classes, and educational counseling. Mainstreaming has also been one of the reasons for increased tracking of students in school classrooms. More recently there have been second thoughts about the whole desegregation movement in special education, with many special educators pointing out the disadvantages of re-integrating children into normal classes (Telford and Sawrey, 1977, p. 97).

The advancement of special education, however, has not been a story of continuous progress. Efforts at treating and educating the mentally retarded suffered when the philosophy of social Darwinism, which holds that the evolution of the social order and social institutions is determined by laws of nature, was dominant. Whenever this philosophy has prevailed or the ideas of genetic determinism have been in the ascendancy, special education efforts, especially for the mentally retarded, have suffered (Telford and Sawrey, 1977, pp. 94–95).

The court battles of the past twenty years have produced a legal and ethical history that is unique in educational history. The basis for the legal efforts was the increasing recognition of the rights of all children. The courts have attempted to balance the rights of children, parents, and society in these decisions. As early as 1869 in *Fletcher et al. v. Illinois* the court attempted to balance parents' rights over their children with children's own rights:

> Counsel urges that the law gives parents a large discretion in the exercise of authority over their children. This is true, but this authority over their children must be exercised within the bounds of reason and humanity. . . . It would be monstrous to hold that under the pretense of sustaining parental authority, children must be left, without the protection of the law, at the mercy of depraved men or women, with liberty to inflict any species of barbarity short of the actual taking of life. (In Suran and Rizzo, 1979, p. 15)

The courts have also recognized children's rights to equal access to educational opportunities, the right of handicapped children to be educated, the need for fair procedures for classifying the mentally retarded, and the need for humane treatment of the institutionalized retarded.

As mentioned above, the *Brown* decision of 1954 was a critical juncture for advancing the rights of minority children to an equal education. In this decision the Supreme Court recognized two principles which have aided in the special education movement: first, individuals in modern society need a decent formal education as a condition for a decent quality of life; second, separating children is harmful to their self-concepts and reduces their achievement. What follows from these principles is that separate educational facilities are inherently unequal and thus prohibited. In subsequent cases this same reasoning has been applied to special children, particularly the appeal in *Brown* to the due process clause of the Fifth Amendment and the due process and equal protection clause of the Fourteenth Amendment.

In 1971 the commonwealth of Pennsylvania, when challenged by the state association for retarded children agreed to provide a free appropriate education for all children with mental retardation, and also to identify all children who had been excluded from public schools. These children, between the ages of six and twenty-one, were to be educated in regular classrooms wherever possible. The Pennsylvania Association for Retarded Children, which brought the case, contended that the state had not given retarded children due process before denying them life, liberty, and property.

In 1972 the *Mills v. the Board of Education of the District of Columbia* decision in the District of Columbia went beyond retarded children to include a broad range of mental, physical, and emotional disorders. The court added that financial considerations were not acceptable for denying education to handicapped individuals. In arguing that lack of money was insufficient reason for not providing services, the court asserted:

> The District of Columbia's interest in educating children must clearly outweigh its interest in preserving its financial resources. If sufficient funds are not available to finance all services and programs that are needed and desirable in the system, then the available funds must be expended equitably in such a manner that no child is entirely excluded from a publicly supported education consistent with his needs and ability to benefit therefrom. (In Berdine and Blackhurst, 1985, p. 9)

In the 1970s Congress took a more active role in asserting the rights of the handicapped. In the Rehabilitation Act of 1973 it stated that "no otherwise qualified handicapped person . . . shall solely by reason of this handicap be excluded from participation in, be denied the benefits of, nor be subjected to discrimination under any program or activity receiving Federal Assistance" (In Howe and Miramontes, 1992, p. 27). The following year the act was amended to make clear that this applied to educational opportunities and that that the act included individuals who had physical or mental handicaps.

The single most important legislation affecting special children has been Public Law 94–142, the Education for All Handicapped Children, which was enacted in 1975 by Congress. This law was designed to ensure free and appropriate public education for all special children between the ages of three and twenty-one. The purpose of the law is "to assure that all handicapped children have available to them a free and appropriate education which emphasizes special education and related services designed to meet their unique needs." The law provided for the federal government to help defray special educational services for handicapped children. This act made federal support contingent on the effort of states to identify all children and mandated the following: (1) free appropriate public education; (2) special education services; (3) related services; (4)

the least restrictive environment (presumed to be the regular classroom); (5) due process protections; (6)individualized educational programs. The act, which has been resisted on the basis of costs, has also given rise to many questions about its implementation (Berdine and Blackhurst, 1985, p. 24).

These legal efforts were prepared for by other governmental efforts at various levels. A United States Children's bureau was created in 1912 to deal with problems of children's health and welfare. A White House conference in 1930 addressed problems relevant to the care of children in areas of nutrition and medical care. In the 1950s parents of retarded children became active in what has become an influential and powerful advocacy organization, the National Association for Retarded Children (NARC).

In the 1960s there emerged at the highest levels of government a movement to ensure that all children receive equal educational opportunities. President Kennedy, no doubt because of his first hand knowledge of retardation within his family, addressed the needs of special children on many occasions. He offered the following rationale for increased efforts in this regard:

> The manner in which our nation cares for its citizens and conserves its manpower resources is more than an index to its concern for the less fortunate. It is a key to its future. Both wisdom and humanity dictate a deep interest in the physically handicapped, the mentally ill, and the mentally retarded. Yet, although we have made considerable progress in the treatment of physical handicaps, although we have made great strides in the battle against disease, we as a nation have for too long postponed an intensive search for solutions to the problems of the mentally retarded. That failure should be corrected. (In Gearheart, 1972, p. 19)

A great deal of legislation was passed in this decade for the benefit of disadvantaged children, including provisions of the Elementary and Secondary Act. Many programs were inaugurated and facilities established during these years. Special education benefited from this movement especially when in 1961 the President's Panel on Mental Retardation was founded to address the needs of the retarded child.

The United Nations has also made a declaration on behalf of special children. In its 1959 *Declaration of the Rights of the Child*, it recognized the rights of children to develop to their full capacity. In Principle 5 it stated that "the child who is physically, mentally, or socially handicapped shall be given the special treatment, education, and care required by his/her particular condition" (In Suran and Rizzo, 1979, p. 17).

In summary, from the judicial decisions and Congressional Acts bearing on special education handed down in the 1970s the following principles have been established:

1. There is a Constitutionally guaranteed right to an education for all children, and this right cannot be abridged by reason of any mental or physical handicap;

2. the education guaranteed by this right must be appropriate to the learner's individual needs, and must be provided at the public's expense;

3. the right to an education at the public's expense cannot be abridged due to a lack of funds;

4. the contention that certain handicapped children are ineducable is not permissible;

5. the least restrictive or most normal atmosphere is to be preferred in providing an education for the handicapped child;

6. the overriding consideration in every decision about what is an appropriate education for a handicapped learner is the absolute Constitutional requirement that its due process clause be followed so that equal protection under the law is guaranteed. (Baker and Bender, 1981, pp. 47–48)

Education for Gifted Children

Although special education for gifted and talented children is a rather recent phenomenon, the identification of gifted and creative children has existed since the work of Lewis Terman who in 1925 began his study of the gifted and talented. Educational approaches include enrichment, ability grouping, acceleration, and promotion of creativity.

Before the 1970s there were few efforts for educating the gifted and talented. New York City had two high schools which enjoyed a national reputation: Bronx High School of Science and the High School of the Performing Arts. Concerted efforts in this area began in the late 1950s because of the launching of Sputnik, the Russian space satellite. Partly in response to this the National Defense Education Act (NDEA) was enacted, which provided money for children who were gifted in science and mathematics. This federal effort sparked the emergence of programs throughout the country. By the early 1960s twenty-one states had programs. By the end of the 1960s many state programs were discontinued, as concern for disadvantaged and culturally diverse children increased. Even ability grouping according to talent was subjected to criticism.

Such programs increased in number in the 1970s when a study commissioned by the U.S. Office of Education contended that there were two million gifted children in the country. In 1972 an Office of Gifted and Talented was established by the Federal government, only to be abolished ten years later. In 1978 Congress passed the Gifted and Talented Children's Education Act which was repealed four years later by the Education Consolidation and Improvement Act (ECIA), which allocated funds for special projects, including those for children with high performance. Although the federal impetus has been important, most of the money available for such programs has been supplied by states and local districts (Meyen and Skritic, 1988, p. 266).

The definition of giftedness has been under great dispute. In the 1978 federal legislation this definition was offered:

> Gifted and talented means children, and whenever possible, youth, who are identified at the preschool, elementary, or secondary level as possessing demonstrated or potential abilities that give evidence of high performance capability in areas such as intellectual, creative, specific academic, or leadership ability, or in the performing and visual arts, and who, by reason thereof, require services or activities not ordinarily provided by the school. (Meyen and Skrtic, 1988, p. 266)

Most programs use a narrower definition, focusing on general academic ability as determined by achievement tests, grades, and teacher recommendations.

Such programs have received recognition in the educational laws of forty-five states. The rationale for such programs is merit rather than need. These programs are also justified on the basis of the national need to develop gifted and talented persons as human capital resources. Philosophic issues related to their education will be treated later in this chapter. Principles upon which such program are based, as well as principles of education for handicapped children have been under constant debate the past twenty years.

In summary, this historical survey has shown that there has been a gradual development of the awareness of society's responsibility towards exceptional children. The harsh treatment found in early years gave way to efforts based on humanitarian grounds. The medical profession first exhibited an interest in and concern for handicapped children. The Enlightenment philosophy stressing the rights of all individuals and the need for basic equality in society gradually led to a more positive treatment of children, including children with disabilities. The compulsory education movement in the United States brought into the schools many children with disabilities. While for many years public education found ways to remove these children from the school or to place them in separate classrooms and institutions, the twentieth century witnessed a revolution in societal attitudes and responsibilities. Following on the Supreme Court's assertion of equal opportunity for all children and the declaration that separate facilities were unconstitutional, a coalition of parents, educators, and politicians in many states pressed the issue of equality for special children. Although legislation has opened public education to all children, there are still many philosophical, ethical, and practical issues that are debated by philosophers and educators.

CONTEMPORARY DISCUSSIONS

In examining contemporary philosophical discussions in special education my attention will focus primarily on issues relating to the disabled and to a lesser degree on issues related to the education of the gifted and talented. This is so because the majority of issues under discussion pertain to this group.

Many areas relating to special education have been subject to philosophical discussion and debate. What is the proper language to be used to refer to exceptional children? What are the responsibilities of the good society towards exceptional children? What is the basis for these responsibilities? What are the goals and aims of special education? How does one best understand the institution and profession of special education?

Need for Philosophical Analysis
in Special Education

Many authors decry the dearth of philosophical analysis in the field of special education. Even though many writers in the field speak of the need for special educators to possess a personal philosophy of education, the standard textbooks contain little philosophical discussion. Tymitz (1983) in a study of the philosophies of forty special education teachers found that most of the educators were unable to articulate a conceptual foundation for their professional activities.

Special education has received little attention from philosophers and special educators have not generally attempted a philosophical approach. Legal and instructional issues have been emphasized. Some discussions, however, have a decided philosophical or theoretical bent. Most of the theoretical discussions are about social theories underpinning the field. But each of these theories does assume a particular philosophical stance. The dominant theories are behaviorist, social interactionist, and critical social theory. Though the behaviorist paradigm still dominates, it has been subjected to criticism from the other two perspectives in recent years.

Behaviorism and Special Education

Behaviorism is clearly the espoused view of the one full-length treatment of philosophy of special education, Edward James Kelly's *Philosophical Perspectives in Special Education* (1971). Kelly recognized that his work was the first attempt to propose philosophical rationales capable of unifying special education as a discipline. Although this work is valuable as a first attempt, it has not fulfilled the promise of the author nor led to the publication of other specifically philosophical works.

Upon close analysis it is clear that only two chapters in the book are explicitly philosophical, the chapter on epistemology and the chapter on ethics. The main argument in the book is over the goals of special education, namely, how one balances the goals of intellectual development with those of adjustment to one's handicap, and relation to others and vocational pursuits. Kelly presents the overall goal of special education as the provision of therapeutic-instructional benefit for its subjects. He contends that the development of the child's full intellectual intelligence is critical only for the gifted and for children with mild to moderate handicaps. It is of secondary importance for children with extreme learning problems. For the latter, adjustive and adaptive goals are more important (p. 88). The adjustive goals are directed to the personal adaptation of children to their own needs and pursuits as well as to their integration into normal functioning situations.

Taking a behaviorist orientation, Kelly argues that special education attempts to "induce desirable behavioral changes which are of eventual benefit to its subjects" (p. 15). Kelly favors methods of programmed learning for intellectual education, modification or extinction of malajustive behaviors, and programmed learning for the reinforcement of adaptive skills. He considers those changes to be desirable which are declared to be so within the social-cultural-teleological context of the therapeutic setting. Thus the question of knowledge and learning is to be resolved by the question of what is valuable in a particular setting. Kelly contends that socioeconomic factors influence our judgment about who is in need of special education. Our view of who needs special education is in practice determined by the nature of tests of intelligence and diagnosis that we use to define, classify, and evaluate handicapping conditions.

Considering that Kelly wrote this book before the major discussions on special education in the mid-1970s, one can applaud his attempt to discuss goals and ethical issues. While many have embraced the behaviorism in pedagogy that he advocates, questions can be raised about the social-cultural-teleological context in which special education takes place. In actual fact discussions about the nature and role of special education easily turn into discussions about the basic values of a society and its institutions as well as the rights of all individuals within this society.

Even though Kelly attempted to provide the field of special education with the philosophical basis of behaviorism, many critics contend that there are serious theoretical problems within the field because of its almost exclusive commitment to behaviorism or positivism (Meyen and Skrtic, 1988). Other scholars contend that the field lacks any guiding theory, arguing that special education is guided not by an explicit theory but by a set of unconscious assumptions which are narrowly based. Bogdan and Kugelmass (1984) summarized these assumptions:

(1) Disability is a condition that individuals have; (2) disabled/typical is a useful and objective distinction; (3) special education is a rationally conceived and co-ordinated system of services that help children labelled disabled; (4) progress in the field is made by improving diagnosis, intervention, and technology. (p. 173)

These assumptions cumulatively accept the philosophy of behaviorism or positivism as the unifying theory for special education because they are compatible with the principles of philosophic behaviorism. The first assumption is based solely on the observation of individuals' behavior, without any attention to individuals' perceptions and without an analysis of the definitions and causes of disabilities. The second assumption is that behavioristically oriented tests of human intelligence are valid and that those who are below the statistical norm are in some way intrinsically deficient. The third assumption, coming from the functional analysis of organizations, places special emphasis on the latent and hidden functions of organizations, without giving attention to the meanings with which individuals invest organizations or the particular ideologies which drive organizational life. The fourth assumption originates in and restates the prevailing view of scientific research and practice. All of these assumptions have been subjected to criticisms by writers in the field, especially by the radical critics whose work will be discussed below.

Another criticism of the behaviorist paradigm of special education is that it has confounded theories. Jane Mercer (1973) contends that biological and psychological theories of deviance are confounded or confused within the clinical perspective of mental retardation. In her view, special educators make use of a pathological model in drawing the distinction between normal and abnormal, a distinction which is based on purely subjective or evaluative judgments about what is normal and abnormal. She points out that biological symptoms are at the basis of these judgments. She also shows that at the same time the field uses a statistical model according to which position on a frequency curve determines normalcy. The latter model is evaluatively neutral. Mercer (1973) explains the results of this confusion:

The implicit logic that underlies this transformation is as follows: Low IQ = "bad" in American society: a social evaluation. "Bad" = pathology in the pathological model. Therefore, low IQ = pathology. Thus, IQ which is not a biological manifestation but is a behavioral score based on responses to a series of questions, becomes conceptually transposed into a pathological sign carrying all of the implications of the pathological model. (pp. 5–6)

This confusion of theories led to the conclusion that mental retardation is an objective condition which individuals have, when it may be in many cases only a matter of statistical difference. Mercer's analysis goes to the heart of school IQ testing, especially as it relates to special children. As indicated earlier, this movement from the Progressive period was largely the work of Lewis Terman of Stanford.

The third theoretical criticism leveled against the behaviorist paradigm is that it concentrates too narrowly on particular academic disciplines to the exclusion of others. Many contend that this approach relies too heavily on behavioral psychology and biology. These theorists contend that prevailing theory places the root causes of disabilities within the individual, without offering consideration of the causal factors existing in larger social and political processes that exist outside the individual. These radical critics, contend that the preferred methods of diagnosis, intervention, and technology do not adequately address the social, cultural, and political aspects of special education (Goffman, 1961; Szasz, 1974). Since the major theoretical criticisms come from this group, the next section will present these criticisms.

Alternative Conceptualization: Social Interactionism

A number of scholars in recent years have attempted to reconceptualize special education. These scholars find the traditional conceptualizations too tied to the medical model which relies on biology and psychology. These theoretical alternative approaches try to address some of the criticisms leveled against the field.

It is the contention of these reconceptualists that the disciplinary base of special education should go beyond psychology and biology to include the social sciences, the humanities, and the arts. These theorists have drawn on recent work in the philosophy of science in attacking the mechanistic paradigm utilized in special education. Their attack represents the principal theoretical debate within special education (Heshusius, 1989).

The first alternative theory in special education, social interactionism, is rooted in the discipline of sociology. Bogdan and Kugelmass (1984) reject what they term a mechanistic model of special education which regards the teacher as a behavioral engineer. They contend that sociology provides an alternative model for viewing special education and the student which it serves. Specifically, they draw on symbolic interactionism to provide the alternative model for special education. In this approach what is essential for understanding social phenomena is not the function of activities in the social order but the particular meanings that people ascribe to their social interchanges. What this entails in education is the interpretion of what is happening according to the meaning that the participants give to their actions. For its research this approach depends not on the quantitative research of the positivist but on qualitative research in life histories.

Applied to education this approach attempts to understand special education from the perspective of the clients. This approach places great importance on insiders' views of services. Studies in this mode have been done on inmates in asylums and on disturbed people. These histories have revealed many aspects of the lives of the people which are not open to quantitative researchers. For example, Becker (1966) has described the behavioral modification, seclusion, and tranquilizing medications administered by staff, procedures which he considers methods of punishment and behavioral control. While the staff speaks in terms of cure and control, clients report boredom, manipulation, and coercion. This approach highlights the subjective meanings of special education.

What this theory adds to our understanding of special education is the importance of self-created meanings and the weakness of the standard definitions and understandings of special education and disability. Societal definitions of disability, even if they are enshrined in laws, mean little in the subjective meaning systems of individuals. The implication of this is that educators should attend more to these subjective meanings and interpretations than they do and not be misled by the so-called objectifications of disabilities. Symbolic interactionism can make educators sensitive to the effects of placing labels on individuals and classifying them in ways which they would not accept. Since these labels may be important when dealing with public policy because they are defined by law, they should not be used in educational settings. Efforts also should be made to limit their use in the public sphere as well.

The symbolic interactionism approach sensitizes educators to the power of prejudice and stereotypes in special education. This perspective has given rise to the term "handicapism" to indicate a form of discrimination against people with disabilities. Forms of discrimination are found in many areas of life: physical and literacy barriers, medical treatment, and portrayal in arts and media.

While symbolic interactionism has provided many insights into the situation of the disabled and into the processes of special education, it does not appear to have the potential to provide a comprehensive alternative theory for understanding all aspects of special education. The theory remains a powerful one for researchers and scholars but it does not have the levels of understanding, interpretation, and generalization needed to include all aspects of special education. It deals well with the highly personal and interpersonal aspects but it is weak in dealing with the social, political, economic, and legal realities of this complex field.

Radical Analysis of Special Education

Just as in others areas of education, special education has its radical critics who raise important philosophical and ideological issues. Radical educational theory attempts to analyze the social, economic, and political factors involved in educational theory and practice. It attempts to point out who benefits and who suffers from present arrangements. It is especially sensitive to forms of domination and oppression in society and its institutions.

Shapiro (1980) applied radical social analysis to the concept of mainstreaming, contending that "the attempt at reform in special education, or in any other areas of the field, has become the attempt to resolve issues arising not simply out of education itself, but out of the broader social domain" (p. 223). Others have extended critical analysis to the entire field of special education.

One such radical analysis has been provided by Sigmon (1987) who questions the existence of a learning disability, contending that this concept is a myth that has led to the misdirection of efforts in special education. In a Marxist analysis which utilizes resistance theory, Sigmon argues that many of those classified under the label of learning disabled are more often the victims of poverty and unemployment that beset their families. Arguing that many of these students have become school resisters he contends that many student resisters have been formally classified with various special education labels such as emotionally disturbed, socially maladjusted, and especially learning disabled—because LD is the easiest to assign a student since it is the least noxious—by a general education system unable to deal with them. (p. 77)

Sigmon does not deny that there are children who need special education because of their real handicaps but he contends that special education often becomes the place for school resisters, a place for accommodating persons of minority classes and races that do not fit easily into public schools. Sigmon also contends that labeling children as learning disabled is a way of gaining additional funds to pay for programs for such stigmatized children (p. 82).

What gives a certain plausibility to Sigmon's contention and that of others is the overrepresentation of certain classes and ethnic groups in special education classifications. Mercer (1973) found that students from lower socioeconomic and non-white backgrounds were disproportionately labeled and that Mexican-American and black students who were so labeled were actually less deviant than whites, that is, they had higher IQs.

Sigmon attacks the very concept of learning disability. This is the essence of his argument. The concept originated in the idea that retarded children were brain damaged. Further, the development of IQ tests provided a scientific reason to explain why some children were not learning and should thus be put in special classes. Finally, with the growth of children so identified, most of whom have only mild disorders, the term learning disability has been used as a justification for "new educational arrangements which have become a massive means of social control in the schools with children and youths" (p. 90). Special children are thus often scapegoats for many of the problems of society and its schools: class differences, disparity of wealth, poor teaching, and political struggles among parents, educators, and politicians. In his opinion the special education tracks are really "an attempt to conserve and perpetuate the culture and its institutions of which the school is an important one" (p. 94).

Thus Sigmon's radical analysis utilizes the logic of the cultural reproduction-resistance dialectic found in the Marxist analyses of social class struggle. For him

This struggle has led to the inadvertent co-optation of special education by including millions of so-called mildly handicapped children instead of concentrating on the best possible education for the moderately and severely impaired (p. 97).

Sigmon's analysis complements the analysis offered by the British sociologist, Tomlinson (1982), who focused on the misuse of the language of "special needs" children. She contends that

The terminology used as a legitimation for the exclusion of more and more children from the normal education system and for placing them in a type of education which does not allow them to compete for educational credentials, and subjects them to even more social control than in normal schooling, is that of special needs. The use of the term is rapidly becoming tautological rhetoric, and its uses are more ideological than educational (p. 72).

Special needs concerns translate for Tomlinson into the ideology of control and power over particular classes in society. What Tomlinson has done is to analyze special education utilizing the insights of the new sociology propounded by the British scholars Michael Young (1971) and Kevin Harris (1977) and used by the United States educator, Henri Giroux (1981; 1983).

There no doubt has been an increase in numbers of children being classified as possessing learning disabilities. Many special educators have begun to make this point. What distinguishes the radical position is its insistence that this practice serves particular political, social, and economic interests. What Tomlinson, Sigmon and others see in this practice is the serving of the particular ideological purpose of social control of large groups of people. This ideology has historical roots in the history of special education.

Finally, a small group of radical special educators have developed an approach to special education that is informed by the theory of education as political conscientization developed by Paulo Freire. Holtzman and LaCerva (1986) have provided an empowering theory and practice of learning. They have also incorporated Vygotsky's theory that postulates higher psychological processes as a series of qualitative transformations that arise through dialectical processes which are sociocultural and historical. In this approach educators attempt to create an environment of social interchanges in which educational methods are adapted to the social and historical situation of the students. Educators make use of the personal, historical, and political experiences of students to help them make these experiences the object of debate and confirmation. Holzman and LaCerva describe their work with learning disability students in a multiracial high school in New York.

Although there are many challenges to the positivist or behaviorist theory that is dominant in special education, one cannot say that any of the alternative theories has succeeded in gaining a large number of adherents. While the critics make many valid criticisms of the prevailing theory and offer some helpful correctives, it appears at times that they have set up a straw person in presenting a rather rigid view of the scientific mentality. Some of the ideas of the critics are congruent with more enlightened perspectives within special education. This debate makes it clear that in education as in other areas of human endeavor it is not possible to understand complex reality and practice merely through one lens.

An Enduring Problem: Definition and Terminology

No field in education has had such a serious problem with definition and classification than special education. Over the years many terms have been used to identify students of special education. Disputes over definition, terminology, and classification are not superficial matters but often cloak serious philosophical issues and issues of public policy. Many groups of people have to be satisfied with the language used: parents, teachers, children, and policy makers. Terminology is necessary for communication purposes; but efforts should be made to avoid terms that have pejorative meanings. Definitions are also important to differentiate among learners and their needs. Terms should be used with special sensitivity and also with an awareness that usages often vary from group to group and from time to time. One can see this in the changes of use of terms over the years to refer to African-Americans.

The matter of definitions is an important issue in special education because of the need to determine which students are eligible for federal and state aid. Some standards of eligibility need to be set. Definitions are needed to clarify who is eligible and who is not. If definitions and criteria for definitions change, there is a danger that students will be denied what they need and what they are entitled to. Because special educators communicate with different publics, compromises are often made in the language of special education.

Educators tend to use the language of *exceptional* or *special* children. In recent federal legislation *handicapped* is used. Advocacy groups most often use the language of *persons of disability* or the *disabled*. The language of *exceptional* is preferred by educators because it emphasizes children at either extreme of the mental ability scales, including the gifted and the mentally retarded. The term *handicapped* does not include the gifted. The general public interprets the word *exceptional* to refer only to the gifted. There is a difference between *handicapped* and *disability*. *Disability* refers to a particular condition while *handicap* describes the consequences of the disability. Thus persons are handicapped because of their disabilities.

There is a consequence connected with definition and terminology that plagues special education. While terminology and classifications are important, when children learn of these classifications, they may serve as self-fulfilling prophecies in their school work. There is also the danger that once the child has been classified, there is little possibility for returning to the regular educational situation.

Radical social critics have directed attention to the politics of labeling in education, including special education. Scott (1972) has described the effects of labeling someone as different or deviant:

> Another reaction that commonly occurs when a deviant label is applied is that within the community a feeling arises than "something ought to be done about *him.*" Perhaps the most important fact about this reaction in our society is that almost all the steps that are taken *are directed solely at the deviant.* Punishment, rehabilitation, therapy, coercion, and other common mechanisms of social control are things that are done to him, implying that the causes of deviance reside within the person to whom the label has been attached, and that the solutions to the problems that he presents can be achieved by doing something to him. (p. 15)

It is a short step to considering this person as morally deficient. According to Apple (1979) this language in school serves only to abase individuals and classes to whom these labels are attached.

While radical critics rightly point out the dangers of labeling in special education, they have shown little sensitivity to the complexity of the issue. It is not an easy matter to come up with definitions and labels that are satisfactory for all interested groups: children, parents, teachers, and policy makers. With all the good will and effort of special educators,

Meyen and Skrtic (1988) note that major problems remain in defining exceptional children and youth:

1. Characteristics of exceptional individuals are not present at birth. They may appear at any time, so identification is difficult. Characteristics also overlap, even among those with the same characteristics, instructional needs vary.

2. Like all people, exceptional children change, and their educational needs change accordingly. The state of flux complicates the use of definitions.

3. Cultural differences cloud the issue. Progress is being made, however, in producing nondiscriminatory assessment and in responding to language differences. (p. 8)

Political Philosophy and Special Education

Because special education has received so much attention from the law, it has also received treatment from social and political philosophers. The major question asked is what should a democratic society do for the least advantaged of its members and for what philosophical reasons should it do this.

Nondiscrimination and equal opportunity

One operative democratic principle is that of nondiscrimination. This principle becomes one of nonexclusion: "no educable child may be excluded from an education adequate to participating in the processes that structure choice among lives" (Gutmann, 1987, p. 127). To this principle must be added the idea of equal educational opportunity which entails that the democratic state should devote the necessary resources to education, especially primary education, and that these should be distributed in such a way that the life chances of all children are maximized. Equal opportunity also entails that resources be used according to natural ability and willingness to learn. None of these interpretations is adequate in itself for resolving this issue of special education.

It is argued that the democratic standard entails education to the point of participation in political life, which is presented as the *threshold of education* (Gutmann, 1987, p. 136–137). What the threshold is must be determined empirically in each social context. This threshold has been recognized by courts when they state that an adequate education must be provided or that a child must be given the education necessary for life as a citizen. Functional literacy is the usual standard given.

It is clear that much more should be done for some children than others to enable them to reach the threshold. This may entail spending more money and providing extraordinary services for a deaf or retarded child, as it does in the case of all disadvantaged children.

What is owed to children with brain damage? These children cannot be given the same democratic opportunities but "we do owe them a good life relative to their capabilities, a life good for them, not simply convenient for us" (Gutmann, 1987, p. 155). What is owed them depends on their capability and our willingness to provide the many things that they need. Gutmann (1987) wisely adds

> This standard leaves room for democratic discretion in deciding on the particular combination of schooling and non-educational services to provide brain-damaged children. Any adequate combination, however, is bound to be more costly and demanding than raising average children up to the normal threshold. (p. 156)

The next question is obvious. How much is the democratic state obligated to provide, given the high costs of such arrangements. In the United States it has been recognized that such costs have to be shared by local, state, and federal governments. The federal government has assumed responsibility but its funding has decreased over the years. There is no doubt that fairness to special children is costly. Many procedures have been introduced to insure this fairness. Critics contend, however, that this has led to a bureaucracy in which all suffer.

The cost question raises important issues especially when one considers the greater share of resources and staff time that might have to be devoted to special children. Combining children in the same classroom may control some of the costs. But dealing with special children often entails more resource teachers and more aides. With limited resources, this often means that the benefit of some children has to be sacrificed to that of others. This may be done fairly if all children achieve the threshold. But it may happen that some children's real needs will have to be sacrificed. Principles of fairness and due process can go just so far in the case of real-world problems.

Another issue under the rubric of equal educational opportunity concerns *gifted and talented children.* The justification for such programs is a matter of debate. There are those who argue that as long as some children are not reaching even the educational threshold, programs for such children are unfair. These programs can be defended on the basis of the benefit to society that will accrue if gifted and talented children are educated to the limit of their ability. However, it is not easy to determine whose education will result in the betterment of society. Another justification offered is that such children have special needs which should be met and if they are not met these children are in risk of suffering harmful effects from school and even of dropping out.

Principle of due process

One of the principles operative in special education to achieve fairness is due process, that is, the right to have one's liberties, rights, or benefits protected through fair and impartial procedures. Attention to due process has come about because of situations in the past where disabled children were removed from schools. With the laws asserting that children shall not be denied "free appropriate education" and have access to the "least restrictive environment," there has been a need to have certain procedural rules. This area is complicated by possible conflicts with the rights of regular children and the reality of different evaluations by different members of a staff.

Due process for special children has been likened to informed consent for medical treatment (Howe and Miramontes, 1993, p. 31). This means that parents and children should be involved in any decisions that are made and should be given a reasonable account of the diagnosis. This diagnosis must be based on the relevant facts of the situation. Professionals in these matters must treat parents with respect and understanding so that they can make the informed consent that is called for.

Special children have a greater right to due process in matters of suspension and expulsion because of the past tendency to remove troublesome children. The law has formalized the rights of special children with regard to due process. They have the right to remain in school while their placement is being negotiated; they may not be suspended for behavior related to their handicapping condition; educational services must not be denied. The law has stated that schools cannot claim lack of resources to provide services, sensitive to past unjust expulsions of special children. Like all cases of expulsion and suspension the presumption is in favor of the students, especially special children.

REFERENCES

Adler, Mortimer et al. *The Paideia Proposal: An Educational Manifesto*. New York: Macmillan, 1982.

Adler, Mortimer. *Reforming Education*. New York: Macmillan, 1988, p. 105.

American Jewish Committee. *Religion and Public Education: A Statement of Views*. New York: American Jewish Committee, 1979.

Apple, Michael. *Ideology and Curriculum*. Boston: Routledge and Kegan Paul, 1979.

Arato, A., and Gebhardt, Eike, eds. *The Essential Frankfurt School Reader*. Urizen Books, 1978.

Aries, Philippe. *Centuries of Childhood*. New York: Knopf, 1962.

Aristotle, *Politics and Poetics*, trans. by Benjamin Jowett and S. H. Butcher. New York: Heritage, 1964.

Aronowitz, Stanley, and Giroux, Henry. *Education Under Siege: The Conservative, Liberal, and Radical Debate over Schooling*. South Hadley, Mass.: Bergin and Garvey, 1985.

Ashner, Mary Jane. "Teaching the Anatomy of Criticism." In Ralph Smith, ed. *Aesthetics and the Problems of Education*. Urbana, Ill.: University of Illinois Press, 1971.

Association for Supervision and Curriculum Development-ASTD. *Religion in the Curriculum*. Alexandria, Va.: ASTD, 1987.

Auerbach, J. et al. "In Gilligan's *In a Different Voice*." *Feminist Studies*, 1985, 11, pp. 149–161.

Ayer, A. J. *Truth and Logic*. London: Gollancz, 1946.

Baensch, Otto. "Art and Feeling." In Susanne Langer, ed. *Reflections on Art*. New York: Oxford University Press, 1961.

Baker, D. Philip, and Bender, David R. *Library Media Programs and the Special Learner*. Hamden, Conn.: The Shoe String Press, 1981.

Beardsley, Monroe. "The Classification of Critical Reasons." In Ralph Smith, ed.

Aesthetics and Problems of Education. Urbana: University of Illinois Press, 1971.

Becker, H. S. Introduction. In C. Shaw, ed., *The Jack Roller*. Chicago: University of Chicago Press, 1966.

Bellah, Robert et al. *Habits of the Heart*. Berkeley: University of California Press, 1985.

Bellah, Robert et al. *The Good Society*. New York: Knopf, 1991.

Berdine, William H., and Blackhurst, A. Edward. *An Introduction to Special Education*. Boston: Scott Foresman and Co., 1985.

Bernstein, Richard. *John Dewey*. New York: Washington Square Press, 1967.

Bischoff, Guntrum G. "The Search for Common Definitions of Religious Studies and Public Education." *Religious Education* 1976, 71, 1, pp. 68–80.

Bloom, Allan. *The Closing of the American Mind*. New York: Simon and Schuster, 1987.

Bogdan, R., and Kugelmass, J. "Case Studies of Mainstreaming: A Symbolic Interactionist Approach to Special Schooling." In L. Barton and S. Tomlinson, eds. *Special Education and Social Interests*. New York: Nickols, 1984.

Borowitz, Eugene. "Judaism and the Secular State." In Theodore Sizer, ed. *Religion and Public Education*. Boston: Houghton Mifflin, 1967.

Bowen, James. *A History of Western Education: Volume 2. Civilization of Europe*. New York: St. Martin's Press, 1975.

Bowles, Samuel, and Gintis, Herbert. *Schooling in Capitalist America*. New York: Basic Books, 1976.

Branscomb, Lewis M. and Gilmore, Paul C. "Education in Private Industry." *Daedalus*, 1975, 104, pp. 222–233.

Bricker, David. *Classroom Life as Civic Education: Individual Achievement and Student Cooperation in Schools*. New York: Teachers College Press, 1989.

Broudy, Harry and Palmer, John. *Exemplars of Teaching Method*. Chicago: Rand McNally, 1964.

Broudy, Harry. "Between The Yearbooks." In Jonas Soltis, ed. *Philosophy & Education. Eightieth yearbook of the Society for the Study of Education*. Chicago: University of Chicago Press, 1981.

Broudy, Harry. "The Arts as Basic Education." In Ralph Smith and Alan Simpson, eds. *Aesthetics and Arts Education*. Urbana: University of Illinois Press, 1991.

Brown, Camille and Cassidy, Rosalind. *Theory in Physical Education*. Philadelphia: Lea and Febiger, 1964 p. 54.

Bruner, Jerome. *The Process of Education*. Cambridge: Harvard University Press, 1963,

Butts, R. Freeman. *The Revival of Civic Learning: A Rationale for Citizenship Education in American Schools*. Bloomington, Ind.: Phi Delta Kappa Educational Foundations, 1980.

Byrnes, Lawrence. *Religion and Public Education*. New York: Harper and Row, 1975.

Callois, Roger. *Man, Play and Games*. New York: Free Press, 1961.

Cassirir, Ernst. *An Essay on Man*. New York: Bantam Books, 1944.

Chapman. Paul Davis. *Schools as Sorters: Lewis M. Terman, Applied Psychology, and the Intelligence Testing Movement, 1890–1930*. New York: New York University Press, 1988.

Charlton, K. "Imagination and Education." In Jane Martin, ed., *Readings in the Philosophy of Education: Study of Curriculum*. Boston, Allyn and Bacon, 1964.

Chavis, I. M. "Historical Overview of Special Education in the United States." In P. Bates and Associates, eds. *Mainstreaming: Problems, Potentials, and Perspectives*, Minneapolis: National Support Systems Project, 1977.

Chazan, Barry. "Indoctrination and Religious Education." *Religious Education* 1972, 67, 4, pp. 243–252.

Childs, John. "Should the School Seek Actively to Reconstruct Society." *Annals of the American Academy of Political and Social Science*, 1935, 182, pp. 8–9.

Clark, Stanley J. "Amateurism, Olympism, and Pedagogy." In Marie Hart, ed. *Sport in the Sociocultural Process*. Dubuque, Iowa: W. C. Brown, 1974.

Clark, Walter. "On the Role of Choice in Aesthetic Education." In Jane Martin, ed., *Readings in the Philosophy of Education: Study of Curriculum*. Boston: Allyn and Bacon, 1964.

Coleman, John. "Sport and the Contradictions of Society." In Gregory Baum and John Coleman, eds. *Sport*. Edinburgh: T & T Clark, 1989.

Copleston, Frederick. *A History of Philosophy: Volume I: Greece and Rome*. Westminster, Maryland: Newman Press, 1953.

Cox, Edwin. *Problems and Possibilities for Religious Education*. London: Hodder and Stoughton, 1983.

Cremin, Lawrence. *The Republic and the School: Horace Mann on the Education of Free Men*. New York: Teachers College Press, 1957.

Cremin, Lawrence. A. *American Education: The Colonial Experience, 1607–1783*. New York: Harper and Row, 1970.

Cremin, Lawrence. *American Education: The National Experience, 1783–1876*. New York: Harper and Row, 1980.

Curti. Merle. *The Social Ideas of American Educators*. Totowa, N.J.: Littlefield, Adams and Co., 1966 (1935).

Denton, David, ed. *Existentialism, Phenomenology in Education*. New York: Teachers College Press, 1974.

Dewey, John. "The Moral Significance of the Common School Movement." 1892, *Middle Works* 4:192.

Dewey, John. "Green's Theory of the Moral Motive." 1892, *Early Works*, 3, 122–158,

Dewey, John. "My Pedagogic Creed (1897)." In *John Dewey on Education*. Edited and with an Introduction by Reginald D. Archambault. Chicago: University of Chicago Press, 1964.

Dewey, John. "Pedagogy as a University Discipline." *University Record*, 1896, 1, nos. 25, 26, pp. 353–55, 361–63.

Dewey, John, *Ethics*, 1908. *Middle Works* 5:6.

Dewey, John. "Education vs. Trade-Training—Dr. Dewey's Reply." *The New Republic*, 1915, 3, 42–43.

Dewey, John. *Democracy and Education*. New York: Macmillan, 1916.

Dewey, John, "Learning to Earn: The Place of Vocational Education in a Comprehensive Scheme of Public Education." *School and Society*, 1917, 5, pp. 331–335.

Dewey, John. *Quest for Certainty*. New York: Minton, Balch, and Co., 1929.

Dewey, John. *Experience and Education*. New York: Macmillan, 1938.

Dewey, John. *Theory of Evaluation*. International Encyclopedia of Unified Sciences, Vol. II. Chicago: University of Chicago, 1939.

Dewey, John. *Art and Experience*. New York: Minton, Balch and Co., 1934.

Dewey, John. *A Common Faith*. New Haven: Yale University Press, 1934.

Dewey, John. *Philosophy of Education*. Totowa, N.J. Littlefield, Adams and Co., 1966.

Dewey, John. "Religious Education as Conditioned by Modern Psychology and Pedagogy." *Religious Education* 1974, 69, 1, pp. 5–11.

Donohoe, John. *Catholicism and Education*. N.Y.: Harper and Row, 1973.

Dubois, William. *The Negro Artisan*. Atlanta: University of Atlanta Press, 1902.

Durkheim, Emile. *The Division of Labour in Society*. London: Routledge and Kegan Paul, 1964.

Dykhuizen, George. *The Life and Mind of John Dewey*. Illinois: Southern Illinois Univ. Press, 1973.

Elias, John L. *Paulo Freire: Pedagogue of Liberation*. Malabar, Fla.: Krieger Publishing Co., 1994.

Engel, David E., ed. *Religion in Public Education*. New York: Paulist, 1974.

Entwistle, Harold. *Education, Work, and Leisure*. London: Routledge and Kegan Paul, 1970.

Erasmus. *The Essential Erasmus*. Edited and translated by J. P. Dolan. New York: Mentor, 1964.

Farrell, G. *The Story of Blindness*. Cambridge: Harvard University Press, 1956.

Finkelstein, Barbara. "Education and the Retreat from Democracy in the United States." *Teachers College Press*, 1984, 86, pp. 280–281.

Fitzpatrick, E. A., ed. *St. Ignatius and the Ratio Studiorum*. New York: McGraw-Hill, 1933.

Flew, Anthony. "Indoctrination and Doctrines." In I. A. Snook, ed. *Concepts of*

Indoctrination: Philosophical Essays. Boston: Routledge and Kegan Paul, 1972.

Frankena, W. *Ethics*. Englewood Cliffs, N.J.: Prentice Hall, 1973.

Freire, Paulo. *Pedagogy of the Oppressed*. New York: Continuum, 1970.

Freire, Paulo. *Education for Critical Consciousness*. New York: Continuum, 1973.

Freyne, Sean. "Early Christianity and the Greek Athletic Ideal." In Gregory Baum and John Coleman, eds. *Sport*. Edinburgh: T & T Clark, 1989.

Gearheart, B. R., ed. *Education of the Exceptional Child: History, Present Practices, and Trends*. Landam, Md.: University Press of America, 1972

General Education In a Free Society. Cambridge, Mass.: Harvard University Press, 1946.

Gilligan, Carol. *In Another Voice*. Cambridge: Harvard University Press, 1982.

Giroux, H. *Ideology, Culture, and the Process of Schooling*. Philadelphia: Temple University Press, 1981.

Giroux, H. *Theory and Resistance in Education: A Pedagogy for the Opposition*. South Hadley, Mass.: Bergin and Garvey, 1983.

Giroux, Henry. *Schooling and the Struggle for Public Life*. Minneapolis: University of Minnesota Press, 1988.

Goffman, E. *Asylums: Essays on the Social Situation of Mental Patients and other Inmates*. Garden City: Doubleday, 1961.

Goldman, Ronald. *Readiness for Religion*. New York: Seabury. 1965.

Goodlad, John. *A Place Called School*. New York: McGraw-Hill, 1984.

Greene, Maxine. "Art, Technique, and the Indifferent Gods." In Ralph Smith, ed. *Aesthetics and the Problems of Education*. Urbana: University of Illinois Press, 1971.

Greene, Maxine. "Literature, Existentialism, and Education." In David Denton, ed. *Existentialism, Phenomenology in Education*. New York: Teachers College Press, 1974.

Greene, Maxine. "Aesthetic Literacy in General Education." In *Philosophy and Education. Eightieth Yearbook of the National Society for the Study of Education*. Jonas Soltis, ed. Chicago: University of Chicago Press, 1981.

Grimmitt, Michael. *What Can I Do in R.E.?*. Great Wakering, Eng.: Mayhew-McCrimmon, 1973.

Grimmitt, Michael. *Religious Education and Human Development*. Essex, U.K.: McCrimmon Publishing Co., 1987.

Gross, Ronald, ed. *The Teacher and the Taught*. New York: Delta, 1963.

Grossman, Walter. "Schiller's Aesthetic Education." In Ralph Smith, ed., *Aesthetics and Problems of Education*. Urbana: Illinois: University of Illinois, 1971.

Gutmann, Amy. *Democratic Education*. Princeton, N.J.: Princeton University Press, 1987.

Habermas, Jurgen. *Communication and the Evolution of Society*. Boston: Beacon, 1979.

Harris, K. *Education and Knowledge: The Structured Misrepresentation of Reality*. London: Routledge and Kegan Paul, 1979.

Hartshorne, H. and May, M. A. *Studies in the Nature of Character*. Columbia Teachers College. Vol. 1: *Studies in Deceit*. Vol. 2: *Studies in Service and Self-Control*. Vol. 3: *Studies in Organization of Character*. New York: Macmillan, 1928–30.

Haskins, Charles Homer. *The Rise of Universities*. Ithaca, N.Y.: Cornell University Press, 1957.

Hauerwas, Stanley. *A Community of Character: Toward a Constructive Christian Social Ethic*. Notre Dame, Ind.: Notre Dame Press, 1981.

Havelock, Eric. "Plato on Poetry." in Ralph Smith, ed. *Aesthetics and Problems in Education*. Urbana: University of Illinois Press, 1971.

Heck, Arch. *The Educational of Exceptional Children*. New York: McGraw-Hill, 1953.

Hellison, D. *Humanistic Physical Education*. Englewood Cliffs, N.J.: Prentice Hall, 1973.

Heshusius, Lous. "The Newtonian Mechanistic Paradigm: Special Education, and Contours of Alternatives: An Overview." *Journal of Learning Disabilities* Volume 22, No. 7, August-September 1989.

Hetherington, Clark. "Fundamental Education." In Arthur Weston, *The Making of American Physical Education*. New York: Meredith Publishing Co., 1962.

Higgins, Joseph R. and Arend, Susan. "Science and Technology of Human Movement Studies: Some Assumptions for the Future." In Raymond Welsh, ed. *Physical Education: A View toward the Future*. Saint Louis: C. V. Mosby Co., 1977.

Hill, Brian. *Faith at the Blackboard: Issues Facing the Christian Teacher*. Grand Rapids, Michigan: Eerdmans, 1982.

Hirsch, E. D. *Cultural Literacy*. New York: Random House, 1987.

Hirst, Paul H. "Public and Private Values and Religious Educational Content." In Theodore Sizer, ed. *Religion and Public Education*. Boston: Houghton Mifflin, 1967.

Hirst, Paul H. "Liberal Education and the Nature of Knowledge." In Jane Martin, ed., *Readings in the Philosophy of Education: A Study of Curriculum*. Boston: Allyn and Bacon, 1970, pp. 157–168.

Hirst, Paul H. "Richard Peters's Contribution to the Philosophy of Education" in David Cooper, ed., *Education, Values and Mind: Essays for R. S. Peters*. Boston: Routledge & Kegan Paul, 1986.

Hirst, Paul H. *Knowledge and the Curriculum*. Boston: Routledge and Kegan Paul, 1974.

Holtzman, L. and LaCerva, A. "Development, Learning, and Learning Disabilities." Paper presented at Eighth International Conference on Learning Disabilities, Kansas City, MO, 1986.

Horkheimer, W. *Critical Theory: Selected Essays*. New York: Herder and Herder, 1972, p. 270.

Howe, K. R., and Miramontes, Ofelia B. *The Ethics of Special Education*. New York: Teachers College Press, 1993.

Huizinga, Johann. *Homo Ludens: A Study of Play Element in Culture*. Boston: Beacon Press, 1950.

Hull, John M. *Studies in Religion and Education*. London: Falmer Press, 1984.

Hutchins, Robert. *The Learning Society*. New York: New American Library, 1968.

Itard, Jean. *The Wild Boy of Aveyron*. New York: Appleton Crofts, 1932.

Jaspers, Karl. *Man in the Modern Age*. New York: Doubleday, 1957.

Jenkins, Iredell. "Aesthetic Education and Moral Refinement." In Ralph Smith, ed. *Aesthetics and Problems of Education*. Urbana: University of Illinois, 1971.

Jordan, Diana. *Childhood and Movement*. Oxford: Blackwell, 1966.

Kaelin, Eugene. "Aesthetic Education: A Role for Aesthetics." In Ralph Smith, ed. *Aesthetics and the Problems of Education*. Urbana: University of Illinois Press, 1971.

Kaelin, Eugene. "The Existential Ground of Aesthetic Education." in David Denton, ed. *Existentialism and Phenomenology in Education*. New York: Teachers College Press, 1974.

Kaelin, Eugene. "Why Teach Art in the Public Schools." In Ralph Smith and Alan Simpson, eds. *Aesthetics and Arts Education*. Chicago: University of Illinois Press, 1991.

Kaestle, Carl. *Pillars of the Republic: Common Schools and American Society, 1607–1860*. New York: Hill and Wang, 1983.

Kant, Immanuel. *Education*. Ann Arbor, Mich.: University of Michigan Press, 1960.

Kathan, Boardman W. "Prayer and the Public School: The Issue in Historical Perspective and Implications for Religious Education Today." *Religious Education*, 1989, 84, 2, pp. 232–248.

Katz, Michael. *Class, Bureaucracy, and the Schools*. Now York: Praeger, 1971.

Katznelson, Ira, and Weir, Margaret. *Schooling for All: Class, Race, and the Decline of the Democratic Ideal*. Berkeley: University of California Press, 1985.

Kelly, Edward James. *Philosophical Perspectives in Special Education*. Columbus, Ohio: Merrill, 1971.

Kleinman, S. "The Significance of Human Movement: A Phenomenological Approach." I. A. Gerber, ed. *Sport and the Body*. Philadelphia: Lea and Febiger, 1972.

Kliebard, Herbert. *The Struggle for the American Curriculum. 1893–1958*. New York: Routledge and Kegan Paul, 1987.

Kneller, George. *Existentialism and Education*. New York: John Wiley, 1958.

Koestler, Arthur. *The Sleep Walkers*. Baltimore: Penguin Books, 1964.

Kohlberg, Lawrence. *Essays on Moral Development. The Philosophy of Moral Development*. San Francisco: Harper and Row, 1981; *The Psychology of Moral Development*: Harper and Row, 1984.

Krug, Edward. *The Shaping of the American High School, 1880–1920*. Madison: University of Wisconsin Press, 1964.

Langer, Susanne. *Feeling and Form*. New York: Scribner, 1953.

Langer, Susanne. *Mind: An Essay on Human Feeling. Vol. I*. Baltimore: Johns Hopkins Press, 1967.

Langer, Susanne. "The Cultural Importance of the Arts." In Ralph Smith, ed. *Aesthetics and Problems of Education*. Urbana: University of Illinois Press, 1971.

Lannie, Vincent P. "The Development of Vocational Education in America: An Historical Overview." In *Vocational Education: Prospectus for Change*, edited by Carl J. Schaefer and Jacob J. Kaufman. Boston: Massachusetts Advisory Council on Education, 1967.

Lawson, Hal A. "From Futures Forecasting to Future Creation: A Planning Model for Physical Education and Sport." In Raymond Welsh, ed. *Physical Education: A View to the Future*. Saint Louis: C. V. Mosby Co., 1977.

Lazerson, Marvin, and Grubb, W. Norton eds. *American Education and Vocationalism: A Documentary History, 1870–1970*. New York: Teachers College Press, 1974.

Lenk, Hans. "Sport between Zen and the Self." In Gregory Baum and John Coleman, eds. *Sport*. Edinburgh: Clark and Clark, 1989.

Leonard, George. *The Ultimate Athlete*. New York: Viking Press, 1975.

Lewis, Guy. "Adoption of the Sports Program, 1906–1939: The Role of Accommodations in the Transformation of Physical Education." *Quest*, 1969, 12.

Lloyd, Genevieve. "Reason, Gender, and Morality in the History of Philosophy." *Social Research*, 1983, 50, pp. 490–513.

Locke, John. "The Second Treatise of Government," In *Two Treatises of Government*. New York: Cambridge University Press, 1960.

Locke, John. *John Locke on Education*. New York: Teachers College Press, 1956.

Lynch, James. *Education for Citizenship in a Multicultural Society*. New York: Cassell, 1992.

MacIntyre, Alasdair. *A Short History of Ethics*. New York: Macmillan, 1966.

MacIntyre, Alasdair, *After Virtue*. Second Edition. Notre Dame, Ind.: Notre Dame Press, 1984.

Mann, Horace. *The Republic and the School*. Edited by Lawrence A. Cremin. New York: Teachers College Press, 1957.

Marcuse, Herbert. *Essay on Liberation*. Boston: Beacon Press, 1969.

Marrou, H. I. *A History of Education in Antiquity*. New York: Mentor Books, 1956.

Martin, Jane Roland. "Needed: New Paradigm for Liberal Education." In Jonas Soltis, ed., *Philosophy and Education: Eighthieth Yearbook of the National Society for the Study of Education.* Chicago: University of Chicago Press, 1981, pp. 37–59.

Marx, Karl. *Selected Writings.* Edited by T. B. and Rubel M. Bottomore. London: Penguin Books, 1967.

McCluskey, Neil G., ed. *Catholic Education in America: A Documentary History.* New York: Teachers College Press, 1964.

Mercer, J. M. *Labelling the Mentally Retarded.* Berkeley: University of California Press, 1973.

Metheny, Elizabeth. "The Third Dimension in Physical Education." *Journal of Health: Physical Education, and Recreation.* March 1954, 25.

Meyen, E., and Skrtic, T. M. *Exceptional Children and Youth.* Denver, Col.: Love Publishing Co., 1988.

Mill, John Stuart. *On Liberty.* Indianapolis: Bobbs-Merrill, 1966 [1859].

Moran, Gabriel. *Religious Education as a Second Language.* Birmingham, Ala.: Religious Education Press, 1989.

Muller, H. J. *The Uses of the Past.* New York: Mentor Books, 1954.

National Task Force on Citizenship Education. *Education for Responsible Citizenship.* New York: McGraw-Hill, 1977.

Newman, John Cardinal. *The Idea of the University.* New York: Longmann, 1960.

Nicholson, Linda. "Women, Morality, and History." *Social Research,* 1983, 50, pp. 514–536.

Nisbet, Robert. *The Social Philosophers: Community and Conflict in Western Thought.* New York: Thomas Crowell, 1973.

Noddings, Nel. *Caring: A Feminine Approach to Ethics and Moral Education.* Berkeley: University of California Press, 1984.

Nozick, Robert. *Anarchy, State and Utopia.* New York: Basic Books, 1974.

O'Hanlon, Timothy, "Inter-scholastic Athletics 1900–1940: Shaping Citizens for Unequal Roles in the Modern Industrial State." *Educational Theory* 1980, 30, 89–103.

Oglesby, Carole. "Who Are We?" In Raymond Welsh, ed. *Physical Education: A View toward the Future.* Saint Louis: C. V. Mosby Co., 1977.

Olafson, Frederick A. "Teaching *About* Religion: Some Reservations." In Theodore Sizer, ed. *Religion and Public Education.* Boston: Houghton Mifflin, 1967.

Orem, R. C. *Montessori and the Special Child.* New York: Putnam, 1969.

Parsons, Michael. "Herbert Read on Education." In Ralph Smith, ed., *Aesthetics and Problems of Education.* Urbana: University of Illinois Press, 1971.

Pennsylvania Catholic Conference. *"Public Education and the Student Conscience: A Dilemma for Concerned Citizens.* Harrisburg: Pennsylvania Catholic Conference, 1976.

Perkinson, Henry. *The Imperfect Panacea: American Faith in Education, 1865–1976*. Second Edition. New York: Random House, 1977.

Peters, R. S. *Moral Development and Moral Education*. London: George Allen and Unwin, 1981.

Phenix, Philip. *Realms of Meaning*. New York: McGraw-Hill, 1964.

Phenix, Philip. "Religion in Public Education: Principles and Issues" In David Engel, ed. *Religion in Public Education: Readings in Religion and the Public School*. New York: Paulist, 1974.

Piaget, John. *The Moral Judgment of the Child*. New York Free Press, 1966 (1922).

Popper, Karl. *The Open Society and Its Enemies*. London: Routledge and Kegan Paul, 1962.

Power, E. *Philosophies of Education*. Englewood Cliffs, N.J.: Prentice-Hall, 1982.

Pratte, Richard. *The Civic Imperative: The Need for Civic Education* New York: Teachers College Press, 1988.

Priestly, Jack G. "Towards Finding the Hidden Curriculum: A Consideration of the Spiritual Dimensions of Experience in Curriculum Planning." *British Journal of Religious Education* 1985, 7, 3, pp. 112–119.

Purpel, David, and Ryan, Kevin. *Moral Education. . . . It Comes With the Territory*. Berkeley, Cal.: McCutchan, 1976.

Rawls, John. *A Theory of Justice*. Cambridge: Harvard University Press, 1971.

Read, Herbert. *Education Through Art*. Third Edition. London: Faber and Faber, 1958.

Report of Harvard Committee. *General Education in a Free Society*. New York: Oxford University Press, 1946.

Rice, Emmet A., Hutchinson, John J., and Lee, Mabel. *A Brief History of Physical Education*. Fifth Edition. New York: Ronalad Press Co., 1969.

Robinson, Edward A. "Religious Education: A Shocking Business." In John Hull, ed. *New Directions in Religious Education*. Basingstoke, Eng.: Falmer Press, 1982.

Robinson, H. B., and Robinson, N. M. *The Mentally Retarded Child*. New York: McGraw-Hill, 1965.

Rockefeller, David, Chairman. *Coming to our Senses: The Significance of the Arts for American Education*. New York: McGraw-Hill, 1977.

Rossiter, Graham M. "The Need for Creative Divorce Between Catechesis and Religious Education in Catholic Schools." *Religious Education* 1982, 77, 1, pp. 21–40.

Rothman, D. J. *Conscience and Convenience: The Asylum and its Alternatives in Progressive America*. Boston: Little Brown, 1980.

Rousseau, Jean Jacques. *The Emile: Selections*. Translated and edited by William Boyd, New York: Teachers College Press, 1956.

Runkle, John. "The Manual Element in Education." In Martin Lazerson and W. Norton Grubb, eds. *American Education and Vocationalism: A Documentary History, 1870–1970.* New York: Teachers College Press, 1974.

Rush, Benjamin. "Thoughts upon the Mode of Education Proper in a Republic." In Frederick Rudolph, ed. *Essays on Education in the Early Republic.* Cambridge: Harvard University Press, 1965.

Ryan, Thomas. "Toward a Spirituality of Sport." In Gregory Baum and John Coleman, eds. *Sport.* Edinburgh: T & T Clark, 1989.

Sandel, Michael. *Liberalism and the Limits of Justice.* New York: Cambridge University Press, 1982.

Scheffler, Israel. *In Praise of Cognitive Emotions.* New York: Routledge, 1991.

Scot, J. "Sport and the Radical Chic." In McGlynn, ed. *Issues in Physical Education and Sport.* Palo Alto: National Press, 1974.

Scott, Robert A., "Proposed Framework for Analyzing Deviance." In Robert A. Scott and Jack D. Doughlas, eds. *Theoretical Perspectives on Deviance.* New York: Basic Books, 1972.

Shapiro, H. S. "Society, Ideology, and the Reform of Special Education." *Educational Theory,* 1980, 30, pp. 211–223.

Siedentop, Daryl. *Physical Education: Introductory Analysis.* Third Edition. Dubuque: Iowa, William Brown, 1980.

Sigmon, Scott B. *Radical Analysis of Special Education: Focus on Historical Development and Learning Disabilities.* London: The Falmer Press, 1987.

Silberman, Charles. *Crisis in the Classroom.* N.Y.: Random House, 1970.

Sizer, Theodore, ed. *The Age of Academies.* New York: Teachers College Press, 1964.

Sizer, Theodore, ed. *Religion and Public Education.* N.Y.: Houghton Mifflin, 1967.

Sizer, Theodore. *Horace's Compromise.* Boston: Houghton Mifflin, 1987.

Slusher, Howard. *Man, Sport and Existence.* Philadelphia: Lea and Febiger, 1967.

Smart, Ninian. *Secular Education and the Logic of Religion.* London: Faber, 1966.

Smart, Ninian. *Religious Education in a Secular Setting.* London: SCM Press, 1968.

Smith, Ralph, ed. *Aesthetics and Problems of Education.* Urbana: University of Illinois, 1971.

Smith, C. M. "The Aesthetics of John Dewey and Aesthetic Education." In Ralph Smith, ed., *Aesthetics and Problems of Education.* Urbana: University of Illinois Press, 1971.

Smith, Ralph. "Teaching Aesthetic Criticism in the Schools." In Ralph Smith and Alan Simpson, eds. *Aesthetics and Arts Education.* University of Illinois Press, 1991.

Soltis, Jonas, ed. *Philosophy and Education. Eightieth Yearbook of the National*

Society for the Study of Education. Chicago: University of Chicago Press, 1981.

Sparshott, F. E. "The Unity of Aesthetic Education." In Ralph Smith, ed. *Aesthetics and the Problems of Education.* Urbana: University of Illinois Press, 1971.

Spencer, Herbert. *Education: Intellectual, Moral, and Physical.* Patterson, N.J.: Littlefield, Adams and Co., 1963 (1903).

Spring, Joel. "Mass Culture and School Sports." *History of Education Quarterly* 1974, 14.

Spring, Joel. *The American School: 1642–1985.* New York: Longmann, 1986.

Spring, Joel. *The Sorting Machine Revisited: National Educational Policy Since 1945.* Updated Edition. New York: Longmann, 1989.

Spring, Joel. *American Education: An Introduction to Social and Political Aspects.* New York: Longmann, 1991.

Starratt, J. Robert. *The Drama of Schooling: The Schooling of Drama.* London: Falmer Press, 1990.

Suran, Bernard G., and Rizzo, Joseph V. *Special Children: An Integrative Approach.* Glenview, Ill.: Scott Foresman, 1979.

Szasz, T. S. *The Myth of Mental Illness.* Rev. ed. New York: Harper and Row, 1974.

Telford, C. W., and Sawrey, J. M. *The Exceptional Individual.* Third Edition. Englewood Cliffs, N.J.: Prentice Hall, 1977.

Thurow, Lester. "Technological Unemployment and Occupational Education." In Thomas F. Powers, ed., *Education for Careers: Policy Issues in a Time of Change.* University Park: The Pennsylvania State University Press, 1977.

Tomlinson, S. *A Sociology of Special Education.* London: Routledge and Kegan Paul, 1982.

Tyack, David. "Onward Christian Soldiers: Religion in the American Public School." In Paul Nash, ed., *History and Education: The Educational Uses of the Past.* New York: Random House, 1970.

Tyack, David, James, Thomas, and Benavot, Aaron. *Law and the Shaping of Public Education, 1785–1954.* Madison: The University of Wisconsin Press, 1987.

Tymitz, B. L. "Do Teachers Need a Philosophy of Education?" *Journal For Special Education,* 1983, 19, 1–10.

Watts, A. G. *Education, Unemployment and the Future of Work.* Milton Keynes, Eng.: Open University Press, 1983.

Weiss, Paul. "A Philosophical Definition of Leisure." In P. Bucher, ed., *Dimensions of Physical Education.* Saint Louis: Mosby, 1974.

Welter, Rush. *Popular Education and Democratic Thought in America.* New York: Columbia University Press, 1962.

Westbrook, Robert. *John Dewey and American Democracy*. Ithaca N.Y.: Cornell University Press, 1991.

White, J. P. "Creativity and Education: A Philosophical Analaysis." In Jane Martin, ed., *Readings in the Philosophy of Education: Study of Curriculum*. Boston: Allyn and Bacon, 1971.

White, J. P. "Indoctrination and Intentions." In I. A. Snook, ed.. *Concepts of Indoctrination: Philosophical Essays*. Boston: Routledge and Kegan Paul, 1972.

Williams, Jesse F. *The Principles of Physical Education*. Philadelphia: W. B. Saunders Co., 1964.

Wilson, John. *Moral Education and the Curriculum*. Oxford: Pergamon, 1969.

Wilson, John. "Indoctrination and Freedom." In I. A. Snook, ed., *Concepts of Indoctrination: Philosophical Essays*. Boston: Routledge and Kegan Paul, 1972,

Woodward, Calvin. "The Fruits of Manual Training." In Martin Lazerson and W. Norton Grubb, eds., *American Education and Vocationalism: A Documentary History, 1870–1970*. New York: Teachers College Press, 1974.

Young, M., ed. *Knowledge and Control: New Directions for the Sociology of Education*. London: Routledge and Kegan Paul, 1971,

Zeigler, Earle F. "Philosophical Perspective on the Future of Physical Education and Sport." In Raymond Welsh, ed., *Physical Education: A View Toward the Future*. Saint Louis: C. V. Mosby Co., 1977.

INDEX OF PRINCIPAL NAMES

INDEX OF
PRINCIPAL SUBJECTS

VITA

John L. Elias, Ed.D., is professor of Religion and Education at Fordham University, New York. Dr. Elias teaches both in the Graduate School of Religion and Religious Education and the Graduate School of Education. He was a visiting research professor at the University of Birmingham and the University of Sussex, England. He is the author of *Paulo Freire: Pedagogue of Liberation, Foundations and Practice of Adult Religious Education, Philosophical Foundations of Adult Education, Studies in Theology and Education, Moral Education: Secular and Religious,* and *Psychology and Religious Education.*